D0090539

DEMOCRACY IN BLACK AFRICA

Democracy in BLACK AFRICA

SURVIVAL AND REVIVAL

John A. Wiseman

Paragon House Publishers
New York, New York

The paper used in this publication meets the minimum requirements
of American National Standard for Information Sciences—
Permanence of Paper for Printed Library Materials, ANSI Z39.48-1984.

First edition, 1990

Published in the United States by

Paragon House
90 Fifth Avenue
New York, NY 10011

Library of Congress Cataloging-in-Publication Data

Wiseman, John A.
    Democracy in Black Africa : survival and revival / John A.
Wiseman. — 1st ed.
      p. cm.
    Bibliography: p.
    Includes index.
    ISBN 1-55778-140-0
    1. Representative government and representation — Africa, Sub
-Saharan.   2. Africa, Sub-Saharan—Politics and government.
I. Title.
JQ1879.A15W57   1990
321.8′096—dc19   89-3179
                                                              CIP

Manufactured in the United States of America

This book is dedicated to my mother and my late father.

Contents

Preface

THE GERMINATION OF THE IDEAS underlying the major argument of this book took a great deal longer than did the process of actually writing it. When I first became seriously involved in the study of African politics nearly two decades ago, the democratic political systems of postcolonial Africa appeared to be in danger of extinction. The conventional academic wisdom was that this was inevitable and that competitive democracy had no future in black Africa. Alongside this was a widespread belief that the decline in democracy was in no way a matter for regret and that more authoritarian types of rule might be able to provide better prospects for solving Africa's problems. The picture I was given was that Africa did not want or need democracy and, anyway, was incapable of making it work.

In 1973 I made the first of many visits to Africa when I went to Botswana to do research for my doctoral thesis. What I found was a political system that was palpably democratic and appeared to exhibit every likelihood of remaining so. Numerous discussions with senior politicians—including those opposed to the government—and with many more humble folk left me in no doubt that democracy was not only valued but well understood. The first African state I had experienced in person seemed to fly in the face of the conventional wisdom I had been taught. But perhaps I had misread the situation in Botswana. Perhaps, despite all my impressions, democracy in Botswana was shortly to crumble away and add further evidence of the unworkability of democracy in Africa. (More than a decade and a half later it would appear that I had not misread the situation.) In any case, my experience was still limited. It was always possible that Botswana was in some way unique and that it represented no more than an outstanding exception to an otherwise-confirmed rule.

In 1974 I went to Nigeria to teach political science in the country's largest university. The three years I spent there were all under military rule. Political parties were banned and un-elected soldiers ruled by decree and the threat of force. Nine months after I arrived, the head of state, Yakubu Gowon, was overthrown in a relatively peaceful coup and six months later, his successor, Murtala Muhammed, was assassinated in a very violent but unsuccessful coup attempt that led to many further deaths. Surely this fitted the picture of African politics I had been given? Of course, in a sense it did, but it was only a part of what was happening in Nigerian politics. It was during this period that the road back to democratic civilian rule was being charted. Although I left Nigeria before the process was com-plete, I was in a position to witness firsthand the great debate within the country about the return to democracy. I was able to discuss the changes that were taking place with my Nigerian academic colleagues, with my students, and with a wide range of Nigerians outside the campus, including the Hausa peasants in the village where I was engaged on a research project. Over-whelming interest in, and support for, the restoration of de-mocracy was apparent in all quarters, and it was genuinely exhilarating to be involved, however much on the periphery, in what was taking place. In retrospect we know that that particular democratic experiment in Nigeria was doomed to failure. The operation of the Second Republic was badly flawed and many of the leading politicians failed to live up to the democratic hopes that preceded its inauguration. Nigerians exhibit a certain amount of justifiable cynicism about their political leaders, but it is clear that for most of them a workable democracy, one in which the citizens participate in choosing their rulers, remains the desired goal.

In 1979 I made the first of many visits to the small West African state of The Gambia, where democracy has been in operation since independence. Even a bloody attempted coup in 1981 failed to undermine the system. Once again I was con-vinced that democracy was understood: the supposed "ignorant masses" are in fact remarkably well informed about what is going on and have a much better understanding than they are usually given credit for.

Thus, the bulk of my personal experience in Africa has been in states where democracy has been continously in operation or where its absence at the time was a matter for great regret coupled with a determination to reestablish it. While I fully realized that these three states did not constitute a representative sample in a statistical sense, they seemed to me to present a strong counterargument to the idea that democracy is unsuitable for, and unattainable in, black Africa. Nor were they isolated examples. By the late 1970s and early 1980s it seemed apparent that the desire for democracy was widespread in other parts of Africa in spite of very real difficulties in implementing it. Even the dark cloud presented by the failure of revived democracies in Nigeria and Ghana could not obliterate this fact, and as the 1980s progressed, the strength of democracy, through the survival of some democratic systems and the revival of others, still shone through.

The picture of African politics presented in the literature on the subject, however, became ever bleaker as the 1980s wore on. While this was not without some substance, it did appear to be rather unbalanced. It seemed to me that what was needed was a realistic but positive reassessment of the role of democracy. It was important that this cover the whole of black Africa and not be limited to particular states or regions. Also, while the entire postindependence period needed examination, especially in those states where democracy had survived, it was necessary to pay particular attention to the past decade or so, which had been the main period of revival. While this reassessment would have to recognize the problems that democracy had faced, it needed to emphasize the successes achieved, rather than just gloomily reiterating the failures, as so much of the literature had done. While one could not claim that black Africa had been an outstanding arena of democratic politics, that fact had to be balanced against the more positive developments that had taken place. This was the thinking that led me to write this book.

Any book covering such a wide range of states is necessarily dependent on secondary sources for much of the empirical material. This book is no exception. Although I have visited a number of the states involved, I can claim research experience only of the three already mentioned. For the rest, I have made extensive use of the work of others with, I hope, due acknowledgment. Because this book represents developments in my thinking over a long period, a full list of those who have given me assistance of one sort or another would be unacceptably long, and so I am forced to highlight a minority. Among scholars of African politics, I am particularly indebted to Bill Tordoff, Dennis Austin, Ali Yahaya, Sam Oyovbaire, J. Isawa Elaigwu, James O'Connell, Arnold Hughes, Dick Crook, and Sulayman Nyang. For help in conducting research in Africa I am greatly indebted to Ba Tarawale, "Uncle Joe" Cates, Rudolph Allen, Ade Fowlis, the peasants of Gimi village (Nigeria), Brian Egnor, Eleanor Gabaake and Lenyeletse Seretse. Financial assistance for my work in Africa has come from the Social Science Research Council in the United Kingdom, Ahmadu Bello and Newcastle universities, the Nuffield Foundation and the British Academy. My wife Gill and my four children have assisted in many different ways. At Paragon House, Ken Stuart, Ed Paige, and Laura Greeney have provided encouragement and help. Here in Newcastle, Suzanne Mullholland has performed wonders in translating my handwritten scrawl into readable text.

Finally, and in a different way, I must acknowledge the efforts of countless black Africans who have struggled, and continue to struggle, often at great personal cost, to make democracy a reality in their home countries. Without them I would have nothing to write about.

None of the above is in any way responsible for any mistakes, omissions, misunderstandings, and misjudgments others may find in this book.

John A. Wiseman
University of Newcastle upon Tyne

Part • One

THE CONTEXT OF THE DEBATE

IN ORDER TO APPRECIATE the case studies of the survival and revival of democracy in black Africa it is necessary to establish the context in which they have operated. This first section of the book will set out the three major aspects of this context.

To begin with the theoretical and definitional context of the debate and its relationship with Africa has to be clearly established. Unless care is taken democracy can be an elusive notion capable of many conflicting understandings. It will be argued that representative democracy, in which the state is governed by the representatives of the people at large, is the only realistically applicable notion of democracy for the large-scale states of modern Africa. It is also argued that in the selection of these representatives the people must have a choice which involves real competition between those who would seek political office. In practice this choice is made manifest by the existence of competing political parties which will put forward their candidates and policies for the approval, or otherwise, of the electorate. The latter must include the entire adult population of the state because a universal franchise is of paramount importance if democracy is to exist. At the same time it has to be recognized that there is an inevitable gap between political theory and what actually takes place in the real world. Political systems are, at best, an imperfect realization of abstract ideals, in Africa as elsewhere. Any discussion of democracy in Africa must come to terms with its imperfections but not at the expense of excluding it from the political agenda.

Debates about democracy in Africa are, by implication, linked to the wider debate concerning democracy in the Third World, especially in relation to the sort of conditions which impede or support its existence. Thus, the second context is a comparative one. A necessarily brief discussion of the political role played by democracy in other parts of the Third World is followed by an examination of the conditions in which African democracy operates. It is argued that while these conditions may be more or less positive, often the latter, they are not deterministic, and that democracy can operate even in seemingly unpromising circumstances. On a broad comparative basis democracy plays a wider role in the Third World than is often realized.

Finally it is necessary to locate the survival and revival of democracy in Africa within the context of the history of African political developments. This context is provided by a broad overview of Africa which suggests a periodization of the historical process. This begins with a brief examination of the profoundly undemocratic period of colonial rule, which itself was instrumental in the creation of the democratizing forces of African nationalism. In the 1960s, the first decade of independence for most states, democracy appeared to be on the decline in black Africa but the evidence presented suggests that since around 1970 the picture has been more promising in a number of states. The combination of the survival of some democracies and the revival of others has meant that this form of rule has remained an important part of the African political scene.

Chapter • 1

Democracy as Choice and Competition in an Imperfect World

THIS BOOK IS ABOUT the real world of African politics, not about the abstractions of political theory. It has no pretensions to make any significant contribution to democratic theory. Over the centuries more ink has been spilled by political writers on the question "What is democracy?" than on any other, and I do not wish to enter this debate at any length. However, because a particular conception of democracy provides the frame of reference for all that is to follow, it is vital to make clear at the outset what that conception is in order to specify the field of study and avoid unnecessary confusion. Readers may agree or disagree with the way in which the term democracy is used, but at least they will be clear as to its intended meaning.

One of the problems in dealing with the concept of "democracy" is that over the years it has become a very value-laden term and there is widespread agreement that it is "a good thing."

Many governments of quite different types wish to describe themselves as democratic. In some cases the term has even been incorporated into the official name of the state, although it is a noticeable paradox that in most cases where this has happened (e.g., the German Democratic Republic, the People's Democratic Republic of Yemen), the states concerned appear singularly undemocratic. That the term *democratic* almost inevitably connotes praise, while *undemocratic* implies censure may simply be a problem that must be lived with.

The long-lived, and perhaps even clichéd, idea that democracy implies government "of the people, for the people, by the people" is still the bedrock of democratic beliefs, though it is inherently problematic for a whole number of different reasons. If *by the people* is taken to refer to direct democracy—as preached, but not practised, in the ancient Greek city states, where the majority of the population, including all women, was banned from participating—then it has little relevance to contemporary large-scale states in Africa or elsewhere.[1] More relevant is the notion of representative democracy in which "by the people" is interpreted as meaning *by the representatives of the people*. This interpretation is used here. This leads naturally to the centrality of how the representatives are chosen. If they are chosen by the people, an inescapable implication is that all the people must have the opportunity to take part in that choice and that a universal franchise must exist. Denial of franchise on the grounds of race, sex, religion, wealth and so on cannot be tolerated if democracy is to exist. That is why, for example, the Republic of South Africa, despite exhibiting some features associated with democracy, could not be described as a democratic system. If we leave aside white South Africa, the question of franchise has not been central to politics in independent Africa. Where elections have taken place, a universal franchise has been the norm despite a few exceptions (e.g., in the first republic in Nigeria, the vote was withheld from women in the Northern Region).

Of much greater relevance in black Africa than the question of who has a vote has been that of what choice has been available to the voters. If the system is deliberately structured so that the electorate is offered little or no choice as to who it can vote for, then the possession of the vote is denuded of most of its significance and the potential for democracy within the system is very dramatically reduced. It is because of this that the notions of choice and competition are central to the conception of democracy used in this book. When the voters elect representatives, the element of choice should be as wide as possible. Intimately related to this is the contention that a wide selection of candidates, free to propose different views, should be allowed to compete with each other in attempting to attract the support of the electorate. It is through competition that choice is made meaningful in an election. Logically, there is no reason why this competition has to be based on political parties, although in practice it tends to be so. As yet no African state has experimented with the idea of allowing openly competitive national-level elections but banning the formation of parties. The result would almost certainly be the creation of all sorts of informal alliances that would rapidly become parties in all but name. It is unlikely that a body of independent representatives would remain unconnected and atomized for very long. Thus, it is part of the conception of democracy used here that it could be no-party or multi-party (meaning two or more). It would, however, quite definitely exclude the notion of single-party democracy on the grounds that it is a contradiction in terms. For readers unfamiliar with the literature on African politics, this may seem a quite unremarkable and uncontentious point but this is far from being the case. Much Western scholarship on Africa has been plagued by the fear of being labelled ethnocentric. Thus many Western observers have bent over backward to try to support the claims to democracy of ruling elites in Africa who were banning all opposition to themselves and denying their peoples the right to choose their representatives in freely competitive elections. As Martin Staniland comments in a recent article on this topic, "the irrelevance of western democracy quickly became the smart orthodoxy".[2] To avoid the charge of ethnocentrism many scholars adopted a bogus Afrocentrism. As Staniland argues, "a very usual expression of Afrocentrism was the adoption of a self-denying attitude toward crusading for democracy in Africa".[3] Although the same people would have been justifiably horrified if their own governments had decided to ban all opposition, they were quite willing to accept it in Africa. Hiding behind the spurious specter of ethnocentrism is a very real racism, however unintentional it may be, based on the idea that different standards of behavior should be adopted in dealing with Africa and that what is unacceptable in Europe or America is quite acceptable for black people in Africa. Historically, the development of competitive democracy originated in the West (so too, of course, did Marxism) but that does not make it irrelevant to Africa. There is nothing inherently un-African about democracy and there is certainly nothing inherently undemocratic about Africans in general (which is not to say that there are no undemocratic Africans). In recent years the debate has become further clouded by ideological bias. Right wing scholars have been looking benignly at the democratic claims of single-party states like Kenya or the Ivory Coast, while left wing scholars have been doing the same for Mozambique. Whatever the merits or demerits of the social and economic policies of these states, none of them fits with the conception of democracy adopted here. Democracy is about how the representatives of the people are chosen and not about what economic policies those chosen support. Of course, it can be argued that governments that are accountable at the ballot box and have to convince the electorate that they offer better policies than the opposition are probably more likely to adopt policies acceptable to at least the majority of the population. The main reason why current South African government policy works against the interests of the majority of the population is that the government is accountable only to a minority. Ultimately this is what the whole struggle in South Africa is about.

Democracy does not presuppose any particular set of government policies. The electorate, provided it is given a choice, will decide which set of governors and policies it wants. Thus, *for the people* is realized through periodic elections in which the mass of the population is able to choose both the policies and the personnel of the future government. In a single-party state this choice is at best limited to personnel. In some of Africa's single-party states (Tanzania is perhaps the best known example), the voters in each constituency are invited to choose between two candidates of the same ruling party. While choice and competition are not entirely absent in such circumstances, they are heavily circumscribed. All candidates represent the same party, must support the same policies, and have been chosen or at least approved by the same ruling group. Elections in some of these states are not meaningless, as the electorate can and does vote out MPs who are perceived to have performed poorly. The replacement representative may be more honest, hardworking, dedicated, or simply more pleasing in personality, but he is bound by the same policy stranglehold as his predecessor. The notion of choice relates to politicians as well as to voters.[4] In a single-party state a politician who feels that the policies of the ruling party are wrong can do one of two things. He can pretend, for career reasons, that he has no objections or he can opt out of legal and constitutional politics altogether by either retiring from political life or joining a subversive organization. It is only in a freely competitive system that he can join another party, or perhaps start his own, and attempt to change the government through the ballot box.

If it is accepted that choice is essential in a democracy, then several other features follow. The mechanisms through which that choice is expressed, most importantly elections, must be as free and uncoerced as possible. In addition, the election must be fair: the official results must correspond with the way votes were actually cast in the polling stations. This may seem an obvious point, but in a continent where election rigging has sometimes been rampant it is an important one. While it may be unrealistic to expect any election to be totally free of malpractice, the overall result should reflect the will of the electorate even if some doubts may be raised over the outcome in an odd constituency. Extending well beyond the period of elections, a high degree of freedom of speech and association must be in operation. If the choice at the polling booth is to be meaningful, those who disagree with the ruling party must be free to organize themselves and make their views known to the electorate as well as they are able. Perhaps ideally, all parties should have equal campaign resources, but it would be unrealistic to see choice as dependent on this. Any restrictions on the freedom to form political parties and groupings can only be justified by a most stringent examination of their necessity in a particular case. (See, for example, the discussion of restrictions on party formation in the Second Republic in Nigeria.) Simply being opposed to the government and ruling party of the day cannot alone be sufficient justification for being banned in a democracy. In fact, the role of opposition is crucial to the functioning of democracy, not only in terms of providing electoral choice and offering an alternative government, but also in terms of subjecting the governing party to constant critical examination in public forums, including that of the legislature. A critical, often very critical, opposition has been an almost constant feature of Africa's democracies. The existence of a situation in which opposition is legally possible but does not arise is very rare in Africa, although it occurred briefly in Malawi and Tanzania before opposition parties were made illegal with the introduction of the single-party state in both countries. The proper functioning of an opposition does not, however, necessarily imply an alternation in power between two or more major parties. Although this has tended to happen in Britain and the United States, there are other well-functioning democracies where it does not, as the dominance of the Social Democrats in Sweden so well exemplifies. The fact that in two of Africa's most successful democracies, Botswana and The Gambia, the same party has been in power since independence is not a negation of democracy. The distinction between a single-party state, in which, it is argued, democracy is virtually impossible, and a hegemonic party state, in which one party is very much stronger than the combined opposition, is a vital one.

One further characteristic of a democracy that needs mentioning is the need for the existence of a relatively autonomous judiciary. Ruling parties and governments make and execute the laws of the land, but in a democracy they do not also have a total control over the adjudication of those laws. This is another area in which the independence of judiciaries in African democracies—often demonstrated by the courts finding against the government of the day—contrasts strongly with the control of judges in single-party and military-ruled states.

In outlining the conception of democracy that provides the frame of reference for the rest of this book, the overwhelming emphasis has been on a set of principles governing the acquisition and use of political power. Virtually nothing has yet been said concerning the precise structure of institutions and their interrelationships that these principles must inform and in which they will operate. One of the main advantages of this sort of approach is the avoidance of the idea that it is only by adopting a carbon copy of the constitution of a Western democratic state that an African state can be described as a democracy. Although the principles of the acquisition and use of political power adopted here are broadly in line with the notion of liberal democracy as understood in the West, they allow for a very wide range of permutations of institutionalization. The principles may operate in a unitary or federal structure with a high or low degree of local government autonomy; voting may or may not be based on proportional representation and can take place in single or multi-member constituencies; the system may be parliamentary or presidential and may or may not embody a clearly demarcated separation of powers; the party system may range from two to many or none at all; chiefs and other traditional leaders may or may not be included in the system in a great range of different ways.

In short, the possible institutional adaptations to particular local circumstances, while maintaining the basic principles, are almost infinite. To be successful, an African democracy must be sensitive to local conditions; the simple adoption of an institutional frame designed elsewhere is unlikely to be successful.

Having outlined a conception of democracy, it has to be borne in mind that the real world is not populated by moralistic philosophers. That there is sometimes a gap between the principles and what actually takes place is hardly surprising and is certainly not unique to democracy. It has to be recognized that governments in democratic societies do sometimes deviate from democratic principles. (One of the most important functions of opposition and the judiciary is to be vigilant over such departures.) Politicians in African democracies, as in the rest of the world, do not always behave in the way they should. There is undeniably a natural tension between democratic principles and the desire of politicians to secure and maintain political power, and clashes with self-interest are unavoidable.

In approaching the study of democracy in the real world of Africa, some pragmatic modification of the conception is necessary. To be a nonpurist is to be realistic. We live in an imperfect world, and here as elsewhere democracies are imperfect, but an imperfectly functioning democracy is nevertheless quite different from a nondemocracy. The question of how far deviation from democratic principles can go before a system ceases to be an imperfect democracy and becomes undemocratic is of course a reasonable and pertinent one. However, rather than attempt to provide an answer at an abstract level, it is more productive to relate the question to particular cases, taking into account all the individual local circumstances. This approach will be adopted later, in the examination of particular case studies. Classifying individual states at particular points in time may be a matter of judgment, and there is a vital need that this judgment should not be too dogmatic.

Finally, it should be emphasized that what is attempted here is a realistic reassessment of the role democracy has played in postindependence Africa to date. It is not intended as an advocacy for democracy and I would certainly not suggest that democracy provides a panacea for all of the many serious problems that contemporary African states are facing. At best, it may suggest ways to help solve some of the problems of some of the states. I know that many of my fellow academic observers adopt a much gloomier view of the prospects for democracy in Africa than the one offered here. I also know, from numerous personal encounters within Africa at all levels of society, that the desire for democracy is great.

Chapter • 2

The Conditions for Democracy?

STUDENTS OF COMPARATIVE politics have generally assumed that competitive democracy is an inappropriate and inherently non-viable system for managing politics in Third World states.[1] The major features of democracy are usually believed to be virtually impossible to achieve and sustain in all but a relatively small number of Western political systems. Because many of the social and economic characteristics thought to be associated with the development of democratic systems in the West are absent in the Third World, it is argued that democracy is un-likely to be anything but an ephemeral rarity. Without stable and developed economies, normally with a strong industrial base, a literate and educated citizenry, a sophisticated com-munications network, and a relatively homogenous civic cul-ture, the essential preconditions for democracy are held not to exist. It is sometimes even argued that an established democratic tradition is an essential ingredient even though this would leave one at a loss to explain the arrival of democracy in the first place.

That there are some elements of truth in such views is perhaps undeniable. Democracy is not the empirical norm within the Third World and the authoritarianism of single-party and military rule has been a widespread phenomenon. Common impressions of Third World states being ruled by bemedalled soldiers or single-party bosses are not without their foundation. Elections in which only one party is permitted to put candidates before the electorate or states in which elections are simply not held are to be found in considerable numbers. Furthermore, it is most likely that this state of affairs will continue in the foreseeable future.

In spite of this, however, the general picture of undemocratic regimes controlling the states of the Third World does remain a partial one. The major argument of this book is that democracy has played, is playing, and is likely to continue to play a significant role as a viable alternative to Third World authoritarianism. The focus here is on the independent states of black Africa, but it is well worth mentioning some of the other notable examples of Third World democracies. Since independence in 1947, India has had a justifiable claim to be the world's largest democracy. Despite its great size, its cultural complexity, and its undeniable poverty, India has, with perhaps a brief exception during the State of Emergency in 1975, maintained what is essentially a free democratic system. That it has done so in spite of its serious conflicts and cleavages is a testament to the skill of several generations of its political leaders from Gandhi and Nehru on. When, in 1977, the Indian electorate voted the Congress Party out of office and turned to the alternative Janata Party, Congress went into opposition and reorganized its strength for further electoral contests. When it returned to power in 1980 it did so in a democratic manner, by convincing enough of the Indian electorate that it was the best fitted to rule. To the south of India the island state of Sri Lanka has persisted with democracy in spite of being plagued by tremendous communal tensions and by a conflict between the majority Sinhalese population and the Tamil minority that constantly threatens its political stability. In Pakistan the election in late 1988 of Benazir Bhutto following years of military dictatorship under President Zia marked a significant revival of democracy.

During the late 1970s and early 1980s the states of Latin America, so long identified with military dictatorships, have witnessed a quite remarkable return to democratic rule.[2] Since 1979 Equador, Peru, Bolivia, Argentina, Brazil, and Uruguay have joined the longer-established democracies of Columbia and Venezuela. Now it is the army juntas of Chile and Paraguay which are in the minority in a continent where most governments owe their position to the freely expressed support of the electorate. Even in these two cases recent events point to the possibility of revival of democracy. Among the small island states of the Carribean, politics may sometimes be a rough business, but for the most part it has been a democratic one. Other examples of Third World democracy lie scattered about the globe. Papua-New Guinea, probably the most culturally diverse state in the world for its size and containing some of the world's most remote and traditional peoples, has had a well-maintained democratic system since independence, as have several of its Melanesian neighbors. In 1986 in the Philippines a quite remarkable demonstration of "people power" brought about a restoration of democracy, even though threats from the army and ultraleft insurgents still pose dangers.

This brief listing, which is not exhaustive, underlines the contention that democracy not only exists in the Third World, but is not even a rarity there. But what of black Africa? It is generally believed that, of all the parts of the Third World, Africa offers the least fertile soil for democracy. In terms of what are generally supposed to be the necessary preconditions for the existence for democracy, black Africa appears to be the most disadvantaged. Of all the continents, Africa is much the least economically developed. Most of the world's poorer states are African and the bulk of its people are among the most poverty stricken. Standards of living, measured by all the usual criteria of health and welfare, life expectancy, infant mortality and so on, are extremely low. Its economies, predominantly agrarian and nonindustrialised, are among the most vulnerable and least developed in the world. For many there is not even the consolation of making even slow progress in the right direction. In a distressingly large number of African states the postindependence era has to date been one of economic decline. When this decline is set along side the highest population growth rates in the world, the consequences in human suffering are inescapable. The terminology that places African states in the category of "developing countries" is, for many, simply misleading: all are underdeveloped but only a few are developing.

Africa also appears to be lacking in terms of the other "preconditions" for democracy. Literacy and general educational standards are universally low. Although all the African states have a small, well-educated elite and some have made good progress in extending basic literacy to wider sections of the population, for most the provision of universal education at the primary level remains an impossible dream. In terms of communications Africa is similarly disadvantaged. Again despite some improvements in some states much of the communication network is rudimentary to say the least. Often the only efficient communication center is the national airport that links the fortunate few to the outside world. While flying from Accra or Bamako to London or Paris is relatively easy, traveling from the capital to the outlying areas of Ghana or Mali is quite a different matter. Traveling to the rural areas where, after all, most of the population lives, is often a very difficult business and the standard of roads is appalling. Even if the roads were better, the shortage of spare parts for broken-down vehicles and of fuel to power them (often due, in both cases, to a shortage of foreign exchange and to distribution problems) makes travel difficult.

Perhaps the greatest problem that African states face is their cultural heterogeneity. Almost all are made up of a large number of ethnic groups with their different languages, customs, and religions and with a singular lack of any common history except perhaps as enemies. Almost all are archetypal examples of "states without nations," lacking the cultural glue to hold them together. This state of affairs is primarily a result of the nature of their origins. The contemporary map of African states is almost entirely of nineteenth-century European colonial construction. During the "scramble for Africa" and especially at the conference of Berlin (1884–1885), the boundaries within Africa were decided on in Europe, by Europeans, and reflected the European balance of power and European interests. Furthermore, the boundaries were often drawn in almost complete ignorance of what they actually meant on the ground, grouping peoples together in an ad hoc and largely accidental fashion. That African states in the postcolonial period have had difficulty in functioning as cohesive units is as unsurprising as it is predictable.

This random linking of heterogeneous cultural groupings also meant the linking of heterogeneous political systems and political cultures. Traditional precolonial African political systems were extremely diverse, ranging from stateless societies in which political leadership was unknown, to highly centralized state systems.[3] At the national level, the newly independent states of Africa lacked not only an established democratic political tradition but any unified political tradition at all. The component groups within the state most certainly did have their own individual political traditions, often highly efficacious and locally well-respected, but for the new state this proved more of a problem than a solution. One of the major problems facing the new states of Africa in the 1960s was precisely the fact that they *were* new, their only history as identifiable units being the history of colonial domination.

Taking all these factors into account, it would seem that Africa represented a supremely difficult test case, even by Third World standards, for the application of democratic systems of rule. It is certainly true that, perhaps especially in the 1960s, democracy faced an uphill struggle for survival in Africa. When faced with governments' collapse into the authoritarianism of single-party and military rule, the early optimism surrounding democracy in postcolonial Africa gave way to a dominant mood of pessimism which has by and large been sustained ever since. In general, the literature on democracy in black Africa has concentrated on its failures. It has been seen by most commentators as a temporary phase just before and just after independence, providing the mechanisms for the transfer of power from colonial rulers to indigenous political leaders, but then withering away. The conclusions drawn are that the conditions for the survival of democracy do not exist and that it is not a viable alternative.

In this book I wish to adopt a quite different emphasis, concentrating more on the successes of democracy than on its failures, more on its continued existence than its collapse. Rather than concentrating on why it has been overthrown in an admittedly large number of states, I intend to concentrate on how, where, and why it has managed to survive. While recognizing the fact that at any given time a majority of African states cannot be described as functioning democracies, a very much stronger emphasis than hitherto will be placed on its continuous survival in a small number of states, and, probably even more importantly, the way it is continually being revived and resurrected in other states following periods of single-party or military rule. In changing the focus from failure to success it is possible to demonstrate that democracy has a greater relevance to African politics than has yet been generally recognized. What have been seen as the social and economic preconditions for democracy may be more accurately regarded as helpful rather than necessary. The fact that most of Africa lacks most of these preconditions has made the attainment of democracy more difficult, but it has not made it impossible.

Chapter • 3

An Overview of Democracy in Africa

The Transfer of Power and Beyond

DEMOCRACY IN AFRICA is often perceived as part of the legacy of European colonial rule. To the extent that this is an accurate picture it is a very limited one. For most of the colonial period the system of rule was resolutely authoritarian and contained little or no democratic content as far as the people of Africa were concerned. It was African nationalism that initially provided the democratic challenge to colonial authoritarianism and that was largely responsible for the democratization that took place in the terminal colonial period. The institutions through which the transfer of power took place and with which the majority of states began the independence period were, by and large, democratic in character. But if they were, to a significant extent, African-initiated, why are they so commonly perceived as a European legacy? It is perhaps in the interests of the excolonizers that this should be so because it seems to absolve them of any responsibility for the diminution of democracy since the hand over of power. Thus the view is commonly expressed that "we" (the Europeans) gave "them" (the Africans) democracy, so it is not our fault if they failed to continue it. Ironically the "European heritage" view also suits the interests of some of those African leaders who sought to protect their own position by abandoning democracy and justifying the move by claiming that the system was an alien importation. This rather odd identity of interest has done much to support the myth of democracy being an inappropriate and alien form of rule in Africa.

The replacement of democracy with single-party and military rule was so common in the 1960s that it is correct to see the collapse of democracy as the dominant political motif of politics in Africa in that period. However, the period since 1970 has shown rather more mixed fortunes for democracy in Africa. Not only has it managed to survive in a few isolated cases, it has attained a wider presence through its reintroduction in a number of states. It is because of this that a reassessment of its role is now relevant. Before looking at individual cases in detail, this chapter will provide a broad overview of the features of democracy in Africa.

COLONIAL RULE AND THE DEMOCRATIC CHALLENGE OF AFRICAN NATIONALISM

Colonial rule is inherently undemocratic. While the degree of authoritarianism it encompasses varies considerably from place to place and from time to time, it is logically incompatible with democracy. The political supremacy of an alien ruling elite is government "of" the people but it is doubtfully "for" the people, and, however one twists the meaning of the word, it can never be "by" the people.

European colonial rule in Africa was not entirely devoid of African participation, but it was not until very late in the day that significant numbers of Africans had any involvement in their own government, and even then such involvement was largely absent in the Belgian and Portuguese colonies. Of course in those colonies where white settlers were numerous, local participation in decision making, by whites only, arrived much earlier. In British Africa the system of indirect rule was largely adopted. Here much of the day-to-day administration was left in the hands of the African traditional leaders, chiefs sometimes being created in those societies that had previously lacked them. Justified by claims of respect for African traditional culture, indirect rule also had the advantages of parsimony. Because the chiefs were ultimately responsible to the colonial authorities rather than to their own people, indirect rule had the effect of subduing the democratic content of many traditional systems because political survival had more to do with keeping the Europeans content than with responding to the needs of the subjects.

With a few rare exceptions the French did not adopt indirect rule. French colonial policy always contained a much more explicit ideology of cultural assimilation (the policy was renamed "association" in 1905), which reached its symbolic apotheosis with young African school children being taught songs about "our ancestors the Gauls". This policy was never as far reaching in practice as it was in theory and the number of Africans assimilated was always relatively small. Nevertheless, it did produce some results that would have been unimaginable in the British context. As early as 1914, Blaise Diagne became the first elected black deputy, on a very restricted franchise, in the French parliament. In the late 1950s, Felix Houphouet-Boigny, later president of the Ivory Coast, was a full member of the French cabinet. One finds it hard to picture a Kwame Nkrumah or a Jomo Kenyatta sitting in the British Conservative cabinet in the same period.

Democratic representation in the government of the colonies remained at a minimal level until late on. Even after World War II the idea of self government and independence, when it was thought of at all, was seen as being centuries away. In some cases a tiny number of Africans, elected on an extremely limited franchise, were present on governing bodies. In others, principally in British Africa, a few selected chiefs were included. However, change was on the way, caused by a combination of two major factors: the relative decline of the European powers on the world stage; and the increasing African nationalist demand for democratization and indigenization of political control. For most of black Africa this change was relatively peaceful. The major exceptions were the Portuguese territories of Angola, Mozambique, and Guinea-Bissau, where major wars of liberation were needed to displace the colonial powers and where the phase of democratization never took place. It is quite probable that, had Britain and France not realized the impracticability of hanging on to their colonies and moved to granting independence, they too would have faced the same sort of hopeless and debilitating wars as Portugal. In the main, the French learned their lessons, albeit expensively, in Vietnam and the British, much less expensively, in India.

In the French territories it was the Loi Cadre of 1956 that marked the major breakthrough to democracy by introducing universal suffrage and a high degree of internal autonomy. This was just four years before independence in all of the states of francophone Africa excluding Guinea, which rejected De Gaulle's proposal for a French Community and became independent in 1958[1], and the microstates of Comoro Islands and Djibouti which stayed under French control until 1975 and 1977 respectively. Although the process in the British territories did not present quite this level of uniformity, the general picture of a move to full democracy shortly before independence is equally applicable. For all the colonies the "democratic heritage" was very much something that was tacked on at the end of what had been anything but a democratic period in Africa's history.

It needs to be stressed that this democracy was not simply foisted on unwilling incomprehending Africans. In almost all cases the nationalist leaders and their followers supported the democratic model and had been demanding freedom of political association and one man, one vote in advance of the willingness of the colonial authorities to grant them. The fact that so many leaders repudiated the idea of a legal and legitimate opposition at a later date must under no circumstances be allowed to obscure this fact. In the negotiations surrounding the transfer of power, demands for single-party domination through the banning of opposition were absent and military rule was not even a cloud on the horizon.

The institutionalization of the mechanisms for the transfer of power and the establishment of democracy were then both part of the same process. The constitutions of the newly independent state were often closely modeled on those of the departing colonial power, presidential systems predominating in francophone Africa and Westminster-type parliamentary systems being adopted in the anglophone states. Retrospectively it is possible to argue that this modeling went too far and that democratic institutions were not as carefully adapted to particular local circumstances as they might have been. In the light of experience this certainly seems the case, and it is noticeable that where democracy has survived or where it has been reintroduced, closer attention has been paid to this point. The 1979 constitution in Nigeria, for example, was far more appropriate than the one with which the country entered independence in 1960. Local adaption of democratic institutions is of course quite different from the large-scale dismantling of democracy that took place. To argue that the precise constitutional arrangements were not always appropriate is quite different from arguing that democracy itself was not appropriate.

The African response to the democratization process in terms of party formation was instructive. In most states the natural unconstrained emergence of parties was sufficient to offer the electorate real choice in terms of alternative policies and leadership, but not so great as to threaten the system. A very small number of states produced highly fragmented party systems, which made the creation of political order very difficult. Zaire and Somalia are the best examples of this phenomenon, the latter producing at one stage no less than 130 different parties, and this in a state with an ethnically homogeneous population of around three million. At the other end of the scale there were an even smaller number of states that failed to produce any significant opposition parties when the latter were permitted, and even here this was a situation of very short duration. In Malawi the Malawi Congress Party (MCP) of Hastings Banda had no significant opposition challenge in the immediate pre-independence period. Shortly after independence serious splits occurred within the party between Banda and some of the younger, more radical members. Banda responded to this threat to his position by expelling his MCP opponents and curtailing their actions by declaring a single-party state. In Tanzania no significant opposition to the Tanganyika African National Union (TANU) existed when the country became independent in 1963. However, by the time of the 1965 election Nyerere had, like Banda, precluded the possibility of an opposition emerging by moving to a single-party state. It is hard to imagine that alternatives to the ruling parties in Malawi and Tanzania would not have come into existence since the mid-1960s had they been permitted to do so. Thus, by the early 1960s democracy was in place over most of the African continent; only in the southern part, with its constellation of white racial minority ruled states, was it absent on a large scale. The intense optimism both inside and outside of Africa that was quite genuinely felt at the time was, however, to be short-lived. African democracy, which had reached its apotheosis in a very short period of time, proceeded to its nadir with even greater rapidity.

THE 1960s

During the 1960s, which for most of Africa's new states was the first decade of independence, the most striking political change was the decline in the number of states practicing democracy. Although, as we have seen, most states started with democratic systems, a majority had moved to single-party or military rule by 1970. Although there was a considerable amount of diversity, the most common single pattern was for a state to move to a single-party system, which was then in turn subject to military intervention. Shortly after independence the ruling political elites became increasingly critical of the role and status of the opposition. Opposition parties were accused of being divisive and of hindering development, but it does not seem unduly cynical to suggest that in many cases the simple desire of the new elites to cling to power was more persuasive. While it is true that independence did not bring the gains promised in advance by nationalist leaders, it is doubtful if opposition parties were to blame. In some cases opposition elites were co-opted into the ruling party, but more often they were banned, imprisoned, or even killed. In many cases (e.g., Ghana, Mali, Uganda, Niger, Burundi, CAR, Congo Brazaville) the attempt of leaders to perpetuate their hold on power by scrapping the democratic and constitutional procedures which could have led to their replacement, was to fail as the undemocratic and unconstitutional procedure of the coup d'etat became a permanent feature of African politics.

While the creation of many single-party states was motivated primarily by a desire to remove the challenge of an opposition, it would be unduly cynical to regard this as the sole cause in all states where this type of system was introduced. President Julius Nyerere of Tanzania was the most cogent supporter of the single-party system[2] and his views were echoed, often with rather less conviction, by the leaders of other states. Even those who disagreed with Nyerere's justification of the single-party state rarely doubted his sincerity. In the immediate postindependence period Nyerere's TANU party faced no significant formal opposition and so the move to a single-party state could not be seen as a crushing of opposition. Nyerere argued that Tanzania was a classless society and that the competitive pluralism of a multi-party state could only represent class groupings. Thus, he argued, Tanzania had no need of more than one party because the single party could transfer the traditional egalitarian communalism of African society to the new state structures. (Some other leaders produced a more quasi-fascistic version of this notion of an undifferentiated society.) One may question both the supposed classlessness of traditional society and also the view that a plurality of parties can only represent class interests, class being but one possible basis of party support. More recent writers on Tanzania would take these doubts further by arguing that the system Nyerere set up itself worked to produce a new dominant class grouping identified as the "bureaucratic bourgeoisie"[3] that owed its position to the uncontestable power of the party.

Nyerere also argued that the new system would be more democratic and allow electors more choice. This position was defended on the grounds that, because no serious opposition parties had emerged, elections, if fought within the framework of a multi-party system, would mean that most constituencies would produce unopposed candidates. Instead of this, the system was to become legally single-party and the sole party would then put up two candidates in each constituency, allowing for at least some limited choice. However, it is difficult to see why Nyerere's view that people needed choice could not have been satisfied within the existing system. There was nothing to stop TANU putting up more than one candidate in any constituency lacking opposition candidates. This would have ensured choice for all voters without precluding the possibility that at some time in the future some areas might have preferred the opportunity of voting for a candidate representing a party other than TANU. Over two decades later Nyerere himself began to have serious doubts regarding the desirability of a single-party system (see Chapter 10).

The establishment of single-party rule was one of the two major changes taking place in this period. It was during the 1960s that the African military began to assume a significant role in politics, a development which at first surprised and shocked many observers. Civilian regimes, both democratic and undemocratic, were subjected to overthrow through military intervention. This feature of African politics has persisted ever since, and many of the case studies presented in later chapters provide examples of this phenomenon. The military coup is now the greatest threat to democracy in Africa.

The fundamental basis of the military coup is the overwhelming coercive power of the army. The use or threatened use of military hardware is the bedrock upon which all coups are founded, whether it consists of the violent elimination of the previous regime and its supporters or the stationing of a couple of tanks outside the presidential palace as an indication of seriousness of intent. Against such power, civilian society is weak, the majority of the population being spatially scattered peasant farmers. Even in the urban areas, formally organized interest groups were weak and embryonic, as were many of the very new public institutions of the state. In short, there was not a great deal that Africans could do to stop their national armies seizing power. Some coups were initially welcomed when they displaced unpopular authoritarian regimes, but popular support was not crucial to the success of the seizure of power, which depended more on strength than on notions of legitimacy. Some commentators suggested an element of contagion; that an appreciable number of coups were copycat actions, as groups of soldiers, seeing that their counterparts in neighboring states could take over the government, proceeded to do the same. Experience rapidly suggested that once the military had installed themselves in power, gaining international recognition was relatively easy.

The leaders of newly installed military regimes have continued to justify their actions by claiming that they are acting in the national interest. However, considerable experience of military rule since the 1960s has led observers to become disenchanted with this sort of explanation, and it would appear that "protection of the national interest" comes fairly far down in the real ordering of motives for military intervention. In reality the interests protected by military intervention are to be found within the armed forces, but they are of different types. The first type emphasizes the particularistic interests involved. In such cases, coup makers can be seen as acting in the interests of some particular regional, ethnic, or communal group or aggregate of groups, often replicating unresolved divisions within the civilian political system. The army can thus be seen in practice as a compilation of armed ethnic or regional groups rather than as a coherent whole, even though its formal structure will not usually reflect this. Coups of this sort will be mounted by army sections with a distinctive ethnic or regional character, usually against a civilian government (democratic or undemocratic) that does not share this character.

In other cases, it is more useful to focus on the military as a corporate group with its own group interests to protect. Analytically, it is not inaccurate to view the armies of Africa as by far the most important and powerful interest groups on the continent. Perhaps unsurprisingly, the main beneficiaries of military coups are often to be found within the army when it comes to the allocation of national resources. In some cases careful attention has to be paid to the personal motives of individuals leading the coup.

In the 1960s democracy was abandoned in a significant number of states as it failed to generate an adequate response to the threats of single-party and military rule.

In the early postcolonial phase, many of Africa's democracies clearly proved to be unstable, although in only a tiny number (e.g., Nigeria, Zaire) was it the case that party competition reached the level of threatening to undermine the integrity of the state. It was the view of many that democracy itself was a destabilizing factor. Largely because of the arbitrary way in which African states had been created by European powers, they were seen as being dangerously pluralistic. Against this background it was argued that the public contestation involved in democracy would only produce instability and could even lead to the breakup of many states. Versions of this argument were not only used by academic observers but by African leaders seeking to introduce more authoritarian forms of rule. The empirical experience of unstable democracies seemed to support such arguments: if African democracies (or at least a sub-stantial number of them) were proving to be unstable, then democracy, it was argued, was an unsuitable form of govern-ment that could only produce confusion. However, it can be argued that the reasoning behind this proposition is faulty.

The early postindependence period witnessed the coinci-dence of two factors which have no necessary relationship. First, many of the new states of Africa with the background of heightened pluralism and severe underdevelopment were ac-tually or potentially unstable. Second, almost all of these states had democratic systems of government at independence. It cannot, however, be assumed that the factors of democracy and instability are necessarily causally linked. I would argue that instability was a feature of many new African states, but that in a causal sense this often had little or nothing to do with the public contestation of democracy. Put simply: if many states are potentially unstable and most are democracies, then many democracies will be unstable but it is not democracy itself which makes them so.

Instability is then a reflection of the nature of the postcolonial state and not of the failings of a specifically democratic system. This line of argument is supported by subsequent events. If democracy had been the sole or major cause of instability, then one would have expected that the more authoritarian nondem-ocratic state structures would have overcome the problems of political instability in Africa. This has simply not happened and the single-party and military-rule state have not led to stability.

Despite all this it is uncontestable that the trend in African politics in the 1960s was away from democracy and towards authoritarianism. Had the direction and momentum of this trend continued the democratic system would have long since been swept away in Africa. Democracy would have been rele-gated to the history books as an irrelevance for students of contemporary Africa. The single most important argument of this book is that this did not happen.

SINCE 1970

Table 3-1 gives an overview of the extent of multi-party dem-ocratic systems in black Africa since 1970.

Table 3–1. Black African Democracies since 1970		
STATE	*PERIOD(S) OF MULTI-PARTY* **DEMOCRACY** *SINCE 1970*	*COMMENTS/DETAILS*
Botswana	continuous	Democracy maintained since independence in 1966.
Burkina Faso (called Upper Volta until 1984)	1978 to 1980	A short but vigorous democratic interlude between periods of military rule in a chronically unstable country.
Central African Republic	February to September 1981	A brief democratic interlude before the military again took over. The country has yet to recover from its deprivations under "Emperor" Bokassa.
Djibouti	1977 to 1981	Not independent until 1977—now a single-party state.
The Gambia	continuous	Full democracy since independence in 1965, in spite of violent coup attempt in 1981.
Ghana	up to 1972 and 1979 to 1981	The only state, so far, where democracy has been restored twice following periods of military rule. On both occasions, democracy was ended by further military intervention.
Lesotho	until January 1970	Qualifies for inclusion here by only a few weeks. When (as is widely believed) the ruling Basotho National Party lost the 1970 election, Prime Minister Leabua Jonathan staged a coup to keep himself in power. In the later Jonathan period opposition parties were permitted, but promises of new elections never materialized. The Jonathan government was overthrown by the military in 1986.
Liberia	1985 to present	A return to democracy following a period of military rule. The conduct of elections was hotly contested by opposition parties who claimed rigging despite winning some seats.
Mauritania	1986 to present	Limited to municipal level.

Table 3–1. continued		
STATE	*PERIOD(S) OF MULTI-PARTY* **DEMOCRACY** *SINCE 1970*	*COMMENTS/DETAILS*
Mauritius	continuous	Full democracy since independence in 1968, despite a temporary state of emergency in 1971. On two occasions (1982 and 1983), opposition parties came to power through victory in elections: these are the only examples so far of peaceful succession through the ballot box.
Nigeria	1979 to 1983	A restoration of democracy following demilitarization in 1979. Another military coup in 1983.
Senegal	1976 to present	The only example so far of a single-party state moving back to democracy without any military intervention. Democratization in stages: at first only three parties allowed, then four, then unlimited.
Sierra Leone	until 1978	Democracy ended by declaration of a single-party state. There was some harassment of opposition parties before they were banned, but they did win a substantial minority of seats in the 1977 elections.
Sudan	1986 to present	Democratization by military junta, which overthrew president Numeiri in 1985. Return to democracy took place under the difficult circumstances of drought, famine, and civil war.
Swaziland	until 1973	Democracy ended when King Sobhuza II assumed supreme power and scrapped the constitution. Extensive use of traditional Swazi forms of rule since then, despite the death of Sobhuza in 1982.
Uganda	1980 to 1985	A dubious case, with many claims of election rigging and harassment of opposition. President Obote overthrown by a guerilla force led by Museveni. Country still suffering badly from the deprivations of the Amin period.

Table 3–1. continued		
STATE	PERIOD(S) OF MULTI-PARTY **DEMOCRACY** SINCE 1970	COMMENTS/DETAILS
Zambia	until 1973	A move to a single-party state occurred when the dominance of the ruling party was threatened, not only by the persistence of opposition parties, but by splits within its own ranks. Prior to this President Kaunda had claimed to be a strong supporter of multi-party democracy.
Zimbabwe	1980 to present	Achieved independence later than most African states. President Mugabe has stated his intention to move to a single-party state in the future.

The compilation of Table 3-1 indicates some of the classification problems referred to earlier. It will always be debatable how extensive the imperfections in a democracy can be before it is eliminated from the category. No doubt some would argue for the exclusion of one or more of those included here. Uganda and Liberia are perhaps the most dubious examples; they will be discussed in detail later on. Equally, however, it might be possible to argue for the inclusion of some that are omitted here. Kenya was constitutionally multi-party until 1982 but the freedom of opposition parties was greatly restricted. At any given time there will be a number of states that have indicated a likely return to democracy in the future (e.g., Nigeria in 1992). These have been omitted on the grounds that the change has not yet taken place, but by the same token Zimbabwe is included even though there seems a strong possibility of a move to a single-party state before too long.

In examining the black African states that have had a multi-party democratic system at some time since 1970, it is possible to divide them into four separate groups. First, are those where democracy has functioned in an uninterrupted manner throughout the period. Only Botswana, The Gambia, Mauritius, and Zimbabwe are of this type. Next are those in which

the democratic system was still in its immediate postindependence phase when it collapsed. In several of these cases,
the explanation for the collapse was due less to the greater
comparative longevity of the democracy than to the fact that
the country became independent later than most. Djibouti, Lesotho, and Swaziland are examples of this type. Then there are
the cases in which democratic systems were reestablished following a period of military rule as part and parcel of the process
of demilitarization. Examples here would include Nigeria, Burkina Faso, and Ghana. In the case of the latter this has happened twice, in 1969 and 1979. The final category is that in
which a single-party state has transformed itself back into a
democracy while the same party remained in power. Senegal
is the only black African state in which this has taken place.

Obviously the existence of democracy in African states is
patchy and intermittent. Although well over one-third have had
some period of democratic rule since 1970, only four have
experienced an unbroken run since independence. However, it
has to be realized that this is as much a reflection of the generally
unsettled nature of politics across Africa as it is of the problems
of the democratic system as such. If a similar chart were composed for other types of political systems in Africa, it would
indicate a not dissimilar picture of fluctuation and change. Indeed, it would show in many cases far greater levels of political
instability (and even total collapse) than the one presented for
democracy.

While it is of course true that democratic states have been
in a minority in Africa since 1970, they have by no means been
negligible. Rather than repeatedly asking why democracy is
frequently overthrown, we should be asking why it has survived
as well as it has. Given what might be regarded as a nonsupportive environment, its survival as an alternative is perhaps
more surprising—and more in need of explanation—than its
overthrow. Such an explanation will require a detailed examination of those states in which democracy has survived or
been revived.

Part • Two

SURVIVAL

EVENTS IN THE IMMEDIATE POSTINDEPENDENCE PERIOD meant that examples of the continued existence of democracy in black African states were severely limited in number. For a variety of reasons many states moved on to more authoritarian forms of rule, although a number have since changed direction yet again and revived democracy. In the literature considerable attention was paid to the decline in democracy but comparatively little attention was given to the states where it continued to function. In understanding democracy in Africa it is thus of crucial importance to examine those states where it has managed to survive. In only three, Botswana, The Gambia and Mauritius, can one clearly demonstrate the continuing role played by free, fair and competitive elections, including a range of lively opposition parties, which allow the people to choose their rulers. In the fourth case, that of Zimbabwe, this has existed so far but at the time of writing appears to be seriously under threat.

This section provides detailed accounts of each state. It examines the social and economic background of each and the ways in which they emerged from colonial rule. This latter development took place in Zimbabwe in a way which was very different from the other three. Most attention however is paid to post-colonial politics.

Gaining independence in the mid-1960s Botswana and The Gambia have continued to operate political systems in which opposition parties have exercised their freedom to contest elections and to openly criticize the government. In neither case have any of the opposition parties managed to secure an overall victory at the polls but in both this has to be explained by the ability of the ruling parties to sustain wider popularity and support. In Mauritius, which became independent in 1968, the competitive nature of elections has twice resulted in opposition parties being elected to govern. In Zimbabwe the absence of democracy sustained for so long by the unwillingness of whites to give up racial minority rule was ended largely as a result of pressure from nationalist guerrillas. In 1980 Zimbabwe emerged as a fully independent and democratic state but it has become increasingly clear that the leadership of the ruling party desires a move to a single-party state. This decision appears unshaken by the misgivings of many in Zimbabwe including members of the ruling party, some of whom have been expelled for expressing their doubts publicly. In early 1989 general misgivings were increased by evidence of serious corruption within the elite of the ruling party produced by the Sandura Commission which had been set up to investigate accusations against government ministers and senior party members. Several very senior men were forced to resign. However, even if democracy were to be terminated it does provide an especially interesting and recent example of the problems and workings of the democratic system in Africa.

These four states are different in many ways but in making comparisons it becomes clear that the role of indigenous political leadership emerges as a theme of very considerable importance in explaining the nature of the political process.

Chapter • 4

The Unambiguous Cases

Botswana, The Gambia, Mauritius

ONE HOT AND HUMID SUMMER afternoon a few years ago I went to interview a relatively minor Gambian politician in his shop in Banjul. As is usual on such occasions, the welcome I received was friendly and hospitable. Sitting on the bales of cloth which were his merchandise I explained, by way of introduction, that I was an academic specialist on African politics doing research in his country. At this he suddenly became glum and apologetic, suggesting that I had, perhaps mistakenly, arrived in the wrong state because, as he explained, "we don't have African politics in The Gambia, here we have democracy." Although the reasoning behind this statement is contrary to the argument which is being advanced in this book that there is nothing inherently appropriate about democracy in Africa this little anecdote does exemplify the awareness and pride felt by many Gambians in the rarity of their achievement in sustaining a democratic political system. It is a sentiment that I have often encountered both in The Gambia and in Botswana. Indeed Gambians and Batswana have often pressed me to venture an "informed" opinion as to which of the states is the "most democratic," a request I usually find it diplomatic to evade.

In the light of the very real problems faced by democracy in Africa, the achievement of these two states and of Mauritius in maintaining the system continuously since independence is real enough and the pride expressed by its citizens seems justified. The democratic trio that will be examined individually in some detail in this chapter have, among them, experienced well over sixty years of democratic rule with regular, free, and fair elections; freedom of opposition; freedom of the press and of speech; and all the other characteristics associated with democracy. It is not to detract from this achievement that the realist must add "so far." Although it may be possible to argue that the long duration of democratic survival in itself increases the survival potential as the system becomes more regularized and familiar, there is no guarantee that overthrow will not take place. Just as the abandonment of democracy in other states has certainly not precluded its revival there, so lengthy survival does not preclude abandonment. That there will be challenges and threats in the future is almost inevitable. Democratic rule in The Gambia has already been seriously threatened: an attempted coup by self-proclaimed Marxist revolutionaries in 1981 was only put down with considerable difficulty. Escalating violence in southern Africa will doubtless pose problems for the survival of democracy in Botswana. Although there appears little threat to democracy from specifically domestic sources, the possibility of a major bloodbath in the region cannot be discounted and its potential repercussions for the political systems of the smaller states are incalculable.

BOTSWANA

Situated in the heart of the troubled southern African region, Botswana is a large sprawling country with a relatively small population. With a total land area of 220,000 square miles, it is about the same size as France or Kenya. However, climatic conditions have led to it being one of the least densely peopled states in the world, with a total population of just 1.08 million

(1985 estimate). This population is unevenly distributed, with some eighty percent living fairly close to the line of rail in the eastern part of the country rather than in the Kalahari desert which dominates most of the rest. Despite comparatively rapid urbanization in the postindependence period, the population is still overwhelming rural in character. Even now, only around sixteen percent live in the towns, making Botswana a predominately village-based society.

The key to the size and distribution of the population is water or, perhaps more accurately, lack of it. Rainfall is not only generally low, but also very unreliable from one year to the next, leading to periodic conditions of severe drought, the most recent dating back to 1982, which can prove devastating to the agrarian economy. The exception to this general aridity is the Okavango Delta in the remote northwest of the country, but there is no remotely economically viable way of transferring this water to other parts. Apart from the Delta there is no permanent surface water supply and most has to be obtained from bore holes dug deep in the ground. The depth of the sand cover in the Kalahari, which covers three-quarters of the territory, makes even this impossible there except in a few limited places. The overall problem of water does much to explain the inclusion of the Setswana word *pula* (rain) in the national crest, as the name of the state currency, and as a cry of greeting in all parts of the country.

Botswana is also completely landlocked. While this condition creates problems anywhere in the world, it is especially onerous in the context of southern Africa. The country is surrounded by the Republic of South Africa, Namibia, and Zimbabwe with a tiny, and at times disputed, border with Zambia. Being very heavily dependent on South Africa for transmission of its imports and exports leaves Botswana extremely vulnerable to pressure from its more powerful neighbor. Additionally, many thousands of Batswana men are labor migrants in the republic and while the remittances from their wages are not quite as crucial as they were, any abrupt cessation of this sort of income would pose problems for many.

In the light of this unpromising background it can come as a surprise to learn that since independence Botswana has been one of Africa's (regrettably few) great economic success stories. Although some economists have expressed concern at the patterns of income distribution in Botswana, there is total agreement on the magnitude of economic growth and development.[1] In every year but two since independence, percentage increase in GDP has been in two figures, the highest in sub-Saharan Africa. Central to this growth has been the development of mineral extraction, especially diamonds, which now accounts for more than two-thirds of export revenue. Agricultural development has also been impressive, although vulnerability to drought remains a constant problem, and even in good years Botswana is a net importer of food. Some eighty percent of the population earn their livelihood in the agricultural sector. Economic progress has led to a dramatic improvement of infrastructure. At independence the territory had no roads, few schools, and its capital had only just been moved from Mafeking in the Republic of South Africa. Since then primary school places have more than doubled, secondary school places have increased seven-fold, a new tarred road stretches north-south and health provision has increased dramatically, especially in the rural areas. Furthermore, facilities such as electricity, piped water, and telephone communications, although by no means universally available, have a record for reliability virtually unmatched in Africa.[2] In support of all this Botswana has a bureaucracy renowned for its competence and its seeming immunity to corruption.

For Botswana the problems of social pluralism have never been as acute as they have been for many other African states. The difficulties involved in creating a unified political system from a wide range of peoples and cultures brought together by the arbitrariness of European imperialism exist in a modified and more tractable form here. Nevertheless, given its small population, a considerable amount of social diversity is in evidence, and one should not overlook the skill of the political elites in their handling of this diversity in such a way as to defuse its potentially more problematic nature.

Central to an understanding of the social makeup of Botswana is the distinction between ethnicity and tribe. These two terms, which are often used synonomously when applied to Africa, each have their own distinct meaning here and should not be confused. People of the same tribe do not necessarily belong to the same ethnic group, and different members of a single ethnic group belong to different tribes, or to no tribe at all. The nub of the distinction is that in Botswana tribe is a political grouping whereas ethnicity is cultural. The most fundamental aspect of the definition of tribe here is that of allegiance to a particular chief, although a territorial dimension is not without importance. Although the political role of chiefs has been eroded to some extent at the national level since independence, chieftaincy still lies at the heart of the meaning of tribe. The great anthropologist of the Tswana, Isaac Schapera, wrote that "all natives living in a particular Reserve acknowledge the supremacy of the chief of its ruling community and constitute a single political unit under his leadership and authority. . . . Such a unit is a tribe. . . . It is evident that membership of a tribe is defined not so much in terms of birth as of allegiance to the chief."[3] Although written over forty years ago, this still holds true, albeit in a modified form. Defined in this way, there are eight major tribes in contemporary Botswana. In order of size these are: Bamangwato, Bakwena, Bangwaketse, Batawana, Bakgatla, Bamalete, Barolong, and Batlokwa. The major ethnic group in the country is the Tswana and all the chiefs of the tribes belong to the Tswana ethnic group. However, each tribe contains large numbers of people (sometimes a majority) who belong to other non-Tswana ethnic groups such as Kalanga, Bayei, Ndebele, and Herero. Thus, the tribes are multi-ethnic and the ethnic groups are multi-tribal. Birth and ethnic homogeneity do not define tribal membership, and individuals and groups may change their tribe while maintaining an unchanged ethnic identity. Each tribe has its own totem (e.g., for the Bakwena it is a crocodile, for the Bamangwato, a duiker) which still serves as an emotive symbol of tribal unity.

The population of Botswana also contains a small but important minority of whites, numbering around 5,000, and a few hundred Asians. The concepts of racial equality and tolerance are embodied firmly and unequivocally in the legal and constitutional framework of the state. This strong commitment of the Botswana government to a policy of nonracialism has meant that this white minority in a black state has fared well since independence, in spite of the racial tensions of neighboring South Africa and the fact that most white Batswana are Afrikaners.[4] Individual whites have figured quite prominently in the Botswana political system and have held important positions in the government but without the development of a distinctive and separate white political grouping. In some cases an overwhelmingly black electorate has returned white candidates to parliament in preference to black opponents.

The emergence of Botswana as an independent state in 1966 could hardly be said to reflect the long-term consistency and coherence of British colonial policy in that part of southern Africa. The original decision to grant British protection in 1885 was taken with considerable reluctance following a period of gross indecision. For much of the decade before 1885, the Tswana chiefs had been making persistent requests for British protection against marauding Boers. Initially these requests were rejected and the view of the Colonial Office was well encapsulated by one official who dismissed the area as "a worthless strip of territory." However, in the following years the territory began to look other than "worthless" from the perspective of British strategy in southern Africa, and Cecil Rhodes's view of it as the "Suez Canal to the North" began to look more realistic. The creation of a German protectorate on the coast of southwest Africa in 1884 raised the possibility of a link up between the Germans and the Transvaal Boers, which threatened to cut the Cape off from the interior. It was this strategic question, rather than any humanitarian feeling of protecting the Tswana, which led to the proclamations of 1885. In this year the British extended their power and "protection" over the whole of Tswana territory but divided it into two segments, British Bechuanaland and the Bechuanaland Protectorate. A decade later the former was incorporated into the Cape Colony and is now part of South Africa. Some sections of it make up the "independent" homeland of Bophutatswana. For many years the status of the remaining segment, the Bechuanaland Protectorate, remained contested as Boer demands for its incorporation into South Africa were repeatedly made. British procrastination, which for a long time did not imply any basic rejection of the South African claim, had the effect of preserving Bechuanaland as a separate unit, but it was not until 1963, just three years before the territory gained independence as the Republic of Botswana, that the idea of incorporation was finally abandoned by all sides.

Considering the reluctance with which Britain involved itself in the area, it is hardly surprising that the British were disinclined to commit themselves to any great expense in administration of the territory. The preexisting tribal structure, centered on powerful chieftaincies, made it ideal for the application of the favored system of indirect rule. Under this system most of the day-to-day administration was left in the hands of the chiefs under the rather loose overall supervision of a small number of colonial officials. For most of the colonial period the chiefs retained their power and authority within the tribal structure which dominated the protectorate. It was not until the early 1960s, with independence in sight, that modern political parties emerged to challenge the political preeminence of the chiefs.

Discussion of the role of chiefs leads naturally to the figure of Seretse Khama, the "founding father" of Botswana and the man who, more than any other individual, was responsible for creating and sustaining the democratic system. Seretse was the son of Sekgoma the Second, chief of the Bamangawto, the largest of the Tswana tribes. At the time of his father's death in 1925, Seretse was only four years old. The tribal authorities recognized him as heir apparent (*Morwa Kgosi*—literally "son of the chief") but appointed his uncle Tshekedi as regent until the time when Seretse was old enough to assume his rightful chieftainship. After completing a B.A. at Fort Hare University College (the "black" university in South Africa) Seretse moved to England, where he spent a year at Balliol College, Oxford and then read law at the Inns of Court. During this period he met and married an Englishwoman, Ruth Williams, a romantic attachment that was not only to change the course of Seretse's life, but also to effect profoundly the course of political change in Botswana. The marriage met with opposition from Tshekedi and some other senior Bamangawto royals, but Seretse overcame this when, in 1949, he won the support of a vast Bamangawto crowd at a tribal gathering. However, opposition to his marriage from other sources was to prove more obstructive. To the newly victorious Afrikaner Nationalists in South Africa, with their policies of rigid racial segregation, such a marriage was anathema, and they pressured the British to act against Seretse and his white wife. To their eternal discredit, both Labour and, after 1951, Conservative governments gave way to South African pressure and Seretse was first of all banished

from Bechuanaland and later stripped of all rights to the Bamangawto chieftainship. After a few years Seretse and his family were allowed back to Bechuanaland as private citizens.

However, while official pronouncements by the British could,
and did, affect Seretse's formal legal position, they had little
effect on the emotional relationship between Seretse and his
people. The unique position of Seretse as the recognized, but
not official, chief of the Bamangawto was to become of central
importance to political developments in Botswana. While enjoying the respect, prestige, and authority owing to the chief
of the largest Tswana tribe, he was able to avoid all the petty
ties and restrictions attendant on the role of a Tswana chief.
While retaining a high level of traditional authority, he was
able to emerge as the leader and symbol of the modern political
system, a position he retained until his death in 1980. By a
supreme irony of unintended consequence, the British, in de-
priving the Bamangawto of their recognized chief, created the
circumstances in which the victim of their actions could become the leader of the whole country and one of the greatest
statesmen postindependent Africa has produced.

In comparison with most of Africa the development of modern political parties began much later in Bechuanaland (Botswana) than elsewhere. Even so, there is still some disagreement
as to which was the first political grouping that could be seriously considered to be a party as such.[5] The best claim is that
of the Bechuanaland Protectorate Federal Party, led by Leetile
Raditladi which was founded in 1959, but this party never
achieved any real momentum and fizzled out within a couple
of years. The first party that survived to make an impact on
the political process was the Botswana Peoples Party (BPP)
founded in December 1960. Its three early leaders were Kgale-
man Motsete, Phillip Matante, and Motsamai Mpho. Within a
short time the party was split into factions representing each
of the leaders. The split was perhaps based partly on ideology,
but more realistically represented a leadership quarrel, with
accusations and counter-accusations of corruption and fraud.
For a short time there were, confusingly, three parties claiming
the title of BPP. In 1964 the Mpho faction adopted the name
of Botswana Independence Party (BIP) and shortly afterwards
the Motsete faction became defunct, leaving Matante the leader

of the sole BPP. As a political movement it had been greatly weakened by these developments.

Of much greater significance than any of these was the Botswana Democratic Party (BDP), which in Botswana is most commonly referred to by its nickname "Domkrag."[6] The BDP was created in January 1962, largely on the initiative of Seretse Khama and his close colleague Quett Masire. The latter has quite a different background from Khama, being a commoner and a member of a smaller tribe, the Bangwaketse. The creation of the BDP was due to two factors. The clear trend in British colonial policy by this stage was to move rapidly toward the total independence of its African territories. The African members of the Bechuanaland Legislative Council realized the necessity of creating a national organization to deal with independence in the near future. The BDP was instituted to deal with independence, not to struggle to bring it about. The new party immediately recruited ten out of twelve members of the Legislative Council and from the very start gave the appearance of being the most likely future government of independent Botswana. The second main reason for the creation of the BDP was as a response to the BPP which, despite its chaotic beginning, appeared to offer a direct challenge to the traditional and modern elites in the country. From the very start the BDP has been the largest, best organized, and wealthiest party in Botswana and the only one which can truly claim to be a national party in terms of support, which extends to all parts of the country, even in those areas where the opposition parties have enough support to win seats. The opposition parties have tended to be confined to relatively localized areas of support often based on specific local grievances against the BDP government.

Since its formation, the BDP has been the dominant party and more than two decades later there are no strong signs that the situation is likely to change in the foreseeable future. Elections have tended to be about where the opposition might or might not make some gains rather than about which party was likely to emerge as the overall winner. In March 1965 the first national elections were held to pave the way for independence the following year. As expected, the BDP won a large majority, with twenty-eight of the thirty-one seats in Parliament. The

BPP won just three seats. Two of these were in the northeast of the country where racial and ethnic issues were important, and the third was in Mochudi, the tribal capital of the Bakgatla, where the local chief opposed the BDP.[7] The BIP failed to win a single seat at this stage.

In September 1966 Botswana became independent, with Seretse Khama as its first president and with a BDP government based on a large parliamentary majority. Since that time the most surprising and unusual thing about politics in Botswana has been just how little of importance has changed to any significant extent. The changes that have taken place both in the formal legal institutions of politics and in the structure and electoral performance of the political parties give the very strong impression of being changes in detail rather than any fundamental reshaping. In the surrounding region change has been dramatic, with the coming of independence to Zimbabwe, Mozambique, and Angola following years of guerilla war and the buildup of forces for change, so far unsuccessful, in South Africa and Namibia. In terms of positive economic growth and development, Botswana itself has changed beyond all recognition, a factor not unrelated to its political stability and continuity.

Changes in the legal structure of the political system have been minimal. The president is chosen by the National Assembly acting as an electoral college, with each candidate in the election declaring his choice of presidential candidate before the election. In practice this has always been determined by the party of the candidate. Until 1972 the individual chosen as president had to be an elected MP or become one within six months. A constitutional amendment in that year removed this requirement by making the president an ex officio member of the National Assembly. Presidential candidates do not have to stand for parliament, but they may do so if they wish. In practice BDP presidential candidates have been confident enough to not bother standing for parliament while opposition candidates have stood for both, knowing that their presidential ambitions were unlikely to be fulfilled, but hoping at least to win a seat in parliament. According to the constitution, any MP who might in the future be elected to the presidency would have to resign his parliamentary seat and create a by-election. The logic behind this change is that the duties of president make it impossible to perform properly the role of constituency MP at the same time. The role of constituency MP is taken very seriously in Botswana.

The only other minor change has occurred in the number of constituencies. For the 1965 and 1969 elections there were thirty-one, for those of 1974 and 1979 this was increased to thirty-two, and in 1984 there were thirty-four. It is generally accepted that the delimitation of new constituencies has been carried out solely to reflect increases in the population and changes in its distribution and not to benefit any particular party: as Polhemus concludes, "gerrymandering has not been an issue in Botswana."[8]

The absence of major constitutional change should not be seen as a purely conservative maintenance of the status quo. Rather, it should be seen as reflecting a very positive commitment on behalf of the political leaders of the country to preserve the democratic political system that has existed since just before independence and to defend the values of a free and open competitive democracy. Both Seretse Khama and his successor Quett Masire have continuously and consistently restated their unequivocal support for this type of system and rejected the idea that democracy could be operated in Botswana through a single-party state.[9] This resolve has been enhanced by the very sharp contrast often noted by Batswana politicians between their own system and the absence of democracy in neighboring South Africa.

The party system and the electoral support of the parties have changed a little more than the legal framework, but again the emphasis has been on continuity. The changes are more a matter of altering details than of making fundamental shifts. Botswana has now had an uninterrupted run of five competitive democratic elections, starting in 1965, so the most convenient place to start looking at parties and party support is the election results.

There is obviously insufficient space here to examine all the details of all five elections but the major features stand out fairly clearly in Table 4-1. However, before looking at what these results indicate about party performance, a couple of other points which have a bearing on the figures need to be made. Firstly, it is only the BDP which has the organizational ability and resources to put up candidates in all constituencies.

PARTY	TOTAL VOTES WON	PERCENTAGE OF VOTES WON	SEATS WON
1965 BDP	113,167	80.4	28
BPP (Matante)	19,969	14.2	3
BIP	6,491	4.6	0
BPP (Motsete)	377	0.3	0
Independents	789	0.6	0
1969 BDP	52,518	68.3	24
BNF	10,410	13.5	3
BPP	9,329	12.1	3
BIP	4,601	6.0	1
1974 BDP	49,047	76.6	27
BNF	7,358	11.5	2
BPP	4,199	6.6	2
BIP	3,086	4.8	1
Independents	321	0.5	0
1979 BDP	101,098	75.2	29
BNF	17,324	12.9	2
BPP	9,983	7.4	1
BIP	5,813	4.3	0
Independents	278	0.2	0
1984 BDP	154,863	68.1	29
BNF	46,116	20.2	4
BPP	14,961	6.5	1
BIP	7,288	3.2	0
BPU	3,036	1.3	0
Independents	1,058	0.4	0

Table 4–1. *Botswana Election Results since 1965*

Normally each of the opposition parties individually puts up candidates in half or less of the seats: because they have usually been unsuccessful at negotiating electoral pacts, many constituencies are contested by two or more opposition candidates. Thus, the overall share of votes won by the BDP tends to be disproportionately high, simply because they have the most candidates. However, there are usually a small number of constituencies, always very safe BDP seats, where there are no opposition candidates. As these are constituencies where the BDP could expect a very high proportion of the votes, the absence of opposition, paradoxically, has the effect of reducing the overall size of the BDP vote. At the same time it reduces the percentage turnout in elections, because in uncontested constituencies no votes are recorded as none are cast. Interestingly, the turnout in elections is one area of the political process in which there have been very considerable fluctuations over the period. The overall percentages of the total of registered voters actually voting[10] are 1965, 74.5%; 1969, 54.9%; 1974, 31.2%; 1979, 58.4%, and 1984, 76%. The pattern is clear; starting with a high voter turnout in the pre-independence election, the figure falls steadily to a low point by 1974 and then starts to climb again, ending with an all-time record in 1984. Both the decline and the rise appear to have affected the ruling party and the opposition parties to roughly the same extent. The post-1974 rise reflects a conscious effort on behalf of the BDP government, which was disturbed by the increasingly low turnout in elections. Leaving aside the question of the desirability of high voter participation per se, the BDP became worried that, to the extent that its legitimacy was based on its success in elections, this legitimacy would be weakened if the numbers voting continued to fall. Thus, it was decided before the 1979 and 1984 elections to devote very considerable effort towards increasing the total vote. Extensive voter registration campaigns took place because it was recognized that old lists rapidly became out of date as old voters died off and younger people reached voting age. Before the elections, the government mounted a massive propaganda campaign through the media, using slogans, jingles, and cartoons to urge people to vote. Importantly, it should be noted that the propaganda was aimed simply at persuading people to cast a vote rather than persuading them to vote for a particular party. The campaigns have obviously paid off[11] although there is a limit to how far turnouts can continue to be increased unless voting was to be made legally compulsory, as it is in some other parts of the world.

The clearest and most important fact that emerges from the election results is the continuing success of the BDP. The party has won a large overall majority of seats in every election. It has never won less than two-thirds of the total vote and in three out of the five elections (1965, 1974, and 1979) it won over three-quarters. The fact that no BDP candidate has ever lost a deposit gives a clear indication of their support even in constituencies where they have failed to win the seat. No serious observer of Botswana's elections has ever suggested that they have been conducted in anything but a scrupulously fair manner, which means that the results can be taken as a completely reliable picture of the real size and spread of BDP support.

The continued electoral success of the BDP is explained in a number of ways. Of prime importance is the fact that the BDP government has an outstandingly successful record to campaign on. The record of economic development and growth was discussed earlier. This has been translated into a massive extension of social services, health, education and so on, especially in the rural areas. Botswana is one of those rare countries in which targets laid down in the national development plan are not only reached but frequently surpassed.[12] The government has an excellent record on human rights and civil liberties[13] and has established a considerable reputation for efficient, noncorrupt administration. A good example of the high level of BDP government performance is the way in which it has managed to cope with a succession of serious droughts. In other parts of Africa the sort of drought experienced in Botswana has led to a mass starvation only partly mitigated by humanitarian aid from the outside world. Where the drought catastrophes in other African states have grabbed the world's headlines, the ability of Botswana to cope successfully through its own efforts has gone largely unnoticed. One exception to this neglect is the essay by Holme and Morgan[14] which details the ways in which the response of the BDP government has averted disaster. The authors make clear their belief that the determination to succeed with drought relief is not just due to bureaucratic efficiency but is directly related to the existence of a freely democratic system. They write that "the attention to the needs of the poor stems particularly from the competitive electoral system. . . . The ruling Botswana Democratic Party has recently come to see drought relief as a very effective means of reinforcing its rural support, the principle source of its majority."[15] They conclude that "the critical role that these programmes have come to play in the BDP's election success may convince less democratic governments that food relief can bring much needed popular support."[16]

Having firm control over the government, and hence over the distribution of state resources, has enabled the BDP to respond positively to the sort of local grievances that could otherwise be used by opposition parties to generate support. In several cases, areas that appeared sympathetic to the opposition have been particularly generously treated when it came to development funding.[17] This undoubtedly gives the BDP an advantage, but as Polhemus notes, "it is difficult to fault a democratic government for attempting to respond visibly to the perceived demands of its people."[18] The BDP has also been very successful in retaining harmonious links with most of the traditional leaders in the rural areas. Although in a couple of cases the party has found itself in conflict with dissenting chiefs (in Ngweketse and Kgetleng), in general it has retained their support, which gives it enormous advantages over the opposition in the rural areas.[19] The BDP also gains particularly in the rural areas from being the best organized and the wealthiest of the parties. To organize a national party in a country the size of Botswana takes considerable resources, which the opposition have lacked. Prosaic factors like the number of vehicles at the disposal of the party make a considerable difference when campaigning in the vast remote constituencies of Botswana.

Up to and including the 1979 election, one of the most commonly advanced reasons explaining BDP success was the leadership of Seretse Khama. Because of his unique background he was seen very much as the founding father of Botswana. Apart from his traditional status and prestige, he was a man of high ideals and great political acumen.[20] In July 1980 Seretse Khama died of cancer. The succession to the presidency of vice-president Quett Masire was peaceful, orderly, and constitutional. Masire had been a close friend and colleague of Khama for many years and was recognized as being very able, but doubts were expressed as to whether the high level of success of the BDP could be maintained without the influence of Khama. Masire wisely followed a policy of continuity and faced his first great test in the 1984 elections, the first for the BDP without Khama as leader. As the results indicate, BDP support slipped a little in 1984 but not dramatically so, and it still retained over two-thirds of the total vote. The party under Masire had passed a crucial test. That this was so does not in any way diminish the importance of the contribution Seretse Khama made: it could well be argued that his greatest achievement was to create a system that could survive his passing.

The explanation for the continued electoral success of the BDP is closely connected to the explanation for the relative electoral failure of the opposition parties. Although the opposition has made a significant contribution to politics in Botswana it has constantly lagged behind the BDP at the national level. The most successful of the opposition parties has been the Botswana National Front (BNF) which was formed in 1966, too late to contest the pre-independence election. Since then, it has enjoyed a steady but rather slow growth in its support in every election except that of 1974, when it dipped slightly. The 1984 election demonstrated that, in terms of total vote and seats won, the BNF had established itself quite clearly as the major opposition party, while the others appear to be in decline. At the local level the BNF has experienced real if limited political power through control of several town councils. During its period of existence the BNF has gone through a number of changes. Established as a radical party, it then became a rather uneasy traditional/radical alliance that was dominated by the traditionalists, but since the mid-1970s the radicals have reasserted themselves and have largely retaken control of the party. The BNF was founded in 1966 by Kenneth Koma and Daniel Kwele, following a failed attempt to unite all the opposition in a single party against the BDP. It made little early progress but the situation changed dramatically in 1969 when Chief Bathoen of the Bangwaketse, one of the government's most hostile traditionalist critics, resigned his chieftaincy to join the BNF and fight the election. The 1969 election victories for the party (which included the defeat of vice-president Quett Masire) were all in the Bangwaketse tribal area and largely dependent on the ex-chief. Bathoen used this position of strength to take control of the party and expel many of the earlier leaders, including Daniel Kwele.[21] In 1977 the major radical figure, Kenneth Koma, replaced Bathoen as party president but the 1979 elections still left BNF parliamentary representation in the hands of the traditionalists, although party support was building up in the urban areas, especially in the capital, Gaborone. In the 1984 election the BNF recorded its best ever performance and won four seats to which a fifth was soon added. After the election results had been declared in Gaborone South an unopened ballot box was discovered and the High Court ruled that the BDP victory in the constituency was invalid. In the by-election in December 1984 Kenneth Koma won the seat for the BNF, albeit with a small majority, giving the party control over both seats in the capital. The projected radical image of the BNF was dented a little by accusations that the party was in receipt of South African funding as part of an ongoing campaign to destabilize the BDP government.[22] Before the election the Secretary General of the BNF, Mareledi Giddie, announced that if his party won the election an Nkomati-type agreement would be signed with South Africa (which the BDP has always resisted) but this was denied by Koma. In spite of its undoubted progress the BNF clearly has some way to go before it can expect to pose a serious challenge to the BDP for control of central government. The ruling party recognizes that the BNF is a potential threat to its electoral dominance but has not attempted to resort to illegal methods to meet that challenge. The freedom of the BNF to operate is nicely encapsulated in a telling anecdote recorded by Polhemus, who writes that Koma is "surely the only leader of an opposition party in Africa whose writings were the sole reading matter for sale in the capital city's airport."[23]

At present the other main opposition parties appear to be in terminal decline. The BPP has been reduced to a single seat in its northeast heartland in both the 1979 and 1984 elections, and there is little sign of any renaissance. Shortly after the 1979 election its flamboyant leader, Phillip Matante, died, removing the party's most charismatic figure. The BIP leader Motsamai Mpho held the Okavango seat between 1969 and 1979 but then lost it to the BDP. He failed to regain it in 1984 when it was won by the BNF. Although largely a one-man party, the BIP did make a significant impact on parliament in the decade that it was represented because of the dedication and ability of Mpho. The latter was an ANC member in South Africa and was a "treason trialist" in the 1950s, spending time in South African prisons before being deported in 1960. He was an excellent constituency MP and a supporter of constructive opposition. He once confided to me that "what we need is good government even if this is BDP government." However, lacking resources and a national organization, the BIP faded and Mpho's contribution, valued on both sides of the house in parliament, was lost.

From the founding of the BNF in 1966 until 1982 no new parties appeared in Botswana and those that have been created since have made little impact. In 1982 a Social Democratic Party was announced but failed to achieve any momentum and quickly disappeared. In the same year the early BNF leader, Daniel Kwele, who had had a sojourn in the BDP, announced the formation of the Botswana Progressive Union. Although the party contested the 1984 election it achieved virtually nothing. A Botswana Liberal Party, founded in 1983 by Martin Chakaliso, did not even put up a candidate. While it is always possible that the opposition might make a significant breakthrough or that the BDP could fragment, it is hard to disagree with Wiesfelder's conclusion that "the smart money is likely to remain on continuity as the odds on favourite."[24]

It can be argued—of necessity in a hypothetical manner— that it is the weakness of the opposition that has preserved democracy in Botswana; that the ruling party has never felt seriously threatened and has therefore never had any need to move away from the democratic process. Though such a contention is impossible to disprove while the BDP remains dominant, it may be overly cynical to argue in this way. Weakness has not saved opposition parties in other African states from being eliminated. Both Khama and Masire have not only given democracy their vocal support but have consistently acted in a way supportive of democratic values. The opposition has been perfectly free to put its case to the voters and it is hardly the fault of the BDP that it has not yet had much success in convincing them. At every election since independence the opposition has warned that if the BDP should be returned that would be the last democratic election, but during the more than twenty years since independence this claim has been proved wrong over and over again. Botswana has an enviable record of political freedom, democratic government, and economic development. It would appear that the major threat to these achievements lies in its vulnerability to the might of South Africa rather than to domestic factors.

THE GAMBIA

The small West African state of The Gambia represents an archetypal example of the arbitrary division of Africa by the European colonial powers. Its area of 4,361 square miles makes it one of Africa's smallest countries and in reality it is little more than the banks of the River Gambia. Apart from its coastline it is completely surrounded by Senegal and although it is some 290 miles long it is rarely more than 15 miles wide. The area's contact with Europe goes back to 1445 when a handful of Portuguese settlers arrived, but the establishment of European control did not begin until 1816 when the British founded a settlement at Banjul (known as Bathurst in the colonial period and now the state capital). The establishment of full control over the rest of the country did not take place until the late-nineteenth century, and for most of this period an exchange arrangement with the French was envisaged, whereby Britain would relinquish control in return for other parts of West Africa or, at one stage, Gabon.[25] However, no agreement was ever reached and The Gambia remained under the British who treated it with benign neglect. Thus, the early history of the country was largely haphazard and unplanned in a way which at times verged on the farcical. It is something of an irony that from this unpromising beginning The Gambia has emerged as one of the most stable, democratic, and well run states of modern Africa.

In spite of being arbitrary at the point of origin, a sense of national identity has been created that is more meaningful than that existing in many other African states. In ethnic and linguistic terms The Gambia is remarkably diverse in relation to its size. With a total population of around 700,000 (the most recent estimate), it contains six major ethnic groups—Mandinka, Fula, Wollof, Jola, Serahuli, and Aku—and a large number of minor ones.[26] The Mandinka are the largest group, accounting for more than forty percent of the population. The country contains no powerful traditional chieftaincies or tribes and the traditional chiefs (*seyfo*) have little autonomous power, playing a minor role in the political system. Most areas are very mixed ethnically: mono-ethnic villages exist, but all the divisions (the administrative units into which the country is divided) are multi-ethnic. Islam is the dominant religion: about ninety percent of the population is Muslim, most of the rest being Christian, with a very small number of traditional animists. Economically the country has made slow progress, with periodic reversal due to drought. The basis of the economy is largely agrarian, with groundnuts providing the major foreign exchange earner and groundnut processing being the main industry. Rice, millet, sorghum, and maize are grown mainly for domestic consumption. One significant area of growth has been the tourist industry, which caters for the West European winter market and black Americans visiting Juffere, made famous by Alex Haley's *Roots*, and now contributes nearly ten percent of the GDP. It is ironic that the hot climate, which in the past was a major barrier to European penetration, now provides the magnet for tourists. The Gambia's ability to cash in on its sunshine has been quite remarkable. Unfortunately, the country has no known mineral resources of any value. Funding for development projects has come mainly from abroad. The Gambia's reputation as an efficient, tolerant democracy has made it attractive to donor agencies in Western Europe and the USA. Its Islamic profile has aided the acquisition of funds from the Arab world, and its strongly anti-Soviet stance has brought considerable aid from the People's Republic of China. In spite of this, The Gambia remains an economically poor and vulnerable country.

Until very late in the colonial period party politics was confined almost entirely to the urban coastal areas.[27] The colonial division of The Gambia into Crown Colony (Banjul and its environs) and the Protectorate (virtually all the rest) had a marked effect on political developments. It was not until 1960 that the franchise was extended to include the rural peoples of the Protectorate. By the early 1950s three parties had emerged in the urban areas. The Democratic Party was formed by a Christian minister, the Reverend J. C. Faye, and a specifically Muslim party, the Muslim Congress Party, was formed by

Alhaji I.M. Garba-Jahumpa. In keeping with the spirit of religious tolerance which has been a feature of The Gambia, these two parties merged to form the Democratic Congress Alliance (DCA). In 1951 another party, the United Party (UP) was created by a Banjul lawyer, P.S. N'Jie. Under his leadership the UP became the dominant party in the urban areas and tried to develop some organizational links with the rural people. In this latter respect the UP was completely upstaged in 1959 by the launching of the Protectorate Peoples Party (PPP), which was formed specifically to contest the political dominance of the urban-based politicians by mobilizing the rural people. With a change of name to the People's Progressive Party, the PPP was to become the dominant party in the terminal colonial period and in the postindependence period. The PPP has been led since its inception by Dawda Jawara, a rural Mandinka who had been a senior veterinary officer in the colonial administration and was at that time one of the very small number of protectorate people who had received higher education. With the extension of the franchise to the rural areas, the PPP was in a strong position in relation to its urban-based opponents, and in the preindependence election of May 1962 won a clear overall majority, with nineteen seats to the UP's thirteen, and one for the DCA (the latter soon joined the PPP). On coming to power Jawara set about turning the PPP into a more truly national party, forming alliances, for example, with the Wollof and Aku elites of Banjul. His marriage to the daughter of one of the main financial backers of the UP did much to undermine the latter. In February 1965 The Gambia became an independent state with Jawara as Prime Minister.

Although there has been considerable political continuity in The Gambia since independence, there has been more change, both in the formal constitutional framework and in the party structure, than was evident in the case of Botswana.

In formal constitutional matters the two greatest changes have been the move to republican status in 1970 and the formation of the Senegambia Confederation in 1982. Immediately after independence Jawara signaled his desire for The Gambia to become a republic and a national referendum was held on the issue in November 1965. On this occasion the proposal narrowly failed to gain the necessary two-thirds majority of the popular vote. Although disappointed, Jawara accepted the

decision of the electorate and the proposal was shelved, while
the British queen remained the official head of state in The
Gambia. In April 1970 another referendum was held on the
issue and the necessary majority was obtained. The Gambia
became a republic with a president replacing the queen as head
of state. As the leader of the majority party in parliament,
Jawara became President. Later the constitution was further
amended in time for the 1982 election, to allow for the president to be directly elected in a separate presidential election,
thus increasing the distinction between the executive and legislative branches of government. With the PPP dominant in
parliament and Jawara being able to win a direct presidential
election, the immediate practical consequences of this change
were slight. Presidential and legislative elections do not have
to take place at the same time, but so far they have done so.
In 1982, following an attempted coup d'etat the previous year,
which had been defeated with the assistance of Senegalese
troups (for details see below). The Gambia formed a confederation with its neighbor Senegal.[28] Under the arrangement,
both states retain their sovereignty but a series of institutions
to promote closer cooperation were established, including a
supernational parliament. Since then The Gambia has been
proceeding remarkably slowly on the confederal issue, much
to the annoyance of the Senegalese. The Gambian attitude to
confederation is ambivalent. On the one hand, fairly close ties
with Senegal make a great deal of sense and have existed on
a less formalized basis since independence: on the other, Gambians are wary of any action by their more powerful neighbors
that might be perceived as reducing Gambian autonomy. From
a Gambian perspective there is a narrow line between the desire
for cooperation and the fear of domination by the more numerous (and French speaking) Senegalese.

As in Botswana, there have also been slight increases in the
number of parliamentary constituencies to reflect increases in
population. The independence figure of thirty-two was increased to thirty-four by the 1977 election, to thirty-five by 1982
and to thirty-six for 1987. There have been no complaints that
delimitation of constituencies has been designed to favor any
particular party. Turnout in Gambian elections has been uni-
formly high, reaching a remarkable eighty-two percent in 1977.

Despite the constitutional changes that have been made since independence, the key feature—the existence of an open and competitive democratic framework through which competition for political power is conducted—has remained fully intact. The government of Dawda Jawara has remained committed to this method of organizing political life and none of the changes were designed to have any significant effect on it. Constitutional evolution has thus had a limited effect.

Changes in the political parties that operate within the constitutional system in The Gambia have been very much more extensive than changes in the latter. This is especially true of the opposition parties. All the current opposition parties have been created in the postindependence period, largely since the mid-1970s, and represent postindependence political developments. All of the opposition parties that existed at the time of independence have faded away, although their remnants exercise a small influence in a narrow range of cases. Continuity has been provided by the continuing dominance of Dawda Jawara and his PPP. However, even this is not as straightforward as it may appear, as changes in party personnel have been very marked. There has been a considerable circulation of political elites between ruling and opposition parties. Many current PPP leaders were once in opposition and many of the present leading opposition figures are ex-PPP. Thus, beneath the surface picture of the continuity of PPP dominance lies a very considerable level of political change and fluidity. It would not be too much of an exaggeration to say that it is Dawda Jawara who has represented the one fixed point in the Gambian political scene.

Following independence the then major opposition party the UP went into a steady decline. Perceived by the rural majority as reflecting urban interests and undermined in the urban areas by Jawara's co-option of the urban elites, its support base was eroded. For a short time in 1970 P.S. N'Jie lost control of the party to his brother E.D. N'Jie but regained it following the latter's death in a car crash later the same year. The 1972 election produced only three seats for the party and this was reduced to two in 1977. In 1982 its candidates all lost and in 1987 it fielded no candidates. Some remnants of the UP have defected to the PPP while others offer support to the newer NCP. The old UP leader P.S. N'Jie remains in splendid isolation, motivated, it would seem, only by a personal detestation of

Jawara.[29] In the late 1960s a group of PPP dissidents broke away to form a People's Progressive Alliance (PPA) but the party gained little momentum and after a period in the wilderness most of the dissidents returned to the PPP fold.

By the mid-1970s The Gambia, despite its democratic political framework, appeared to be heading toward a de facto single party state as the old opposition withered. However, in the mid-1970s a new opposition party, the National Convention Party (NCP), emerged. In attempting to create a truly national government Jawara had alienated a number of rural Mandinka, especially in the Baddibu area of North Bank Division, who had previously been among his keenest supporters. Many felt that his power-sharing with other ethnic groups had led to a neglect of the interests of his own group. In addition, the relationship between President Jawara and his vice-president, Sherif Dibba, had deteriorated badly. In 1973 Dibba, a fellow Mandinka, was demoted, following a scandal involving his brother, and as Hughes reports, "he came to be seen among some Mandinka as a victim of the president's policy of favouring non-Mandinka."[30] Seen by Jawara as a potential rival for leadership of the PPP, Dibba was expelled from the party in 1975 and went on to found the NCP, which has since developed as the major opposition party. The negative ethnic image of the party has not been helped by the fact that, along with Dibba, most NCP leaders are Mandinka, in the 1977 election, for example, twenty-five out of thirty NCP candidates were from this ethnic group. However, there is more to the NCP support than Mandinka ethnicity. While the party has done well among the Baddibu Mandinka, it has also done well in the urban areas of Banjul and the suburbs of Bakau and Serekunda. Survey evidence from the latter clearly shows that the Mandinka element is not strongly evident in NCP support there.[31] In the 1977 election the NCP won five seats, and although this dropped to three in 1982 it was back up to five in 1987 when the party won twenty-seven percent of the popular vote. One serious problem for the NCP was that in 1982 and 1987 Dibba failed to win the Central Baddibu constituency he had won in 1977. In 1982 five Independent candidates also won seats but these were all PPP men who had clashed with their local party organizations, and they did not represent a new party formation. In 1975 a Banjul lawyer, Pap Cheyassin Secka had formed an ideologically radical party, the National Liberation Party (NLP). The party, however, performed disastrously in the 1977 elections and ceased to exist soon afterwards.

In late July and early August 1981 an event, or series of events, took place which at the time appeared to shatter The Gambia's record of stability and political tranquility. On July 30 a mixed group of discontented urban youths and lower-rank members of the Gambia's para-military Field Force[32], using the guns of the latter, took control of certain key points in and around the capital, including the radio station. From here they broadcast the announcement that they had overthrown the government and proclaimed a "dictatorship of the proletariat." At this point, part of the Field Force jumped on the bandwagon of the rebellion and part stayed loyal to the government. Jawara, who was in Britain for the royal wedding, announced that he was immediately returning to West Africa, although his own family had been taken hostage by the rebels. As the latter controlled The Gambia's only airport, he flew direct to neighbouring Senegal, where he secured from President Diouf the support of Senegalese troops to help crush the rebellion under the terms of a mutual defense pact between the two countries. There followed a week of fighting in and around Banjul in which it is officially estimated that up to a thousand lives were lost. (Unofficial estimates rise as high as double that number.) Much of the killing involved neither the rebels nor the loyal troops and their Senegalese allies but resulted from the release and arming of convicts in Banjul Prison, who then went on a spree of looting and murder.[33] Gradually the tide turned in favor of the loyal Gambians and Senegalese soldiers and the rescue of the hostages, miraculously unharmed, signaled the final crumbling of the coup attempt. The remaining rebels fled as best they could. Up to a thousand people were detained, although many were subsequently released without being brought to trial. The legal system of The Gambia could not cope with this number of detainees, so judges and lawyers were imported from other Commonwealth countries. This had the additional effect of demonstrating that the due processes of law were being followed. Among those charged was Sherif Dibba, who was later found not guilty and released. There was very little to connect the opposition parties with the coup attempt, although the coup leader, Kukoi Samba Sanyang, had been a (completely unsuccessful) NCP candidate in 1977, but had played no prominent part in the party. The coup appears to have been unrelated to party competition.

It is strongly rumored that, following this bloody nightmare, some elements within the ruling PPP attempted to persuade Jawara to clamp down on opposition and terminate the democratic system. Others argued that it was precisely as a result of the existence of democracy that the attempt generated little support in the country as a whole. Whatever the truth of these rumors, Jawara made it clear that he had no intention of using the coup as a pretext for abandoning democracy in The Gambia, and less than nine months later the 1982 general election took place on schedule, contested by the opposition. If the 1981 coup attempt indicated the vulnerability of Gambian democracy, the fact the system did manage to survive the trauma indicates a certain resilience in the system that might have been doubted in advance. It is perhaps only when a system is severely challenged that one can assess its true strength. In January 1988 rumors of a significant coup plot surfaced in Banjul but proved exaggerated, although three Gambians were later imprisoned for conspiring to overthrow the government.

In 1986 two new political parties were formed. The first was The Gambia Peoples Party (GPP) led by Assan Musa Camara who, like Dibba, had previously been vice-president. Following the 1982 elections, when it was believed that he had been covertly supporting some of the Independent candidates, he had been downgraded by Jawara, by being dropped, first from the cabinet and then from the party secretariat. The final humiliation came with the twenty-fifth anniversary celebrations of the founding of the PPP. Various activities were planned to celebrate a quarter century of the PPP, but the only one in which Camara was invited to take part was a football match.[34] Although he was increasingly alienated from the PPP, his personal relationship with Dibba was such that defection to the NCP was not an attractive proposition. In 1986 he finally set up the new party. At first the GPP had some success and attracted a number of heavyweight Gambian politicians into its ranks, including two former senior PPP ministers and one of the 1982 Independent MPs. Camara was believed to have a considerable personal following and as a Fula was the only non-Mandinka party leader. Both factors appeared to pose a threat to the other parties. However the new party had insufficient time to build up a strong party organization in time for the 1987 elections and was further hit by some defections of early supporters. As it turned out, the GPP did poorly in the election, gaining only thirteen percent of the presidential vote and sixteen percent of the parliamentary. It failed to win any seats, although it did run the PPP a close second in a number of constituencies.[35] It remains to be seen whether the GPP can expand its modest but not insignificant support base in the future so as to seriously challenge the PPP.

The other new party to be created in 1986 was the People's Democratic Organization for Independence and Socialism (PDOIS) formed by Halifa Sallah and Samuel Sarr, both of whom had been briefly detained after the coup attempt.[36] With a distinctive socialist approach, the new party offered a clear ideological choice to the other parties. (In terms of ideology there is not a lot of difference between the PPP, NCP and GPP.) The PDOIS is a small party and is felt to be rather too intellectually remote from the mass of the population. In the 1987 election the party put up only five candidates and did very badly, the best result being twenty percent of the vote in one constituency. Although the party leaders see this as the small beginnings from which a successful party will grow, there must be doubts as to how far it can expand beyond a protest vote mainly in the urban areas. Overall, the 1987 elections suggest that the combined opposition parties have some way to go before mounting a successful electoral challenge to the ruling PPP. While they play an important part in the democratic process, none realistically looks like an alternative government.

Having examined political developments since independence it would be useful to draw together some of the factors that help to explain the survival of democracy in The Gambia. No single explanation appears satisfactory, and it is only by taking into account a variety of features of Gambian politics and society that the reasons may be discerned.

In recent years the analysis of African politics has paid increasing attention to the role played by individual national leaders and to the enormous influence they frequently have on the conduct of politics in their home states. Such notions as "personal rule"[37] and patrimonialism seek to explain the sources of this influence. Most frequently, personal rule has been associated with essentially authoritarian political systems. However, it can be suggested that in The Gambia the personal-rule elements of the system have worked in a way that is supportive of democracy rather than of authoritarianism. This seeming paradox needs explanation. The centrality of Jawara's role in the Gambian political system can perhaps best be categorized as quasi personal rule and quasi patrimonialism. The use of the qualifying prefix "quasi" is needed to avoid overstatement. Whereas personal rule is normally defined as an alternative to constitutional rule, the Gambian case exhibits a mixture of both. In The Gambia, constitutionalism has been an important ingredient in the political process and has been adhered to even when it did not coincide with the aspirations of the national leadership. However, to view Gambian politics in solely constitutional terms would be to leave out the vitally important role of the national leader. As noted, Jawara has been the one fixed point in a Gambian political system that has otherwise been marked by a rapid circulation of elites. Personal relationships with the president play a large part in the rise and decline of members of the political elite. Considerable fluidity is in evidence among elites close to, but not at, the top of the system. The dominance of the national leader has, however, had one unusual consequence. Sir Dawda Jawara has consistently shown a strong personal commitment to an open, competitive, multi-party system even at times when it has not enjoyed unanimous support amongst all his party colleagues. Thus Jawara's personal dominance of his party has helped to ensure the continuation of democracy within the political system as a whole. The key role of Jawara is not limited to his dominance and personal commitment to a democratic system. Commitment would be irrelevant without the ability to make the system work. Jawara is, above all, a very highly skilled political leader. Essentially pragmatic by nature, his political skill has shown itself in his complex balancing of interests and power-sharing between different ethnic and regional groupings, in his ability to retain a large measure of popular support in the country, and, at times, in a certain ruthlessness (which does not extend to physical coercion) with political opponents. The latter characteristic is combined with a tremendous capacity to forgive and forget when reconciliation appears the most appropriate course of action.[38] This combination of personal skill and per-

sonal commitment on the part of Jawara has been an inescapable element of the survival of democracy in The Gambia. It
may also be seen as a point of potential weakness. To the extent
that the system depends on one man (though it does not only
depend on one man), it can be seen as vulnerable to the frailties
of human existence. However, it should be remembered how
well Botswana coped with the death of Seretse Khama after
similar misgivings had been expressed while he was in power.

The Gambia is a small country with a small population. All
parts of the country are readily accessible from the capital and
nowhere is more than a short day's drive away. This has meant
that it is possible for government leaders to tour the country
with ease, which in turn enables them to keep in touch with
grassroots feeling and react to problems before they become
too serious. In his very frequent "meet the farmers" tours, Jawara
makes himself available to just about the entire citizenry. There
can be few Gambians in the rural areas who have not had the
opportunity of seeing the president and putting questions to
him on several occasions. It is easy, not only for government
leaders to go to the peasant farmers but also for the latter to
go to the former. When visiting ministries in Banjul, I have
often been impressed by the way in which ordinary peasant
farmers are able to call in and discuss problems with the relevant minister. In The Gambia, central government is not the
distant, faceless entity that it often seems in much larger states.
Small size not only affects elite-mass contacts but also intra-
elite relationships. If one included all MPs, senior party figures
not in parliament, top civil servants, and businessmen and
leaders of nongovernmental organizations, it would probably
be accurate to say that the political elite of The Gambia at the
national level is not more than about a hundred persons.[39] At
the local level a few senior traditional leaders (*seyfolu*) could
be added. It is not surprising, therefore, that these people tend
to know each other quite well and not infrequently are related
through ties of kinship (not unusual even between "government" and "opposition" figures). This makes conciliation and
compromise rather easier to obtain than it would be among a
much larger group (although it does not guarantee it). Compromise and conciliation can be seen as features of a functioning democracy. Of course small size may assist democracy,
but by itself it does not make it inevitable. Equatorial Guinea

has an even smaller population than The Gambia but under Macias Nguema it produced one of the most violent and coercive political systems Africa has witnessed. Dawda Jawara is no Macias Nguema.

Despite its small size, The Gambia exhibits a high degree of social pluralism. In other African states this type of pluralism has often been associated with political instability and the collapse of democracy. In The Gambia, however, the boundaries between the plural segments are not as sharp as they sometimes are in Africa. Friendship and intermarriage between groups are relatively common.[40] In several Gambian ethnic groups, over half the marriages are exogamous. Most Gambians have kin in religious and ethnic groups other than their own which reduces the chances of political conflict between highly separate and monolithic groups. This relative looseness of plural boundaries is reflected in the political system. Although such factors as ethnicity do on occasion play a political role, they have never dominated the system. The political parties all have a plural support base. No single ethnic group is big enough to strive after political dominance, and the Muslim majority over the Christians is so large as to prevent any serious contest for political dominance. Nor are there any powerful semi-autonomous chieftaincies in The Gambia that could form a contemporary basis for political divisions. Thus, The Gambia exhibits social pluralism but, so far, without the political consequences associated with it in some other African states.

The exact relationship between economic development and the existence of democracy is far from clear in Africa. If a high level of economic growth were necessary to sustain democracy, it would be hard to explain the situation in The Gambia. Since independence the Gambian economy has not made dramatic progress. However, if very significant economic progress is not necessary for democracy to survive, the avoidance of total economic collapse certainly is. Evidence from many other African states strongly suggests that where the economy collapses, democracy is most unlikely to survive. Although The Gambia has had, and continues to have, serious economic problems,[41] it has been far from disaster. Many people, especially in the rural areas, are poor, but in The Gambia they do not starve. The country has not experienced the collapse of services and infrastructure that has occurred elsewhere in Africa. All this may sound a fairly modest achievement but it is one that not all African states have managed, and it has probably provided a minimum level necessary for the survival of democracy.

Since independence the rule of the PPP has not been threatened by the political system; the very serious threat posed by the 1981 coup attempt came from outside the system. Although the party has often lost individual constituencies in elections, the possibility of overall electoral defeat has never looked a likely prospect. Could one say then that the reason that President Jawara has never abandoned the system is that he has never had any compelling reason to do so? One could of course note that in many African states, rather weak opposition parties that did not seem to pose any electoral threat were often banned and that it is rather easier to ban a weak opposition than a strong one. Also, the role of opposition is not only to win elections but to offer public and parliamentary criticism of government performance, either in general or in relation to specific issues, a task which the Gambian opposition has performed. It is true that the ultimate test of commitment to democracy is to maintain it when faced with electoral defeat. As this has never looked likely in The Gambia no definite answer to this question can be given. Under the circumstances the best one can do is to speculate. The question about what Jawara would do if he lost an election is not infrequently raised in private in The Gambia. Having discussed this with a number of politically well informed Gambians, including opposition leaders, I can report that the consensus of opinion is that Jawara's natural inclination would be to stand down. Given his role within the party it might be thought unlikely that the PPP would attempt to cling to power unconstitutionally if the leader did not wish to do so. I offer this not as factual proof (for none is possible) but as informed opinion.

Finally, it is not too tautological to suggest that the longer it survives the more likely it is to continue to survive; that to some extent it has become routinized and self-reproducing. Over twenty years of democratic experience in The Gambia have demonstrated, for that country at least, the fallacy of the argument (most frequently put forward by leaders seeking to justify the banning of opposition to themselves) that in the African context multi-party competition can only lead to divisiveness and the eventual dismemberment of the state. No matter how critical of the government they may be, Gambians do appreciate the freedom they have and would be reluctant to give it up. If the legitimacy of the rulers of The Gambia is based on their ability to win majorities in freely contested elections, abandonment of the system would undoubtedly undermine the legitimacy of those who undertook it and make their long term survival a doubtful proposition.

MAURITIUS

The island state of Mauritius lies some 1,250 miles from the East African coast (or 500 from Madagascar). The state includes the main island of Mauritius, where the bulk of the population live, the smaller island of Rodrigues with a total of just over 30,000 inhabitants, and a number of tiny islands with around 500 inhabitants between them. Despite the intrinsic interest of its social and political systems, it has been largely ignored by political observers who tend to operate within sharply defined regional boundaries. Its regional marginality has meant that, for the most part, both Africanists and Indianists have been doubtful about regarding it as part of their sphere of interest.[42] Yet in many ways it is clearly African, and not just because it is nearer to Africa than to any other landmass. Since independence in 1968, the country has played its part in African affairs. With the ending of colonialism it immediately joined the Organization of African Unity (OAU) and in 1976 the OAU summit meeting was held in its capital of Port Louis. The then prime minister of Mauritius, Sir Seewoosagur Ramgoolam, was chairman of the OAU from 1976 to 1977. In 1970 it also joined the Organisation Commune Africaine et Malagache (OCAM), the francophone grouping of African states.

As a nation state Mauritius is very unusual in having no historically indigenous population. The rich and complex weaving of racial and ethnic groupings that makes up the present population of Mauritius is a result of permanent settlement begun only in the eighteenth century.

Evidence suggests that Arab sailors visited the island as early as the tenth century, but never settled. The first Europeans to discover Mauritius were the Portuguese in 1510 but still no attempt was made at settlement. There were then two short-lived attempts at colonization by the Dutch in the seventeenth century, but they soon abandoned it. Their only remaining influence is in the name of the state which is of Dutch origin. The first permanent settlement began with the arrival of French colonists in 1710. The latter soon began to import slaves from the East African mainland to act as an agrarian labor force. These two groups—white French settlers and black African slaves—provided the starting point for the Mauritian population. In 1810, during the period of the Napoleonic Wars, France lost control of the island to Britain, which remained the colonial power until independence in 1968. The increasing growth of sugar plantations created an enormous demand for labor, and with the ending of slavery, large numbers of Indians were recruited from India to work as indentured workers. The Indians were predominantly Hindu, but also included a significant Muslim minority. To complete the racial mixture, smaller numbers of Chinese moved to Mauritius mainly to work in the retail trade.

The present population of Mauritius, numbering just over one million, is made up of all the above groups in the following proportions: sixty-nine percent Indian (Hindu fifty-two percent; Muslim, seventeen percent); twenty-five percent Creole (people of African or mixed European-African ancestry); four percent Chinese; and two percent whites of European ancestry. It is interesting to note in passing that although the proportions are quite different, Mauritius has the same racial mixture as the Republic of South Africa. Fortunately for Mauritius, the political consequences of this have been quite different from those in the Republic. Marked similarities with this population mix are to be found in many states of the West Indies.[43]

Cultural diversity in Mauritius is even greater than racial diversity. The colonial inheritance is both British and French. English is the official language, but French is also widely spoken, and Creole is the language of the street. Several Asian languages, including Hindi, Tamil, Urdu, Gujerati, and Chinese are also used. All the major world religions—Christianity, Islam, Buddhism, and Hinduism—have significant numbers of adherents. Socially, Mauritius has almost a complete set as far as the human species is concerned. However, intermarriage is common and none of the groups is homogeneous. Like many African states Mauritius is essentially a mono-crop economy, with strong external orientations. Sugar is very much the dominant crop and sugar plantations cover some ninety percent of cultivated land. Until recently sugar accounted for over two-thirds of export earnings. A considerable amount of sugar refining takes place on the island. The size of the sugar plantations varies enormously. Over half of the sugar produced comes from around twenty large estates, including some government-owned, accounting for a high proportion of the paid labor force. There is also substantial production from over 30,000 estates owned by "small planters."[44] Tea, grown in the humid highlands, is the next most important crop, produced mainly by small holders grouped into cooperatives. Tobacco is grown as a cash crop but used mainly in the local production of cigarettes. The government has attempted to increase industrial production, particularly with the creation of the Export Processing Zone (EPZ), which offers attractive tax concessions to investors, both Mauritian and foreign. Although there are problems in the Mauritian economy, especially a high level of youth unemployment, Mauritius ranks as one of Africa's most prosperous states and its per capita GDP is one of the very highest. Because of its strong economy and the relatively high proportion (by African standards) of the labor force in wage employment, the trade union movement is stronger in Mauritius than it is in most African states and has played a significant role in Mauritian politics.

Modern politics in Mauritius can be said to have begun with the creation of the Mauritius Labour Party (MLP) in 1936 by Maurice Cure, a Creole doctor. To some extent modeled on the British Labour Party, it sought to challenge the position of the white Franco-Mauritian planter elite which had, up to that time, dominated the island. The MLP appealed largely to the poorer sections of the community, especially the smaller planters and laborers in the sugar industry, most of whom were Indian. In 1936 and 1937 major strikes occurred among sugar industry workers who made explicitly political demands. In 1938 the (mainly Creole) Port Louis dockers went on strike and the colonial governor, Bede Clifford, declared a state of emergency. During this period the MLP leadership strongly emphasized the class base of the party and its distaste for racial or ethnic communalism. In 1940 Cure stressed that "the workers, Creole or Indian, are all basically the same colour with the same interests united under the same banner. . . . Today the leader of the Labour Party is a Creole: tomorrow it will be an Indian."[45] This competition between class and communalism as rival bases for political organization and support in Mauritius has continued up to the present time. Although at particular times and in particular circumstances one or other of these bases has emerged as predominant, the tension between the two is an ongoing feature of Mauritian politics.

Pressure for political change continued, although it was overshadowed for a time by World War II. Once the war was over, change became inevitable, and in 1947 a new constitution introduced profound modifications to the way the island was governed. This constitution made provision for a legislative council with an elected majority and a large extension of the franchise to include all adults over twenty-one who could pass a literacy test in any language. The wider franchise effectively brought to an end the national dominance of the white Franco-Mauritian elite and increased the power of the Indian community which, if united, was in the majority. The leadership of the MLP passed to an Indian doctor, Seewoosagur Ramgoolam, who was to become the principal actor in Mauritian politics for many years. Under Ramgoolam the MLP was able to combine strong urban trade union support with Hindu rural support.

This period produced a large number of new parties, some of which were distinctly communal in orientation. A Muslim party, the Comitte d'Action Musulman (CAM) was of this type, as was the Independent Forward Block (IFB) based solely on Hindu farm labor support, although both later allied to the MLP. Other communally based parties, such as the Tamil United Party, formed alliances in opposition to the MLP. The main opposition to the MLP came from the Parti Mauricien Social Democratique (PMSD), led by a dynamic young Creole lawyer named Gaetan Duval. The PMSD was supported by the white Franco-Mauritian elites but also by the Creole working class and by some Indians. Parties which could work on the basis of coalitions of communal groups were more successful than those which appealed to a single community.

During the 1960s Mauritius moved towards independence, but this was not quite the foregone conclusion that it may appear in retrospect. In line with events elsewhere in Africa the British favored fairly rapid moves toward full independence for the island. The PMSD, backed by the TUP, was opposed to full independence and favored some sort of permanent "association" with Britain. Full independence was supported by an alliance of the MLP, the CAM, and the IFB. The 1967 election produced a clear majority for the alliance, favoring full independence, although the PMSD did well in the urban areas. In March 1968 Mauritius became Africa's latest new state, with Ramgoolam as the first prime minister. Immediately after independence Ramgoolam brought Duval and other PMSD politicians into a coalition government. This move did not end political opposition to the Ramgoolam government, if that was what it was intended to do, and from 1970 a much more formidable opposition party arose in the shape of the Mouvement Militant Mauricien (MMM). The party was led by a young white Franco-Mauritian, Paul Berenger, who had been much influenced by events in Paris in 1968 when he was a student there and was attracted by Marxism. The MMM appeal was solely a class one and rejected racial or ethnic platforms. It called for widespread land reform and full nationalization of the sugar industry, and gained widespread support among all the communal groups especially among their younger members. Perhaps more worrying for Ramgoolam, the MMM began to successfully recruit support among the trade unions, which had previously backed the Labour Party. By the end of 1971 the MMM controlled three of the most important sugar industry unions, as well as those of the teachers and transport workers. The relationship with the dockers was more ambiguous. Many of the dockers were MMM supporters but not actually controlled by Berenger. In August 1971 they went on indefinite strike that threatened the economy of the externally oriented island, and Berenger failed when he tried to persuade them to return to work. The Ramgoolam government reacted to the threat by declaring a state of emergency and bringing in strike breakers. Berenger and other MMM leaders were detained for twenty days. Although Ramgoolam was acting constitutionally, the state of emergency represented the one significant dent in the democratic record of Mauritius. But it was short-lived. The MMM continued to gain in strength at the same time as the MLP-PMSD coalition broke down and Duval left the government. In the 1976 election the MMM gained the largest number of seats of any single party but Ramgoolam managed to put together a coalition with a majority over his main rivals. Despite bitter opposition to Ramgoolam during the elections, the PMSD once again joined the coalition.

This coalition held up until the time of the next general election in 1982, but it was a turbulent time in Mauritian politics with considerable labor unrest. Part of the MLP broke away under the leadership of Harish Boodhoo to form the Parti Socialiste Mauricien (PSM). In the run-up to the 1982 election the Ramgoolam government started to look weak against a background of strikes, increasing unemployment and inflation, and the prospects for the MMM in a new coalition with the PSM began to look good. Before the election few realized just how strong support for the MMM-PSM coalition really was among the voters of Mauritius. Although Ramgoolam was expected to lose the election, few would have predicted just how badly he would lose or how great the landslide toward the opposition coalition would be. In the election of June 1982[46] the MMM-PSM coalition won all the seats, and after years of presiding over Mauritian politics Ramgoolam was swept from power.

There is no doubt that this represented a landmark in Mauritian politics, but in a very real sense it was also a landmark in the wider arena of African politics. It marked the first occasion in the postindependence period in which the government was changed as a result of the defeat of the ruling party in a free and competitive election. Peaceful political succession through the ballot box had unequivocally arrived in African politics. In the run-up to the election, Berenger had given the chairmanship of the MMM to Aneerood Jugnauth, an ex-minister in the Ramgoolam government, as an attempt (successful as it turned out) to convince the Hindu voters that the party was not in communal opposition to their interests. After the election victory Jugnauth became prime minister and Berenger minister of finance.

It was not long, however, before strains appeared in the new coalition and within the MMM itself when it was faced with the problems of actually governing Mauritius. Berenger unwisely began to campaign for the adoption of Creole as the official national language, and in April 1983 Jugnauth, still prime minister, broke away to form yet another new party, the Mouvement Socialiste Militant (MSM), taking with him a number of MMM politicians. In May the PSM of Harish Boodhoo merged with the new party and in June a new election was announced for August. In the run-up to these elections the new MSM formed an electoral alliance with the MLP and the PMSD of Gaetan Duval to fight against the MMM. The main losers in these political changes were the MMM, and the election proved that Berenger had been out-maneuvered by Jugnauth. The MSM and its coalition partners proved to have great electoral appeal over a wide range of ethnic, racial, and class groupings and emerged with more than two-thirds of the parliamentary seats, with the rest going to the MMM. Thus, in just over one year the MMM had become the first party in postindependence Africa to gain power by defeating the incumbent ruling party at the ballot box and the second to lose power in that fashion. The MMM returned to its previous role of major opposition party and in the municipal elections of 1985 indicated its continued electoral viability by making substantial gains and winning fifty-seven percent of the total vote.

Within two years, however, the political pendulum once again swung against the MMM and in favor of Jugnauth's ruling coalition. In 1987 the economy was in an extremely buoyant state due largely to the success of the Export Processing Zone. The number of companies involved had risen to 425, and export earnings from manufactured goods were rising dramatically. Jugnauth decided to call a general election a year ahead of the expiry of his five year term and the Mauritian electorate went to the polls on August 30. The major contestants were Jugnauth's MSM-dominated coalition, which included the PMSD and the MLP, and an MMM-dominated coalition, calling itself the Union for the Future, which included two smaller left-wing parties. Although Berenger continued to lead the MMM, the party candidate for the premiership, in an attempt to win a larger share of Hindu support, was a high-caste Hindu, Dr. Prem Nababsingh. The election resulted in a fairly comfortable majority for the incumbent ruling coalition, which obtained forty-six seats in the Assembly as against twenty-four for the opposition. Jugnauth was once again prime minister, and his cabinet, announced in September 1987, included an MSM majority, with some positions going to his partners, including

Gaetan Duval who was named deputy prime minister and minister of employment.

The rapid changes in Mauritian politics, brought about by new party formations and splits, defections and reconciliations, coalition-making and coalition-breaking, naturally appear somewhat bewildering to the observer. They might appear even more bewildering if, in the analysis above, I had not chosen to ignore the large number of tiny and ephemeral parties that flitted across the Mauritian political stage from time to time during this same period. But it is vital to remember that, in the midst of all this change, the basic institutions of the political system remained the same as they had been since independence from colonial rule was declared in 1968. The roller-coaster ride of individual politicians and parties cannot hide the central feature, which is the survival of the system: the survival of a democracy which has, so far, produced two peaceful and constitutional changes of government through the ballot box. Whatever the Byzantine maneuverings of the politicians, in the end it is the Mauritian electorate that has had the final say on what has taken place. In trying to draw together those features of the Mauritian political system that explain why democracy has survived, Mauritius's combination of class- and communal-based politics—a combination unique in Africa—is of prime importance. The Mauritian economic system is more developed along capitalist lines (rather than state capitalist lines) than almost any other in Africa. Perhaps only the South African economic system compares with it. However, in the case of South Africa the racial category has been imposed on the system to such an extent by the white ruling elite that the development of class-based political divisions has been greatly weakened. In Mauritius the system has not been purposefully structured in racial and ethnic terms and class has emerged as more of a force in its own right. Economic reality, reinforced by a strong trade union movement and a high level of literacy among the population, has produced a significant level of genuine class-consciousness which is not in evidence in most of the rest of Africa. Thus, attempts by politicians to organize along class lines and to appeal to class in mobilizing political support have a genuine force because they correspond with the political perceptions that exist within the population. In most of the rest of Africa, class-based appeals for support are more alien in form for most of the population and do not have the same impact, except in rather limited areas. However, the descriptive analysis of the development of Mauritian politics already presented indicates that although it is necessary to stress the class element, it would be quite misleading to depict the politics of Mauritius as being solely class-based because the reality is far more complex. Alongside and intermingled with this class consciousness is a consciousness of racial and ethnic pluralism that also makes a significant contribution to the political process. Interests may be perceived in class terms but they may also be perceived in racial and ethnic terms. Similarly, politicians may use the communal divisions as bases for political organization and the building of political support. Appeals along these lines also have a real basis in the political consciousness and perceptions of the population. Mauritian politics at elite or mass levels cannot be seen as simply class-based or simply community-based but as a mixture of the two. At certain times and in certain places one or the other may become predominant. Thus, for example, the rise of the MMM, and particularly its spectacular success in the 1982 election, may be seen as indicating the temporary ascendancy of class politics which then waned, subsequently leading to the electoral defeat of the party the following year. The evidence of the postindependence period suggests that politicians and parties that are able to blend together both types of political identification tend to be more successful more often than those that appeal to one and exclude the other. Parties such as the CAM or the TUP, playing only the communal card, end up as impotent or minor partners in alliances dominated by more broadly based parties. Conversely, the class-based MMM, while emerging victorious in 1982, was subsequently outflanked by parties and leaders more sensitive to the communal divisions of politics.

This combination of class and communalism has important implications, not just for the rise and fall of individuals and groups, but also for the survival of the system. The creation of two quite different types of cleavage within the political system results in the existence of large numbers of crosscutting ties, so that individuals divided by one form of cleavage are united by another form of cleavage. Thus, for example, Indian plantation laborers are communally separated from Creole dockers but share common class identifications. The existence of these crosscutting ties militates against the creation of monolithic political blocks seeking to dominate the system through a zero sum (lose all–win all) approach to politics. The class divisions reduce the danger to democracy of an unrestrained communal conflict that might otherwise threaten it. The evidence presented by postindependence politics in Mauritius indicates that it would be unwise to adopt any highly deterministic evolutionary view suggesting that in the long run either class or community must predominate to the exclusion of the other. Such a situation is always possible but it is not a necessary or, in the foreseeable future, a likely outcome.

One of the recurrent themes of this book is that politics cannot be understood solely in terms of a clash of impersonal social and economic forces that determines the shape and outcome of the political process. Individual political leaders also have a hand in shaping political developments and are not simply corks bobbing about on a sea of forces that they do not control. In explaining the survival of democracy in Mauritius one must also point to the role played by Mauritian political elites. The latter have, in the main, shown themselves to be pragmatic and skilful and quite willing to accept the sort of compromises and temporary setbacks which democracy often entails. Sir Seewoosagar Ramgoolam, described by one observer as "a master of the politics of accommodation,"[47] provides an outstanding example of this sort of approach, but many others could be included and events suggest that Aneerood Jugnauth is following the same path. Even the Marxist-inspired Paul Berenger never attempted to impose an intolerant authoritarianism on the system despite the overwhelming success of his MMM in the 1982 election. As with previous examples of democratic survival, this approach is facilitated by the small size of the country and its political elite. It is these political elites that have made the system work.

Chapter • 5

Democracy under Threat

Zimbabwe

IN SOME WAYS it may seem a little odd to include in a survey of the survival of competitive democracy a state that appears to be moving irrevocably towards the extinction of such a system. If President Robert Mugabe continues on his present course it would appear that competitive democracy will cease to exist in Zimbabwe by 1990. Indeed if he chooses to act unconstitutionally, the demise of the system could possibly come even earlier although this would require a very sharp break with his preference, so far, for acting within the constitution. Thus it may well be that the democratic period in Zimbabwe will be relatively short. Having been resisted for so long by white supremacists it may well be abandoned by their successors. The former denied democracy by restricting the size of the electorate, largely along racial lines. The latter may well deny it by restricting the choice available to the newly enlarged electorate with the introduction of a single-party state. The previous system allowed free choice of parties but only so long as the majority of the population were not in a position to exercise that choice. The future system may well allow the whole population to choose, but only so long as they do not have a free choice to make. Only the present system, which has existed since the downfall of the white supremacists in 1980, allows for reasonably free choice for all of the population. And yet the fact that it does exist at the present time necessitates its inclusion here. If the guaranteed indefinite survival of a type of political system were an essential prerequisite for discussing it, political scientists would never have anything to write about, given the inevitable flux and change in what they observe. At the time of writing there does appear a high probability that competitive democracy will be extinguished in Zimbabwe, but so long as it lasts it does have a role in the politics of that country and needs examination.

The developments and events which led to the establishment of a democratic political system in Zimbabwe in 1980 are relatively well known but will need some elucidation here to give historical context to the discussion. The nature of colonial rule and control in what is now Zimbabwe was different from that which existed in most parts of anglophone Africa. This difference is explained by the fact that it was one of the few African territories that attracted significant numbers of white settlers. Up until 1923 the territory was effectively administered by Cecil Rhodes's British South Africa Company. In that year a high level of autonomy was granted to the white Rhodesian settlers. Although the 1923 constitution granted Britain a veto power over racially discriminatory legislation, it was not a power that was significantly used by the British who, for most of the period, were content to let the settler government run things as they wished. Strictly speaking, the franchise was nonracial but voting qualifications based on literacy, property ownership, and a minimum annual wage meant that in practice the electorate was almost entirely white. Participation in the political system was virtually restricted to whites, and successive governments acted in white interests. The greatest impact of the racial imbalance in political power was on the question of land allocation. Most of the best farming land was allocated to white settlers and the vastly more numerous African farmers were restricted to the poorer land, which was insufficient to sustain them. This created circumstances in which many Africans were forced to accept wage labor on white farms, and later in white-owned industry, to survive. Land alienation was the most crucial aspect of white control and was later to provide the basis of rural support for the guerilla armies seeking to overthrow white rule.

The almost complete disenfranchisement of the overwhelming bulk of the population remained a feature of the political system in the ensuing decades. In 1953 the Central African Federation was formed to include Southern Rhodesia (later Rhodesia, later Zimbabwe) and Northern Rhodesia (later Zambia) and Nyasaland (later Malawi). The CAF was supported by the white settlers of the territories, most of whom lived in Southern Rhodesia: Nyasaland and Northern Rhodesia had very much smaller white settler populations. The Federation was opposed by the growing African nationalist movement in all three component territories because it was seen as a device by which white settlers, mainly white southern Rhodesians, sought to preserve dominance. Amid growing African opposition, the Federation survived for ten years until 1963. Following its breakup, Northern Rhodesia and Nyasaland rapidly moved to independence under majority rule in 1964 as the new states of Zambia and Malawi. White resistance to the principle of majority rule was to delay formal independence for Rhodesia for more than a decade and a half. British insistence on NIBMAR (no independence before majority African rule) was unacceptable to the majority of the white settlers and in 1965 Prime Minister Ian Smith, whose political party the Rhodesian Front (RF) had won substantial victories in the elections of 1962 and 1965, decided on a total break with Britain. On November 11 the Unilateral Declaration of Independence (UDI) was announced. Britain declared this action illegal and economic sanctions were imposed on Rhodesia. Negotiations between Ian Smith and the British prime minister, Harold Wilson, held on HMS *Tiger* (in 1966) and on HMS *Fearless* (in 1968) failed to produce any settlement. A new constitution in 1969 precluded the possibility of any real progress towards democracy via the enfranchisement of the majority of the population. The majority black population was supposed to be represented by ten chiefs who had minimal power under the constitution.

If anything, the inclusion of the chiefs only served to reduce still further the legitimacy they had already largely lost through being identified as agents of white political control.

With Britain huffing and puffing impotently on the sidelines, real opposition to the white minority government of Ian Smith came more and more to be focused on the African nationalist movements of the territory. At that time the nationalist movement, which had a lengthy pedigree, was somewhat divided, with two major groups competing for support. These were the Zimbabwe African People's Union (ZAPU) formed in 1961 by Joshua Nkomo and a breakaway movement from the latter, the Zimbabwe African National Union (ZANU), formed in 1963 by Ndabaningi Sithole with the support of, among others, Robert Mugabe. Both movements were banned and their leaders were either arrested or fled into exile to organize continued opposition to the Smith regime.

In 1971 a new agreement was worked out by the British government and Ian Smith which, although modifying white domination slightly left no real prospect of majority rule in the foreseeable future. The acceptability or otherwise of these proposals to the African population was tested in 1972 with the arrival in Rhodesia of the Pearce Commission. African opposition in the country to the proposals was organized by a new political grouping formed for that purpose, the African National Council (ANC), led by a Methodist bishop, Able Muzorewa. In advance many people believed that the Pearce Commission had been set up to try to give a cloak of legitimacy to the proposals that would have given the Smith regime legality and ended Britain's (by now rather unwilling) participation in the conflict. The Commission, however, was not a whitewash and was determined to test opinion as genuinely as it was able to. Its report in May 1972 made it clear that the proposals were not acceptable to the mass of the population. The opposition organized by Bishop Muzorewa had been successful and the proposals were abandoned, leaving the conflict undecided.

Further negotiations, now involving other powers like the United States, continued in a desultory fashion but it was becoming apparent that armed opposition from the African guerilla opponents of the regime was to be the crucial component of the struggle for democracy in Zimbabwe. The guerrilla struggle was enhanced by the breakup of the Portuguese African empire in 1974. The latter meant independence for neighboring Mozambique which was willing and able to assist the guerrillas, particularly by provision of a safe base. International pressure played a subsidiary role. Attempts to form a single military organization from the ZANU and ZAPU guerrillas by the creation of the Zimbabwe People's Revolutionary Army (ZIPRA) largely failed, and for most of the civil war period the two nationalist groups remained apart and somewhat hostile toward each other. Supported by the Shona majority in the population, ZANU was a much more formidable force than ZAPU, backed by the minority Ndebele. Using the bases in Mozambique, Mugabe's ZANU guerrillas came to dominate much of the countryside, especially in the east. Two recent books by Terence Ranger and David Lan[1] have added significantly to our understanding of the relationship between the guerrillas and the rural peasantry at this time. It was the support of the latter for the former that facilitated the eventual victory of the rebels and ended white minority rule. Contrary to white regime propaganda, the mass of the peasantry supported the aims of the guerrillas. As Ranger demonstrates, support was based on the development of an overtly radical peasant consciousness which was "highly conducive to mobilisation for guerrilla war."[2] But this was radicalism of a particularly peasant type. At its heart was a profound opposition to the land alienation and the administrative interference in production that had characterized the white-ruled state. Because of the overwhelming importance of the land question there was sufficient affinity between the peasant perspective and the guerrilla perspective to provide the basis for unified political and military action. Of course, the radicalism of the nationalist guerrillas, or at least of their leaders, contained added strands of a socialist and collectivist nature, but these were played down or neglected in dealings with the peasants. Ranger reports that he "found no evidence to suggest that . . . the guerrillas preached the virtues of collective or even of co-operative farming."[3] This needs to be borne in mind when assessing the support for collectivist policies in Zimbabwe. Lan's work also stresses the question of land alienation as the crucial factor in determining peasant support for the guerrillas. His focus is on the role of spirit mediums in providing a basis of legitimacy for the armed struggle of the guerrillas. Through possession, the mediums provide a link with the ancestor spirits, most importantly with those of the *mhondoro* (royal ancestors) during highly elaborate possession rituals. As government policy had the effect of turning living chiefs into relatively minor civil servants and state functionaries, so the authority of the ancestors became even more crucial and the political role of the mediums who provided the only link with them grew. The reconciliation of the legitimacy of the long-dead ancestors with that of the guerrillas, which the spirit mediums were uniquely able to bring about, was based more than anything on the issue of land. Guerrilla promises of a return of ancestral lands stolen by whites were highly compatible with the role of the *mhondoro* spirits in protecting the land for their descendants.

The successes of the guerrillas began to put great strains on the Smith government. The war was damaging the economy, costing a million dollars a day to maintain, and white males were finding themselves almost permanently conscripted into the army.[4] Despite the herding of more than half a million African peasants into "protected villages" to try to deny the guerrillas their support, the government was losing control of the rural areas and many white farmers were forced to abandon their farms. In an attempt to stave off the inevitable, Ian Smith patched up an "internal" settlement with cooperation from Bishop Able Muzorewa and Ndabaningi Sithole but this failed to gain international recognition or to stop the civil war. The enormous damage that association with the settlement did to the political careers of Muzorewa and Sithole became evident in the 1980 elections. Although the settlement offered many more concessions than Smith had previously offered, it became obvious that without the involvement of Nkomo and Mugabe, now rather tenuously united in the Patriotic Front (PF), it could provide no solution.

In May 1979 the Conservative Party under Margaret Thatcher won power in Britain. Commonwealth leaders persuaded her not to recognize the internal settlement but to work for an agreement which would include the PF. It was to be one of the great ironies of history that a particularly right-wing British government was to pave the way for the election of a self-proclaimed Marxist as prime minister of Zimbabwe. All the parties to the dispute met at the Lancaster House Conference and against the expectations of many (certainly including this author) an agreement was hammered out that was to pave the way for a democratically elected government in an independent Zimbabwe.[5]

The constitution that was agreed upon accorded well with democratic principles, although the notion of equal representation was modified to guarantee whites disproportionate representation, at least until 1987.[6] The Zimbabwean House of Assembly was to consist initially of eighty members elected on a common African role and twenty on a separate white role. There was also a Senate consisting of ten members elected by the whites in the House of the Assembly, fourteen elected by the African members, ten elected by the Council of Chiefs and six appointed by the president on the advice of the prime minister. A British governor was appointed to supervise the transition to independence and organize the elections, and the period of UDI was formally brought to a close.

Much to the surprise of many, the guerrillas collected at sixteen designated assembly points, where they were supervised by a joint British and Commonwealth force. The elections were held in February 1980 under the supervision of 500 British police and a Commonwealth observer group to make sure that they were free and fair. Perhaps the strongest proof of the impartiality of British supervision of the election was the fact that the least favored candidate of the British government won the election. The Commonwealth observer group also concluded that the election was free and fair.

One question to be faced by the successful guerrilla leaders was whether to fight the election under their collective PF banner or to fight as separate parties. Nkomo maintained that the unity of the PF should continue into the election, but Mugabe was unwilling. It is ironic, in the light of Mugabe's later support for the notion of a single-party state, that he could have had what de facto would have been close to that in 1980 if he had so wished, as the two segments of the PF won nearly all the black-role seats. It was obvious that, to the extent that Mugabe was willing to share power, it was only in a situation which he himself could dominate and in which he could dictate the terms. Nkomo chose to retain the PF banner into the election while Mugabe fought as ZANU (PF). The addition of PF to the title ZANU was as much as anything to distinguish it from the party of Sithole which was still using the ZANU label. In the end, while the two parties dominated the black-role elections, the results indicated a split that rather ominously coincided with the ethnic groups of the separate leaders.[7] Nkomo's PF won twenty seats with twenty-four percent of the vote, but its support was largely confined to Matabeleland, where the Ndebele are the largest ethnic group. Nkomo is Ndebele. Across the rest of the country, which is Shona-speaking, ZANU (PF) emerged with fifty-seven seats and sixty-three percent of the total votes cast. Mugabe is Shona. Able Muzorewa's United African National Congress (UANC) was left with eight percent of votes and just three seats. A variety of smaller parties emerged with no seats and a minimal share of the votes. All twenty of the white-role seats were won by Ian Smith's Rhodesian Front: in most constituencies they were unopposed.[8] With a clear majority, both in parliamentary seats and in the proportion of the total vote, the 1980 election was a decisive victory for ZANU (PF) and its leader Robert Mugabe, and Zimbabwe finally emerged as an internationally recognized state with Mugabe as prime minister and Canaan Banana as president.

Thus, after decades of undemocratic white minority rule and a bitter civil war, democracy finally emerged in Zimbabwe. There is no doubt that the 1980 elections were democratic. Apart from the anomaly of the separate white role, which gave whites a disproportionate number of parliamentary seats, the election results broadly reflected the wishes of the Zimbabwean people and the balance of political support that the parties had. For the first time the whole citizenry of Zimbabwe was able to freely choose their representatives from a wide range of competitive alternatives and had exercised that choice.

How then has the democracy that was finally established fared in the postindependence period? Although its long-term future is clouded by the distinct possibility of the creation of a single-party state, the record so far is a complex mixture of democratic survival and authoritarian impulses and action. In terms of a competitive party system that offers the Zimbabwean electorate a real choice, the system has largely survived, and for the 1985 elections that choice was still available. In broad outline the party system has not changed much since independence. The white party of Ian Smith that changed its name first to the Republican Front (the previous name Rhodesian Front could hardly be maintained) and then to the Conservative Alliance of Zimbabwe (CAZ) continues to have majority support among the shrinking white electorate. Precise figures are difficult to obtain but it is estimated that at least half of the whites (around 100,000) have stayed in the country since independence and recent reports suggest that many who initially went to South Africa are now returning, as the conflict in that country becomes more violent. The shrinkage of the white electorate had the effect of making the twenty reserved seats even more disproportionate. An increasing number of whites, however, are turning away from the leadership of Ian Smith as a thing of the past and adopting a more conciliatory attitude toward the black rulers. This is in response to efforts made by Mugabe himself to push for racial reconciliation and harmony following the horrors of the war. In party political terms a significant number of whites broke away from Smith to form the Independent Zimbabwe Group (IZG) in time for the 1985 elections. Relationships between the two major black parties, ZANU (PF) and the PF (still thought of by most Zimbabweans simply as ZANU and ZAPU) alternated between reconciliation and sharp hostility, but both were still around in reasonable shape for the 1985 election. Other smaller black parties have come and gone without making much impact on the political system, but several continue to exist.

The results of the general elections of 1985 provide a good picture of the strength of party support and the changes that had taken place since 1980.[9] While recognizing that the second election was not as free of intimidation and violence as that of 1980, these defects need to be kept in perspective. The political violence that did take place in the run-up to the elections, however regrettable, was relatively small-scale and certainly not enough to invalidate the results, which still give a reasonably accurate portrayal of the state of play in Zimbabwean politics. In the black-role elections Mugabe's ZANU (PF) emerged with an even larger majority than before, with seventy-six of the total votes and sixty-three seats. This was increased to sixty-four following a by-election that resulted from the death of one of its candidates prior to the election. Although the PF lost some of its share of the vote, it still retained its support base in Matabeleland where it won all fifteen seats, while losing the handful it had previously had outside of that region. The Sithole faction of ZANU won one seat and all the others, including Muzorewa's UANC, won none. In the white-role elections Ian Smith's CAZ won fifteen of the seats, but his support was much less monolithic than in 1980. The more progressive and conciliatory IZG won four seats and the final one went to an Independent candidate. Mugabe expressed dismay that so many whites were still prepared to vote for his old archenemy Ian Smith and was disappointed at the failure of his party to make any significant headway in Matabeleland, but overall the results represented a sound, if not overwhelming, victory for ZANU (PF). The party remained the dominant majority party even if support for it was not ubiquitous.

In trying to assess the performance of democracy since independence, it is necessary to look beyond the rise and fall of parties and their electoral successes. However important these may be they do not tell the full story. The major arena of conflict in postindependence Zimbabwe has been that involving, on the one hand, Robert Mugabe, his ZANU (PF), and the central government, and on the other, Joshua Nkomo, his PF, and Matabeleland. On neither side of the conflict do the component parts listed overlap to such an extent as to make them synonymous. Joshua Nkomo is certainly not Matabeleland and he is not even PF, but his relationship with Mugabe's government cannot be understood outside of that context. One is dealing with broad constellations of forces.

In the immediate postindependence period, reconciliation was the prime aim. Mugabe brought Nkomo into his cabinet and gave him the important Home Affairs portfolio (the cabinet also included a couple of whites not closely tied to Ian Smith). The relationship, however, steadily deteriorated and Nkomo was demoted first to public service minister and then to minister without portfolio. By 1983 the relationship was so bad that Nkomo fled Zimbabwe to temporary exile in Britain, claiming that his life was being endangered by central government forces.[10] This was not simply a personal clash between two forceful individuals, but has to be related to what is known as the "Matabeleland problem."[11] For some time armed bands of dissidents had been operating in Matabeleland attacking and robbing government outposts and many private individuals. The Mugabe government claimed that they were Nkomo supporters intent on bringing down the government and backed by South Africa. Nkomo claimed that they were nothing to do with him, had no links with the PF or ZAPU, and that the problem was being exacerbated by Mugabe's hostility to the Ndebele and unfair favoring of the Shona. Mugabe overreacted to the perceived threat, fearing the development in Zimbabwe of an antigovernment terrorist movement similar to RENAMO in Mozambique and with similar South African backing. The North Korean-trained Fifth Brigade, seen by many as Mugabe's private army, were sent to Matabeleland. Abundant evidence exists to support the contention that the Fifth Brigade launched a campaign of terror in Matabeleland, harassing and killing many ordinary peasants who had nothing to do with the dissidents. Supporters of Nkomo and his party officials often seemed to be singled out for especially brutal treatment by the Fifth Brigade, although it was never altogether clear that this was inspired by official government orders. That a genuine threat to national security which required the use of government force existed in Matabeleland cannot be denied. Fear of, and vulnerability to, neighboring South Africa may partly explain why the government reacted as it did, but it is hard not to conclude that the campaign was also aimed at intimidating political opponents who were simply part of the legal opposition and not pursuing a policy of armed confrontation with the government or threatening state security. Politically, the campaign may well have been counterproductive and increased the alienation of the Ndebele. It is certainly the case that the arbitrary violence involved "only antagonised Matabeleland's inhabitants further and made peaceful rapprochement more difficult and distant."[12]

Throughout 1986 and 1987 talks between the two major parties concerning their possible unification continued in an episodic fashion subject to frequent breakdown and restart. In 1987 the government escalated its pressure on Nkomo's party. In June the party was banned from holding rallies in Matabeleland. In September its offices in Matabeleland were forcibly closed and the six district councils that it controlled were dissolved. In October one of its MPs, Mr. Francis Mukombwe, was detained. These actions were excused by continuing, but still unsubstantiated, assertions that the PF was responsible for dissident activity in Matabeleland. Seventy-year-old Nkomo was in an impossible situation. Party activity was becoming increasingly curtailed and Mugabe's intention of banning all opposition parties in 1990 left little if any scope for future development. In December 1987 the veteran nationalist leader agreed to his party being absorbed into the ruling party. In spite of public rhetoric from both sides on the benefits for national unity, and the awarding of cabinet posts to Nkomo and two of his colleagues, Maurice Nyagumbu and Bernard Chidzero, it is hard to see the move as other than an enforced takeover which, in practice if not in law, brought Zimbabwe closer to being a single-party state.

A more positive (in a democratic sense) assessment of developments in postindependence Zimbabwe can be made when judging other aspects of the polity. The rule of law has been in the main upheld and the judiciary has shown a considerable independence of the ruling group. There are a number of clear examples of judges finding against the government and ensuring adherence to the constitution.[13] Considerable press freedom has existed and numerous criticisms of the government have emerged. The Catholic Commission for Justice and Peace in Zimbabwe has been particularly forthright in defending human rights: Mugabe is himself a Catholic.

Thus it can be argued that, broadly speaking, democracy has just about survived in Zimbabwe since independence even though the workings of the system have been rather patchy in democratic terms in relation to some issues and events. The survival of democracy in the medium term is, however, very much in doubt due to Mugabe's expressed desire to create a single-party state. If he continues to act in accordance with the constitution this would be most unlikely to take place before 1990, as the change would require total unanimity among all 100 members of the House of Assembly. It is always possible that a change to a single-party state could be engineered unconstitutionally, but so far Mugabe has exhibited a clear adherence to constitutional correctness and has actually stated that the proposed change would only take place "in the fullness of time and in accordance with the law and the constitution."[14] It would, however, be wrong to personalize the single-party-state issue by relating it solely to the wishes of Mugabe. In fact, the latter has already gone to considerable lengths to restrain the hardliners in his own party who have advocated a crushing of the PF and other opposition parties and an immediate introduction of the single-party state. Perceptions of Mugabe as a hardline Marxist intent on building a totalitarian Marxist state in Zimbabwe are far from accurate. As the national leader he has been subjected to highly conflicting pressures from all sides and has, if anything, tried to steer a middle course. Because of this he has been criticized every bit as much from the left as from the right, both inside and outside Zimbabwe. On economic matters he has been very pragmatic and conciliatory, especially in his dealings with the economically vital large-scale white farms. Politically, he has been less pragmatic and conciliatory, but even here the picture is very mixed.

The justifications advanced for the introduction of the single-party state in Zimbabwe[15] are an odd mixture of traditionalism, nationalism, and Marxism, but it is hard not to conclude that dislike of opposition by the incumbent ruling group provides the main motivation. Many Zimbabweans, and not just members of the opposition, have expressed grave doubts about the advisability and justice of the proposed change, but at the time of writing it would appear that although these voices may be heard they are less likely to be heeded.

In conclusion, one would have to say that it looks likely that the survival of democracy in Zimbabwe will be of shorter duration than the other examples of democratic survival thus far examined. It is not clear yet exactly what form single-party rule may take. Mugabe has said that it will be possible for nonparty Independents to compete in elections which would enlarge the element of choice for the electorate beyond what is normally permitted in such systems. The extreme volatility of the crisis in the whole southern African region makes any precise political prediction of any degree of certainty unusually difficult. The main explanation as to why the survival of democracy, so long denied by the white supremacists, may be short lies with the attitudes of the ruling elite. When Mugabe argues that "ZANU (PF) will rule in Zimbabwe forever, there is no other party besides ours that will rule this country,"[16] it can hardly be seen as conducive to democracy. Unfortunately, it also carries enormously strong echoes of similar statements in other parts of Africa from rulers and parties long since consigned to the scrap heap of history.[17] Those who make peaceful change impossible make violent change inevitable, as the fate of the white rulers of the past in Zimbabwe testifies with abundant clarity.

Part • Three

REVIVAL

THE CASES OF CONTINUOUS SURVIVAL of democracy in Africa are limited in number and can be seen as the exceptions which prove the rule, although it is arguable how many exceptions can exist before a rule is subverted rather than proved. However, the extent and influence of democracy is not confined to these survivors. At any given moment in time they form only a part of the overall strength and extent of democracy in Africa. Particularly since the late 1970s, democracy has been revived in a number of states in which it had previously been replaced by more authoritarian types of rule. Any assessment of democracy in Africa has to take the revivals fully into account. In some cases the revivals have not survived, and democracy has been undermined by a failure of consolidation. However, across Africa as a whole the pattern has been for the failed revivals to be replaced by others and even in many states where revival has yet to take place the early stirrings of a movement back to democracy can be seen.

The most common circumstances in which the revival of democracy in Africa has taken place have been part of a process of demilitarization. Military governments anxious to return the states which they have governed to civilian rule revive democracy as a mechanism for facilitating the transfer of power back to civilian leaders. This process, in which rule in an authoritarian state is democratized in its terminal period to pave the way for the transfer of power, has very striking parallels with what happened at the end of the colonial period. Most of the examples of democratic revival to be examined here occurred in this way. Nigeria and Ghana are examined as case studies. In both cases competitive democratic systems were revived after periods of military rule, as it happens, both in the same year, 1979. In neither case was democracy consolidated. The governments which the elections produced experienced extensive problems, many of their own making, and were subsequently deposed again by the military, in Ghana on December 31, 1981, and in Nigeria two years later to the day. The next three cases to be examined are Uganda, Liberia, and Sudan. These three present more doubtful cases of democratic revival, although the reasons for the doubts are different in each case. The Central African Republic, Burkina Faso, and Mauritania are then briefly examined as ephemeral or partial revivals. The final case to be examined is one in which the military has not been involved in any way in the process of democratization. Senegal provides a unique case, so far, of the revival of a competitive party democratic system emerging directly from a single party system without any military involvement. It can also be regarded as the most successful revival to date.

Some of the revivals may have been relatively unsuccessful, but the very fact that they took place is a testament to the continuing desire for democracy on the part of many Africans. In each case undemocratic alternatives were available. The fact that the democratic alternative was chosen in preference to a more authoritarian one indicates the continuing strength and influence of the former. This remains an observation which has ongoing importance in African politics even when a revived democracy is imperfectly realized and later collapses. Single-party and military regimes quite frequently collapse, but nobody would argue that this indicates they are irrelevant to Africa because of this. Neither does the evidence of the collapse of democracy in particular states indicate its irrelevance.

In the terminal colonial period the colonial elites were a part of the process that produced democratic political systems. Although I have previously argued that the adoption of such systems owed much to the democratic forces of African nationalism, the influence of the colonial powers would still have to be taken into account as part of the equation. In the cases of revival this factor is no longer present. The desire for democracy and the establishment of democratic systems is based entirely on indigenous African forces. Where democracy results in such circumstances, it can be seen as a result of pressures, desires, aspirations, and beliefs which lie entirely within African political systems a quarter of a century after the end of colonial rule.

Chapter • 6

Democratization without Consolidation

Nigeria and Ghana

NIGERIA

NIGERIA IS THE GIANT of black Africa in more ways than one. Its vast territory (over 356,667 square miles) is the home of perhaps one in four of the total population of the continent. Apart from saying that Nigeria has the largest population of any African state nothing else can be said with certainty about Nigeria's population total. Every postindependence census has been distorted, often for political reasons, and its most recent, in 1973, was later abandoned. Recent estimates vary from 70 million to 120 million, but all contain a large amount of guess work. Physically, Nigeria ranges from the dense rain forests of the south to the dry and dusty fringes of the Sahara in the far north. In social and economic terms it exhibits enormous diversity. Ethnically it is the most diverse state in Africa, with around 250 different ethnic groups. Some, like the Hausa-Fulani of the north, the Yoruba of the west, and the Ibo of the east, are very large, but it is a mistaken simplification to see Nigerian politics as entirely revolving around these larger groups. The so-called minority groups (a term usually used to describe all but the big three) are also extremely important and many comprise larger numbers of people than the total populations of Africa's smallest states. Nigeria also exhibits a religious division between Christians and Muslims. The observation that the Muslims dominate the north and the Christians the south also hides numerous exceptions. Many of the southern Yoruba are Muslim and the population of the so-called Middle Belt (the southern part of the north) includes many Christians. Indigenous local religions also have many followers and frequently Islam and Christianity exhibit localized characteristics as they blend in with the local to produce syncretistic variants. The colonial division of Nigeria into a Northern Region, Western Region and Eastern Region has often blended in with ethnic and religious factors to produce a high level of regional conflict, although the evidence does suggest that this was less of a problem in the Second Republic than it had been earlier. Due partly to the nature of colonial rule, the north has always been regarded as the least developed of the regions and although this is less true than it was, the problem of uneven development has continued to be an issue in Nigerian politics. It has to be recognized that conflict based on ethnicity, religion, and regionalism often has an important economic, but nonclass, basis. Because of its higher level of economic development than most other African states, the role of class has become more prominent in Nigerian politics, but at the national level it has yet to challenge the dominance of ethnicity, religion, and region and still plays a more minor part in the political process. Economically, the development of Nigeria has been dominated in the postindependence period by oil. Although commercial extraction of oil in Nigeria began in 1957, in Nigeria it was not until the 1970s that it became dominant, through a combination of a major increase of production and a major increase in oil prices following the success of the OPEC cartel in forcing up world oil prices. By the mid-1970s oil was producing the bulk of government revenue and ninety percent of export earnings. At the same time eighty percent of the population was still engaged in agriculture, mainly of a small-scale peasant type. While the oil money poured in, relatively little was used to diversify Nigeria's economic base, a failure for which the country is now paying the price. Just as Nigeria had benefited enormously from the rise in world oil prices, so it has suffered equally enormously from the decline in those prices since the early 1980s. With a declining price per barrel of oil and greater restraints on production forced on Nigeria by OPEC membership, the Nigerian economy has moved from boom to slump. Although still richer than many African states, the Nigerian economy was, by the late 1980s, in a state of crisis with little prospect for any significant change in the situation.

In comparison with other African states, Nigeria has produced a vast social science literature, increasingly written by Nigerians, which it is impossible to do justice to here.[1] Apart from a brief background, the focus will be squarely on the events leading up to the revival of democracy in 1979 and an examination of how it functioned and how it came to be overthrown by yet another military coup.

Nigeria as a defined political unit has existed for rather less than a hundred years, although the societies which it encapsulates have a long and complex history. The process of welding these societies into a workable and enduring institutional framework is still in some ways incomplete. Since 1960 the task has been in the hands of Nigerians, but it must be accepted that they have not been greatly assisted by their colonial inheritance. For most of the colonial period the British rulers hardly saw their role as one of producing a cohesive independent state and even when this task was accepted, late in the day, it was indifferently performed.

The name Nigeria was first proposed by Flora Shaw in an article in *The Times* in 1898 to refer collectively to several British protectorates on the river Niger. The amalgamation of the protectorates was completed by Lord Lugard in 1914 when, in theory at least, a single governmental system, with a single Governor, was established for the territorial area of Nigeria. This development fell far short of total fusion, and different parts of the territory continued to be administered separately and in different ways. The use of indirect rule, of which Lugard was the great exponent, was dependent on preexisting political systems and these varied enormously. The politically centralized emirates of the north were well-suited to the system but it worked much less well in the west and was virtually impossible to apply in the east, where stateless societies, lacking powerful traditional chiefs, were the norm. The 1946 Richards constitution established a nation-wide legislative council, with some elected representation, but also consolidated the Northern, Western and Eastern Provinces (later Regions) with their own councils. Although the latter had little power, they provided an unfortunate basis for the destructive rivalries that flourished after independence. As Crowder notes, "their creation has subsequently been severely criticised as being the foundation of tribalism in Nigerian politics."[2] Such criticisms are exaggerated, but they are not without a basis in reality. The 1954 Lyttelton constitution advanced the process with the creation of a tripartite federal system based on these regions.

Few Nigerians would disagree with the view that the rivalries of the political system are best dealt with through a federal structure. However, in retrospect, this particular federal system, which survived into the independent period (with a further unit, the Midwestern Region, created in 1963), appears little short of a recipe for disaster. The design of an appropriate federal structure for Nigeria is a process that still continues but there can be little doubt that the one inherited at independence was wholly inappropriate.

Nigeria became an independent state in 1960. In the period of the First Republic, which lasted until 1966, the political system was formally that of a competitive party democracy but it is doubtful whether, even if the notion of imperfectly functioning democracy is used, one could describe the operation of the system as democratic in any meaningful way. Although there existed a large number of political parties there were three main ones: the Northern People's Congress (NPC), the Action Group (AG), and the National Council for Nigeria and the Cameroons (NCNC–later called the National Council of Nigerian Citizens). None of these parties, or indeed most of the minor ones, could be categorized as a national party. Each was dominated by a particular ethnic group and received the overwhelming bulk of its support from the region where that particular ethnic group was dominant. Although complications and ambiguities existed, one could say broadly that the Hausa-Fulani in the north supported the NPC, the Yoruba in the west supported the AG, and the Ibo of the east supported the NCNC. The consolidation of regional control by the different parties was reinforced by their willingness to use a high level of violence against parties from another region. In the north, for example, the level of thuggery and obstruction was such that few candidates from outside the region were even able to lodge their nomination papers for elections. Relations between the regions were often so hostile that "negotiations between them often took on the aspects of foreign relations rather than co-operation between parts of the same system."[3] This was despite the fact that many of the party leaders had previously been leaders of Nigerian nationalism. As Oyediran puts it, "Azikiwe had ceased to be Zik of Africa but Zik of the Ibo nation . . . and soon Awolowo emerged as champion of Yoruba nationalism."[4] Although the party system was structured around regional-ethnic groupings, it represented a mixture of both cultural particularism and material interest. An example of this mixture can be seen in the case of the NPC, which was almost totally dominant in the Northern Region and, because the latter could claim a majority of the population (this was open to argument), was also the main governing party in Nigeria as a whole. The party was organized by the powerful traditional leaders in the north who used the traditional frameworks of social organization and administration for the party machine. Support for the party was engendered through appeals to tradition, especially to Islam. As Whitaker notes, "parties which in effect declared their intention to transfer authority from a traditional to secular and democratic base were regarded by the emirs not as legitimate opponents but as heretical and subversive elements."[5] This applied even to the other main northern party, the Northern Elements Progressive Union (NEPU), led by Aminu Kano. Support for the NPC was not based only on the traditional heirarchy and appeals to ethnic loyalty. Economic interest was also important. At independence the north was grossly disadvantaged in economic and, especially, educational terms. As entry to most senior jobs in the public sector, including the upper ranks in the army, was based on educational qualifications, the majority of senior posts were filled by southerners even in the north. The picture emerged of a numerically and politically dominant north attempting to use its control of central government to promote northern interests and northern control of the state. A further negation of democracy in this period was that in the Northern Region women did not have the vote, so half the potential electorate were disenfranchised.

As the political crisis grew, the Western Region became virtually ungovernable. Anxious to extend its control, the NPC had used their local man, Chief Samuel Ladoke Akintola, to split the AG and jail Awolowo. Elections degenerated into massive violence and a state of emergency was declared. By 1966 democracy had broken down completely in Nigeria and the political system showed every sign of falling apart. In January 1966 the first Nigerian military coup d'etat took place but this did nothing to resolve the crisis; if anything, it made it more serious. It was quite apparent that the army was no more unified than the civilian sector and mirrored the same tensions and splits. In the January coup six of the seven major plotters were Ibo, the officer who emerged as head of state (although there is no evidence that he was directly involved in the coup plot), Ironsi, was an Ibo, and most of those killed were northerners including the leader of the NPC, Ahmadu Bello, and the prime minister, Abubakar Tafawa Balewa. The coup was followed by large-scale revenge massacres of Ibo civilians in the north and, in July, a specifically anti-Ibo counter coup in which Ironsi was assassinated. Events continued on their disastrous course, leading to the proclamation of secession by the Ibo east to form the state of Biafra and to a bloody civil war that lasted nearly three years. Had secession succeeded, the Ibo dominated Biafra would have been a very wealthy state because it included most of the major oil-producing areas. Like most civil wars, the one in Nigeria was fought with incredible bitterness and atrocities on both sides. Eventually, in 1970, the forces of the federal government, led by General Gowon, defeated the Biafran secessionists and the war came to an end. Gowon embarked on a policy of reconciliation ("no victors—no vanquished") which is generally recognized as having been remarkably successful. He also promised a return to civilian rule by 1976, but in October 1974 announced that this was not possible and that because of problems within the country it was to be postponed indefinitely. Against a background of increasing government corruption and inefficiency (although Gowon himself was not corrupt) this indefinite prolongation of military rule was extremely unpopular within the country. It came as no great surprise when, in July 1975, the Gowon regime was toppled by a further coup. The leaders of the coup promised a return to civilian rule by 1979 and set out a clear and coherent time-table as to how this was to be achieved. To their credit, the military rulers stuck to their schedule despite the assassination of the new head of state, Murtala Muhammed, in a botched attempt at a counter coup in February 1976. Nigerians gen-erally accepted that the comparatively lengthy period between the announcement of demilitarization and its coming into ef-fect represented a desire to see that the process ran smoothly rather than an attempt by the military to prolong their control of the state for a few more years. Before initiating the process of working out the mechanisms of the postmilitary political system, the regime took a number of decisions that, although not directly part of that process, were closely associated with it. The division of Nigeria into states that constitute the com-ponents of the federal structure was at the time a contentious issue. Gowon had divided Nigeria into twelve states, but the demands for this number to be increased had met only with procrastination by him. Just a week before his assassination, Murtala announced a new nineteen-state structure and while this did not satisfy everybody, it did take enough heat out of the issue for a return to civilian rule on this basis to be seriously contemplated. (In September 1987 two more states were added, but a continued demand for more states will be a feature of Nigerian politics for some time to come.) The 1973 census which Gowon had hoped would pave the way for civilian rule, but which was widely known to have been rigged, was aban-doned by the new regime. The latter also agreed to undertake the sensitive task of reducing the grossly inflated size of the army.

Most of the detailed work on the drawing up of the new constitution which would structure the Nigerian political sys-tem was left in the hands of civilians. Although the military leaders offered some general points for consideration (for ex-ample, that the constitution should reflect the "federal charac-ter" of the country) and retained a final veto power, they were not much involved in the day-to-day deliberations. Two main stages were included in the constitution-making process. Be-tween 1975 and 1976 a Constitution Drafting Committee (CDC) was given the task of producing an initial draft which provided the basis for the final version to be produced by a Constituent Assembly (CA). The CDC was a relatively small body of fifty individuals appointed by the military government. Membership of the CDC included two "representatives" from each state and a number of academics from such disciplines as law, political science, history, and economics, who were seen as possessing special expertise in political matters. The CDC included a number of senior politicians who had been prominent in the first republic but who had not been too closely associated with the malfunctions of the system. These included Aminu Kano, the NEPU leader, Bola Ige, the publicity secretary of the AG, Richard Akinjide, former federal minister of education, and Nuhu Bamali, the former foreign minister.[6] Of all those appointed, only Chief Obafemi Awolowo declined the invitation to serve, claiming that he did not have the necessary skills in legal draftsmanship. The CDC was chaired by Chief F. R. A. Williams, a leading Nigerian lawyer. The draft produced by the CDC was then submitted to the CA, which was established in 1977. The CA was a much larger body than the CDC and the bulk of its membership was elected rather than appointed, as had been the case of the CDC. Two hundred members were elected through electoral colleges based on the newly democratized local government structure. They were divided among the states in such a way as to recognize population differences but at the same time include members from all parts of Nigeria. Most states had around ten members on the CA; Sokoto had most with fourteen and Niger least with seven. Twenty other members were nominated by the supreme military council along with the seven subcommittee chairmen of the CDC to ensure some continuity. The chairman of the CA was Mr. Justice Udo Udoma, with Mr. Justice Buba Ardo, another CDC member, as his deputy. The CA included five women, of whom four were nominated and one was elected.

The meetings of the CDC were held in private while the CA was much more open to public view. Partly because of this, the deliberations of the CA were marked by far more argument and disagreement than those of the CDC. Also, as an (indirectly) elected body the members of the CA were more identified with constituency interests, which they sought to protect. In the end, despite many heated debates, the conclusions of the CA were little different from the original CDC draft. One issue over which the CA differed from the CDC and the one over which the most heated debate took place (including a walkout and a boycott for three weeks in April 1978) was concerned with the precise role of the Islamic Sharia Federal Court of Appeal. The anti-Sharia group argued that the CDC provisions discriminated against non-Muslims who should not be subject to Muslim law. The pro-Sharia group accepted defeat in the end, but promised to reopen discussion in the future. Nigeria's status as a secular state was preserved intact.

Probably the least contentious issue faced by the CDC and the CA was whether or not a competitive party system should form part of the Second Republic. Support for a single-party state was negligible and there was a consensus that Nigeria was much too complex and diverse to even consider this possibility. Even a radical "minority report" from two left-wing academics on the CDC, Olusegun Osoba and Yusufu Bala Usman, did not challenge this consensus and argued that politicians should be even more accountable to the mass of the population.[7] The general attitude to multi-party democratic competition can be summed up by quoting from Professor B. O. Nwabueze, Nigeria's leading constitutional lawyer, who was a member of the CDC, chairman of one of its subcommittees and a member of the CA. Nwabueze writes that:

> *Freedom of political association is important to democratic government because, while free discussion assures to the community information and participation in public affairs, freedom to form a political party enables those who are politically inclined and share common ideas about government to associate and organise together in order to make their advocacy of their ideas more effective, and to seek, ultimately, an opportunity to implement them by persuading people to vote them into power on the basis of those ideas. . . . democracy has little meaning without a free competition between associations of persons with opposing ideas about government. . . . without an organised party in opposition, government may tend to take the people for granted and may become unresponsive to their feelings. . . . the political responsibility of the government to the governed can only be realised in the context of an organised opposition party alert to expose to the public*

the weaknesses and failures of the government, and ca-
pable of accepting the mantle of office should the people
be inclined to bestow that upon it.[8]

Survey evidence presented by Margaret Peil[9] suggests that
Professor Nwabueze's views on this matter are reflected in the
mass of the population. She reports that "one-party proponents
always take third place to those who prefer several or two
parties. . . . there is a widespread fear that a single party will
lead to dictatorship."[10] Thus, available evidence suggests that,
far from being a misunderstood alien import, competitive democracy has widespread popular support among the Nigerian
population at all levels of society. On more than one occasion
Nigerians have had good reason to be dissatisfied with the way
democracy has operated in their country, but their attachment
to it as a system is genuine and it is not surprising that this
issue was the most easily agreed upon by the CDC and CA.

However, while there was a broad consensus amongst the
makers of the 1979 constitution that a competitive party system
should operate, the constitution makers also had to face up to
the political problems this could create. The experience of the
First Republic, in which political parties were based almost
entirely on sectional communal interests, could possibly be
repeated if no action were taken to try and prevent it. As the
sort of party conflict that had taken place between 1960 and
1966 had come perilously close to tearing Nigeria apart, it was
decided that this time certain restraints on the operation of
parties would be needed and that these restraints should be
included in the constitution. The major logic behind these constitutional constraints was that parties contesting for power
should all be national parties and that the sort of parties that
had operated by appealing to particular regional, ethnic, linguistic, or religious sectors of the community should not be
allowed to contest elections. Although the initial formation of
political parties was unrestricted, the constitution laid down
certain provisions that had to be met if a party wished to contest
elections. These provisions are laid out in section 202 of the
1979 constitution.[11] No party was permitted to contest elections
unless: a) the names and addresses of its national officers are
registered with the Federal Electoral Commission (for details
of the Commission see below); b) the membership of the as-

sociation is open to any citizen of Nigeria irrespective of his place of origin, sex, religion, or ethnic grouping[12]; c) a copy of its constitution is registered in the principal office of the Commission in such form as may be prescribed by the Commission; d) any alteration in its registered constitution is also registered in the principal office of the Commission within thirty days of the making of such alteration; e) the name of the association, its emblem, or motto does not contain any ethnic or religious connotation or give the appearance that the activities of the association are confined to a part only of the geographical area of Nigeria; and f) the headquarters of the association is located in the capital of the federation. These provisions represent a clear attempt to balance the freedom of party activity against the centrifugal tendencies inherent in Nigeria's diversity. A few Nigerians did argue that it would be best to ignore divisions of this type in the hope that they might go away of their own accord and that to include some brake on them in the constitution was to encourage them. This was however very much a minority view and failed to gain significant support. There are, of course, limits to how far legal constitutional constraints can correct the divisive tendencies in Nigerian politics, but as will be seen later in discussions of party support patterns, it does appear that constitutional engineering of this issue did have some degree of success. While there would obviously come a point at which restrictions on party formation would become so overbearing as to negate the idea of competitive party democracy, the 1979 Nigerian constitution was a long way from that point. Rather it should be seen as an adaptation to fit local circumstances in which the basic principles remain intact.

Apart from the rules relating to political parties, a further constitutional attempt was made through provisions relating to the election of the president to force the political leaders to cultivate a national rather than a sectional appeal. The constitution provided for the direct election of an executive president which was a departure from the First Republic, in which the presidency was a largely honorific position. As a constitutional safeguard against candidates attempting to win by securing monolithic support in a particular region, it was decided that the winning candidate, apart from securing the highest number of votes, needed to gain at least one quarter of the votes in at least two-thirds of the states. Thus, it was hoped that the situation in the First Republic in which the NPC could control the system purely by dominating the Northern Region could not be repeated in the Second Republic. As will be shown later, the rather imprecise meaning of "two-thirds of nineteen" led to considerable controversy.

In concentrating on those aspects of the constitution relating to democratic competition and political parties that most concern our present interests, there is only very limited space to mention other aspects. There are, however, several good full-length studies of the constitution written by leading Nigerian academics[13] which should satisfy the appetites of those interested in the details of constitutional law. Here, only some of the major points can be briefly highlighted. In terms of supervizing the organization and conduct of elections, the role of the Federal Electoral Commission (FEDECO),[14] which had been set up by the military government, was crucial and politically sensitive. FEDECO had widespread responsibilities concerning all aspects of the elections. It was responsible for delimiting the constituencies, the voter registration, the examination and registration of parties, running the elections and the arbitration of electoral disputes where they might occur. Even if FEDECO had not been dealing with matters subject to strong partisan interest, the logistical problems alone would point to the enormity of their appointed task. Assessments of the performance of FEDECO under its chairman, Chief Michael Ani, do vary but the conclusions of Jinadu are probably fair when he writes that "credit must be given to the Commission for its limited success. . . . it succeeded by and large in establishing confidence. . . . the election might not have been 'hitch free,' but the results were generally accepted."[15]

The legislative structure of the Second Republic represents a separation of powers between the federal and state levels within a federal system. At the federal level there is a house of representatives and a senate, with the former being more important. Each state of the federation has its own legislature and governor. Certain powers relating to national concerns were restricted to the federal level through an exclusive legislative list. The state houses of assembly had powers to make laws on every matter not included in the exclusive list. There was also a concurrent legislative list that included matters like postprimary education and electric power where both levels of government had legislative powers.

The 1979 Nigerian constitution is often categorized in the literature as an "American-style" constitution. This seems to me to be a rather misleading categorization in some ways. Certainly there are obvious similarities between the United States and the Nigerian Second Republic. Both are federal systems with a directly elected presidency, and an overlap in nomenclature is evident in "senate" and "state governor" and so on. The U.S. has no monopoly on these features. There seems an inherent danger that somehow, by implication, the U.S. is then seen to be included in the blame for the failures of the Second Republic. The U.S. was not involved in any way in the drawing up of the constitution, nor was any other foreign state. No doubt many on the CDC and CA, perhaps especially the academic members, were familiar with the American system of government, but there was no attempt to copy it. The 1979 constitution was an outgrowth of a debate in Nigeria by Nigerians and was designed to provide solutions for what they (in the main correctly) saw as the political problems of the First Republic. It was these perceptions of the Nigerian historical experience that shaped the constitution, and parallels with other systems need to be seen as coincidental. Personally, I find the implication that Nigerians merely sought to copy a foreign blueprint not only misleading but offensively patronizing.

In September 1978 the ban on political parties that had been in force during the military period was finally lifted and they were free to form. It is recognized that covert discussions had been taking place among groups of politicians before that date. The initial result of the lifting of the ban was a rapidly escalating proliferation of parties that formed, merged, and split almost by the hour. Many of them were quite schizophrenic in their desire to be all things to all men. The mood of the moment was brilliantly caught by the Nigerian satirical columnist Candido who writes for the daily newspaper *The New Nigerian*. He announced that the "comrade chief doctor Alhaji Candido was establishing a party dedicated to democratic dictatorship and capitalistic socialism." Among the individuals and organizations which supported the "party" were "Chief B.

O. Smugla and the Nigerian Smugla's vanguard, General P. S. Nairaflow (dismissed), millionaires anonymous, Master Yaro Wayo, the child genius who had won his first 10,000 Naira contract at the age of 10 and comrade J. J. Marx-Keynes, Nigeria's first millionaire socialist importer and exporter."[16] At one stage something like fifty parties of varying size and complexion were in existence, but by December, when FEDECO began its deliberations to decide which met the constitutional provisions for entitlement to contest the elections, nineteen were put forward for examination. Of these just five were eventually recognized as fulfilling the requirements and being sufficiently national in character and organization.[17]

As the parties were forming there was intense speculation as to how much they would be the lineal successors of the old First Republic parties. As it happened, this turned out to be only partly the case. Those who had expected completely new political groupings to emerge were surprised at the level of continuity, while those who had expected a simple reincarnation of old alliances were surprised at the level of change. The first party to be launched was the Unity Party of Nigeria (UPN), led by the veteran Yoruba politician, Chief Obafemi Awolowo. The UPN was the party in which the clearest lines of lineal descent from the First Republic could be traced. In terms of organization and, to a large extent, personnel, the UPN appeared as a reborn version of the AG, although not all the former AG leaders could be tempted into joining. The fact that the party was formed just one day after the ban was lifted indicated the extent to which it had been organized in an informal manner in the period leading up to the legalization of parties. Although Awolowo attempted to project the party as a national party and included many non-Yoruba in the leadership, perceptions of the UPN as Yoruba-dominated persisted. Attempts to persuade senior northern politicians into the party largely failed. The UPN described itself as democratic socialist and promised universal free education and health care if elected. However as Dudley noted, "the UPN's claim to be democratic socialist in orientation has to be seen as one in which, for tactical purposes, the 'democratic' and the 'socialist' components of the party's ideology are packaged in different mixes with each mix being sold to different segments of the population in the hope of maximising total electoral support."[18] The party also exhibited a strong personal element and it was no surprise when it adopted Awolowo as its presidential candidate with Philip Umeadi as his running mate.

The National Party of Nigeria (NPN), which soon appeared the most formidable of the parties, was quite different from the UPN in this respect, as it had no "ready-made" leader at its formation. The core of the NPN consisted of many of the northerners from the constituent assembly and some heavy-weight ex-NPC men. One of the reasons for the absence of an obvious leader was that so many of the very top NPC men had lost their lives in the 1966 coup. However, although northerners clearly appeared as the dominant group in the NPN, the party was able to ameliorate its regional image by recruiting support on a wider base in Nigeria. As Dudley remarked "the former regions of north, east, and west had been pulled together in a new consensus that was being forged by the NPN."[19] Ideolog-ically, the NPN was fairly conservative, although by no means as reactionary as the old NPC. In a competitive struggle[20] Shehu Shagari, an ex-NPC federal minister who had also served as a federal commissioner under the Gowon regime, emerged as party leader and presidential candidate. Alex Ekwueme, a wealthy Ibo architect, was chosen as Shagari's running mate and a Yoruba, Chief Akinloye, became chairman of the party.

The People's Redemption Party (PRP) was formed by a mi-nority of the members of the group that launched the NPN. It was led by Aminu Kano, the old NEPU leader who had been the main opponent of NPC in the north in the First Republic. Although the NPN accused the PRP leaders of forming the party only as a result of their failure to gain the top posts in the NPN, the explanation of the divergence is more clearly associated with ideological differences. Aminu Kano had always been among the most radical of the old northern politicians, al-though his radicalism was of a nationalist populist style rather than scientific socialist. He drew into the party many of the younger radicals, particularly northerners, but also a signifi-cant number of southerners. In some ways the PRP looked like an academic party given the number of young social scientists and historians it attracted to influential positions. Many of these people were more coherently Marxist-oriented but were willing to accept the looser radicalism of Aminu Kano and the PRP when it became obvious that the party was likely to be the most left wing of any with a realistic chance of gaining a share of political power. As will be seen when the election results are examined, the national support for the party reflected perceptions of it being a Kano party rather than having much to do with its ideological orientations. Ideology was more important to the leaders of the party than its supporters. Within Kano, however, there is evidence to suggest that ideological and class-based perceptions of the PRP did effect electoral support for the party and that here it was seen by many as representing the interests of disadvantaged peasants and workers.[21] In terms of the traditional rivalry between Sokoto and Kano (the city, not the man) the PRP was perceived in opposition to the NPN of a Sokoto man, Shehu Shagari.

The remaining two parties recognized by FEDECO emerged from a split in what initially was a single party. The Nigerian People's Party (NPP) started as a tenuous coalition of the anti-Sharia, anti-Awolowo members of the CA and representatives of many of the minority ethnic groups. Soon after its formation it split into two factions, one led by Alhaji Waziri Ibrahim and one by Chief Adeniran Ogunsanya. The Waziri Ibrahim faction broke away to form the Greater Nigerian People's Party (GNPP) with him as its leader and presidential candidate. The Ogunsanya faction retained the NPP title and chose the old NCNC leader Nnamdi Azikiwe as its presidential candidate.

If these five parties were to be placed on an ideological spectrum, it would read, from left to right, PRP, UPN, NPP, GNPP, NPN. This would have to be recognized as a very loose categorization and probably only for the PRP was ideology an important part of its raison d'etre. All the parties pledged their support for national unity, but this was only to be expected. Perhaps the most immediately outstanding feature of the parties is that all of them were led by veteran politicians of the First Republic and even earlier. In fact it seems that, apart from those actually killed off in the various political turmoils of Nigeria, all the old politicians were back and in commanding positions. This surprised a number of people, especially as Azikiwe and Awolowo were well into their seventies. Neither appeared in a "senior statesman" role on the fringes, but as active participants at the heart of the political struggle. Many younger Nigerians, especially among the intellectuals, were dismayed by this outcome as they had hoped for a cleaner break with the past. In retrospect, this development may not be too surprising. Under the constitution the parties could not be sectionalist, at least at the official level, so bids for popular support in that direction were at least severely restrained. Equally, appeals for support in terms of class would be unlikely to produce mass support or financial contributions. So, given that appeals for support on either vertical or horizontal cleavages within society were both muted, the issue of the personality of the leader necessarily became important and the chances of young unknowns emerging as party leaders receded. In addition, thirteen years of military rule had given younger politicians little opportunity to achieve national prominence.

The strength and location of support for the parties can be seen in an examination of the 1979 election results. The elections took place in July and August, starting with those for the senate followed by those for the house of representatives, state legislatures, state governors and finally for the presidency. The logistical problems of holding five sets of elections in a short period (with nearly 2,000 offices at stake) were, in the main, competently handled by FEDECO and there was general agreement that they were largely free and fair. They thus present a reliable picture of party support as it existed in 1979.

Tables 6–1, 6–2, 6–3, 6–4, and 6–5, provide a somewhat aggregated version of this picture.

Although it is a little hazardous, I shall attempt to summarize the major trends. In terms of party support over the country as a whole, the outstanding result was the emergence of the NPN as the closest Nigeria had seen to a truly national party: that is, one which could gain support from all, or at least most, parts of the federation rather than being limited to a regional base. At the federal level, the NPN emerged as the largest party in both the house of representatives and the senate, although it did not achieve an overall majority in either. More indicative of the widespread nature of its support was that it was placed first or second in all states apart from Lagos State. Also, although it did especially well in the north, it picked up the middle belt state of Benue and the southeastern "minority" (non-Ibo) states of Cross River and Rivers. In the presidential election, Shehu Shagari emerged as the winner but only after a constitutional dispute regarding the definition of "two-thirds of nineteen." Shagari gained 5,700,000 votes compared with

Table 6–1. House of Representatives Election Seats						
STATE	TOTAL	NPN	UPN	NPP	PRP	GNPP
1. Anambra	29	3	—	26	—	—
2. Bauchi	20	18	—	1	—	1
3. Bendel	20	6	12	2	—	—
4. Benue	19	18	—	1	—	—
5. Borno	24	2	—	—	—	22
6. Cross River	28	22	2	—	—	4
7. Gongola	21	5	7	1	—	8
8. Imo	30	2	—	28	—	—
9. Kaduna	33	19	1	2	10	1
10. Kano	46	7	—	—	39	—
11. Kwara	14	8	5	—	—	1
12. Lagos	12	—	12	—	—	—
13. Niger	10	10	—	—	—	—
14. Ogun	12	—	12	—	—	—
15. Ondo	22	—	22	—	—	—
16. Oyo	42	4	38	—	—	—
17. Plateau	16	3	—	13	—	—
18. Rivers	14	10	—	4	—	—
19. Sokoto	37	31	—	—	—	6

just under 5,000,000 for Awolowo, his nearest rival. Shagari topped the poll in nine states and won over twenty-five percent of the vote in a further three. In the thirteenth state, Kano, he received twenty percent. His opponents argued that, as he had failed to win at least twenty-five percent in thirteen states (two-thirds of nineteen to the nearest whole number), his election was not valid. Eventually, it was decided by a special Presidential Election Tribunal and upheld by the Supreme Court that in a strict mathematical sense it was only necessary to win twenty-five percent of two-thirds of the vote in the thirteenth

Table 6–2. State Assembly Election Seats						
STATE	TOTAL	NPN	UPN	NPP	PRP	GNPP
1. Anambra	87	13	—	73	—	1
2. Bauchi	60	45	—	4	2	9
3. Bendel	60	22	34	4	—	—
4. Benue	57	48	—	3	—	6
5. Borno	72	11	—	—	2	59
6. Cross River	84	58	7	3	—	16
7. Gongola	63	15	18	4	1	25
8. Imo	90	9	—	79	—	2
9. Kaduna	99	64	3	6	16	10
10. Kano	138	11	1	—	123	3
11. Kwara	42	25	15	—	—	2
12. Lagos	36	—	36	—	—	—
13. Niger	30	28	—	—	—	2
14. Ogun	36	—	36	—	—	—
15. Ondo	66	1	65	—	—	—
16. Oyo	126	9	117	—	—	—
17. Plateau	48	10	—	35	—	3
18. Rivers	42	26	1	15	—	—
19. Sokoto	111	92	—	—	—	19

state, and so Shagari just squeezed in and was declared to have been legally elected as president. Shagari was clearly the most popular candidate, both in terms of his total vote and the wide regional distribution of that vote: Awolowo won in five states with over twenty-five percent in only one more and these were all confined to the west of the country. It was unfortunate that an unnecessary vagueness in the constitution should achieve such prominence in the first election. Support for the NPN in the south of the country was especially important due to its inability to dominate the north in the manner of the old NPC.

Table 6–3. Senate Election Seats						
STATE	*TOTAL*	*NPN*	*UPN*	*NPP*	*PRP*	*GNPP*
1. Anambra	5	—	—	5	—	—
2. Bauchi	5	5	—	—	—	—
3. Bendel	5	1	4	—	—	—
4. Benue	5	5	—	—	—	—
5. Borno	5	1	—	—	—	4
6. Cross River	5	3	—	—	—	2
7. Gongola	5	1	2	—	—	2
8. Imo	5	—	—	5	—	—
9. Kaduna	5	3	—	—	2	—
10. Kano	5	—	—	—	5	—
11. Kwara	5	3	2	—	—	—
12. Lagos	5	—	5	—	—	—
13. Niger	5	5	—	—	—	—
14. Ogun	5	—	5	—	—	—
15. Ondo	5	—	5	—	—	—
16. Oyo	5	—	5	—	—	—
17. Plateau	5	1	—	4	—	—
18. Rivers	5	3	—	2	—	—
19. Sokoto	5	5	—	—	—	—

The NPN lost in three northern states, Kano, Borno, and Gongola and in a fourth, Kaduna, there was the anomaly of the electorate choosing a PRP governor while returning a state house of assembly with an NPN majority, the personality of the candidates being decisive in the election of the governor.

If the NPN can be said to have broken away from the regionally based politics of the First Republic the same cannot be said of the UPN. The party gathered overwhelming support in the Yoruba-dominated west, but performed very moderately elsewhere. It easily won the Yoruba states of Ogun, Oyo, Ondo

Table 6–4. Nigerian Presidential Election Results, 1979					
STATE	GNPP	UPN	NPN	PRP	NPP
Anambra	1.68	0.75	13.49	1.20	82.88
Bauchi	15.44	3.00	62.48	14.34	4.74
Bendel	1.23	53.23	36.19	0.74	8.61
Benue	7.98	2.57	76.39	1.35	11.71
Borno	54.05	3.36	34.71	6.52	1.35
Cross River	15.14	11.76	64.41	1.02	7.66
Gongola	34.09	21.68	35.53	4.34	4.36
Imo	3.00	0.64	8.80	0.89	86.67
˙Kaduna	13.81	6.68	43.13	31.66	4.72
Kano	1.54	1.25	18.58	77.71	0.92
Kwara	5.71	39.49	53.62	0.67	0.52
Lagos	0.48	82.30	7.18	0.47	9.57
Niger	16.16	3.61	75.42	3.72	1.09
Ogun	0.53	92.61	6.23	0.31	0.32
Ondo	0.26	94.51	4.19	0.18	0.86
Oyo	0.57	85.78	12.75	0.34	0.55
Plateau	6.96	5.40	33.39	4.07	50.18
Rivers	2.18	10.34	72.66	0.47	14.35
Sokoto	27.16	3.39	65.21	3.32	0.92
TOTAL VOTE	10.08	29.28	33.58	10.29	16.77

and Bendel and was victorious in the more cosmopolitan Lagos State. This regionally based pattern of support for UPN was not only against the general trend, but also suggested an even greater degree of ethnic-regional political unity in the west than had existed in the First Republic when the AG had been subjected to serious factionalism and splintering which ended with Awolowo being imprisoned by his political opponents. In third place Azikiwe's NPP won the Ibo-dominated states of Anambra and Imo but gave indications that it was not a narrowly based

Table 6–5. Nigerian State Governors Election Results, 1979*					
STATE	GNPP	UPN	NPN	PRP	NPP
Anambra	21,136	6,735	187,388	28,790	772,061
Bauchi	208,845	25,624	438,016	132,766	18,777
Bendel	—	386,758	279,599	5,844	57,756
Benue	23,947	12,323	404,438	9,021	88,290
Borno	385,340	19,507	245,560	40,480	6,605
Cross River	159,592	80,863	428,089	—	46,615
Gongola	309,775	72,982	225,310	15,973	26,715
Imo	59,163	7,400	122,331	20,500	881,499
Kaduna	129,580	—	551,252	560,605	—
Kano	14,804	8,568	218,751	909,118	—
Kwara	—	174,415	188,228	—	—
Lagos	4,049	559,070	45,572	3,335	67,594
Niger	65,822	10,448	248,463	10,469	—
Ogun	—	643,229	44,275	—	—
Ondo	—	1,007,491	48,975	—	6,485
Oyo	7,306	995,138	163,460	—	5,527
Plateau	19,220	10,294	174,708	17,526	412,112
Rivers	7,406	6,227	619,715	2,388	169,594
Sokoto	422,381	—	768,618	33,042	—
				*winners underlined	

ethnic party by also winning the non-Ibo Plateau State. The two other parties had more limited support. The PRP won only Kano State, the home base of its leader, and succeeded in gaining the governorship of Kaduna State. The GNPP won just Borno State, again the home base of its leader, and the ethnically mixed and rather remote Gongola State.[22]

On October 1, 1979, Nigeria once again had a democratically elected government freely chosen by the voters of Nigeria from a range of competing alternatives. After thirteen years of military rule and a horrendous civil war the soldiers returned to the barracks. Having arranged the transfer to civilian rule without attempting to determine their successors, they had fulfilled the undertakings they had given in 1975. The Second Republic in Nigeria lasted a little over four years. It survived long enough to hold the second general election in 1983 but was overthrown by a military coup on New Year's Eve that year. Before examining the elections and the coup, a brief examination of the period is necessary. From one point of view the outstanding feature of the Second Republic was what it did not represent. In spite of many people's fears, it did not represent a return to the violent fratricidal political conflict between regionally based party monoliths that had been seen in the First Republic and that the makers of the 1979 constitution had sought to avoid. In the main, conflict between the parties, however acrimonious, was conducted within the constitutional framework. Party control at federal and state levels (which involved all parties) was not used to attempt to physically harrass opposing parties out of existence as it had been before. The experience of de facto one-party regions in violent conflict with each other was not repeated, and political parties continued to operate in parts of the country where they did not control the organs of government. Although the greatest hopes of the Second Republic were unfulfilled, so were its greatest fears. As will be shown, criticisms of government and party performance certainly cannot be avoided but they have to be balanced against the more positive aspects for which the comparative framework must be Nigeria's historical experience.

In drawing up the constitution, one of the prime considerations was the creation of a series of checks and balances, so lauded in liberal-democratic political theory, designed to avoid an over-concentration of power. The checks and balances certainly worked to check arbitrary power, but also inhibited decision-making and legislative output. In the first eighteen months parliament passed just eleven bills, compared with an average of eighty decrees (the equivalent under military rule) per year in the military period. Relationships between the federal center and the constituent states were still being worked out in practice throughout the period. There were considerable tensions between the central government and state governments not controlled by the NPN (a majority) especially those ruled by the UPN. Each side was constantly testing the other's strength and attempting to carve out larger spheres of influence. State governments especially resented the fact that control of the police was in federal hands, and some even advocated the setting up of a parallel state police along the lines of the old Native Authority police of the colonial period. Early on, President Shagari attempted to strengthen links between the center and the states by appointing his own presidential liaison officers in each state but the move was clumsily handled. The liaison officers were all NPN men, including several who had failed to win elective office, and this was bitterly resented in the states, most of whom ignored them. The anomalous position in Kaduna State, with a PRP governor facing an NPN majority in the state assembly, resulted in a virtual legislative stalemate which was complicated even further by splits within the PRP (see below). Some states, most notably the UPN-dominated Lagos State under its talented governor, Lateef Jakande, gained the reputation of being particularly well run. The period was also marked by an increase in civil liberties protected by an independent judiciary. The independence of the judiciary was well illustrated by what became known as the "Shugaba affair." In this case the majority leader of the GNPP in the Borno State Assembly, Alhaji Shugaba Abdulrahman Darman, was arrested and deported on the grounds that he was not legally a Nigerian citizen. It was never clear if this was an attempt by the central government to weaken the opposition, but certainly many Nigerians believed this to be the case. The affair was taken to court, with the result that Shugaba was declared to be a Nigerian citizen and was awarded substantial damages; the court also ordered the payment of costs against the federal government. The hasty expulsion of some two million illegal immigrants, mainly Ghanaians, in early 1983 certainly earned the Nigerian government considerable human rights criticism in the world media, but the government was acting legally, if not very humanely.

The later stages of the Second Republic were plagued by economic problems on a massive scale. Throughout the 1970s and early 1980s the Nigerian economy had expanded on the back of the tremendous profits occasioned by the oil boom. In April 1982 the bubble burst as oil prices slumped. With successive governments (both military and civilian) having failed to use oil money to diversify the economy or revive flagging agricultural production, the collapse of oil prices had a disastrous effect on oil dependent Nigeria. Income from oil exports, which had provided over ninety percent of Nigeria's foreign earnings, fell from $23 billion in 1980 to under $10 billion in 1983. The effects of this massive reduction in income were exacerbated by serious government mismanagement of the economy. Probably most significant in the effects it had on the legitimacy of the regime was the frightening rise of corruption that accompanied economic decline. With standards of living falling for most of the population, certain individuals closely associated with the government and the parties (including the opposition parties) were seen to be openly accumulating personal wealth through exploiting the positions they held. In his heartfelt book, *The Trouble With Nigeria*,[23] the Nigerian novelist Chinua Achebe attacks corruption as the major problem facing Nigeria and hazards a guess that "sixty percent of the wealth of this nation is regularly consumed by corruption."[24] This is probably an overestimate, but it gives a good idea of the scale of the problem. While there was nothing new about corruption in Nigeria, the ostentatious flaunting of corruptly acquired wealth against the backdrop of economic decline and mass suffering was deeply harmful to the system. Thus, as the 1983 elections approached there was little doubt that the democratic system in Nigeria was under strain.

The parties that contested the 1983 elections were largely the same as in 1979. One new party, the National Advance Party (NAP), led by a radical Lagos lawyer, Tunji Braithwaite, was sanctioned by FEDECO to make the elections a competition between six parties. The PRP had experienced sharp divisions, mainly between the supporters of Aminu Kano and some of the younger radicals, and was in a poor state. Aminu Kano himself had died of natural causes earlier in 1983. The NPN benefited from some defections from the opposition, most notably Ishaya Audu, who had been the vice-presidential candidate for the NPP in 1979. In May 1982 the Biafran secessionist leader, Chukwemeka Ojukwu, had returned from exile in the Ivory Coast and his support for the NPN seemed likely to undermine Ibo support for the NPP.

The election campaigns and the election itself passed off more smoothly than many had feared but there was a marked deterioration from the high standards of 1979. Considerable electoral violence took place, but in the main this was confined to Oyo and Ondo states where attempts by the NPN to dislodge the UPN led to great tension. There were also widespread allegations of electoral fraud and malpractice, although as things have turned out it may never be possible to evaluate the extent of this. In a sense the elections in some cases appeared to be fought in two stages: the first at the polling booth and the second in the courts, as losing candidates challenged the legality of their defeat. The election of the governor of Ondo state was reversed by the courts, but the whole process was still under way when it was brought to an end by military intervention. Because of this it is difficult to know how far the 1983 results provide an accurate picture of support. As all parties were involved in electoral malpractice it can be argued that they canceled each other out to a large extent and that overall national support was accurately reflected in the results even if, in some individual constituencies, the declared results made a mockery of the way people had actually voted. A major irony for the NPN is that it is widely accepted that it would have won the 1983 election without any resort to unfair tactics because it was the best organized party with the widest base of support. From this perspective NPN attempts at electoral malpractice were totally counterproductive in reducing the legitimacy gained from an electoral victory which they would have won anyway. Even if one makes allowance for some inflation of success in the figures, the 1983 results represented a clear win for the NPN. In the presidential election Shagari won twelve million votes, four million more than Awolowo, his closest rival. The NPN won sixty out of ninety-six senate seats and 264 out of 450 house of representative seats and gained control of thirteen of the nineteen states. In spite of obvious problems Nigeria's democracy seemed to have survived the elections. Shagari's second term in office was, however, to prove short. He was sworn in on October 1, 1983, but was deposed by a military coup led by Major General Muhammadu Buhari on December 31 and Nigeria was returned to military rule. In trying to explain the overthrow of Nigeria's democratic revival it is very tempting to point to the failures of the practice of democracy in the Second Republic. It is obvious that the widespread and overt corruption that existed did do something to undermine the legitimacy of both the regime and the system. The fact that the 1983 election was not completely fair also damaged legitimacy and for this the politicians themselves were to blame. The catastrophic fall in the world price of oil was outside their control but undoubtedly economic recession could have been handled better. By 1983 Nigerian democracy was functioning imperfectly but it was still functioning in a recognizably democratic way. In explaining its demise it is quite possible that to focus on these imperfections is quite misleading. In justifying their seizure of power the leaders of the new military regime certainly laid stress on corruption, electoral fraud, and economic mismanagement as the factors that had persuaded them to act. However, the time has now long since passed when observers of African politics are willing to take at face value the gloriously altruistic explanations of military intervention that inevitably come from the military. The coup d'etat has come to be explained primarily through the corporate interest of the army and the individual interests of the coup leaders.[25] From this perspective the "failing" of Nigerian democracy had little or nothing to do with its overthrow. Unlike earlier Nigerian coups, the one in 1983 is difficult to portray as resulting from ethnic-regional tensions: a northern-led civilian government was overthrown by a northern-led coup, but neither exhibited the homogeneity of 1966. There is considerable evidence to suggest that the 1983 coup was, in part at least, a preemptive coup led by senior officers to head off the possibility of one led by junior officers or noncommissioned soldiers. The examples of the Doe coup in Liberia and the Rawlings coup in Ghana had already shown clearly that such coups were quite possible in the west African context and that the consequences for senior officers were very severe indeed, often fatal. Thus by seizing power, the Buhari group was able to establish a highly authoritarian style of rule to head off threats from this direction. For Buhari himself this authoritarianism proved counterproductive and he was overthrown in yet another coup in 1985 led by Major General Ibrahim Babangida.

If it is doubtful that the imperfections of democracy led to its overthrow, would it be possible to argue that an undemocratic single-party system introduced in 1979 would have functioned better and denied the military the pretext for intervention?

Although any answer to this question is necessarily hypothetical, I must say I regard this type of argument as lacking all credibility. To argue that, if the government of the Second Republic had not had to face the challenge of opposition and had not been restrained by the checks and balances of the system, it would have been less corrupt, not only lacks any evidence to support it but is counterintuitive in view of Nigerian experience. Democracy certainly did not prevent government corruption in the period of the Second Republic, but it is not unreasonable to argue that its absence would, in all probability, have produced an even worse result. Nor can it seriously be argued that if opposition had been banned following the 1979 election, a stable political consensus would have emerged in Nigeria. To conclude, the problems of the Second Republic existed in spite of democracy and not because of it.

The military government of Babangida declared its intention to step down and hand power back to civilians in 1990 but later changed the date to 1992. In April 1988 a constituent assembly was established to draw up the new constitution. At the time of writing there can be no guarantee that this further revival of democracy will take place. Past promises of recivilianization made by military regimes in Nigeria have a mixed record of fulfillment: Obasanjo kept to his schedule but Gowon did not. The behavior of future civilian leaders in Nigeria can make it easier or more difficult for the military to intervene again, but there is nothing they can do to make it impossible. A drastic reduction in corruption and a scrupulous adherence to the constitutional rules of democracy could not guarantee an immunity to the coup d'etat: such is the reality of Nigerian politics.

GHANA

At the time of its independence in 1957, Ghana appeared to many observers to be one of the best placed for a postcolonial takeoff in terms of economic and political development. It had a strong and fairly diversified economy, healthy foreign exchange holdings, and a large pool of well-educated labour. Although regional and ethnic cleavages were evident in the political system, they did not appear as deep or divisive as those in Nigeria. The reality of independence has been a tragic denial of all the early hopes, and instead of being lauded as one of the success stories of Africa, Ghana is more often used as an example of just how badly things can go wrong. Economically, its collapse has been nothing short of catastrophic which is one of the reasons why so many Ghanaians have sought to make a living outside of the country in spite of the problems which this often brings them (for example, the mass expulsions from Nigeria on more than one occasion). Politically, Ghana has been very unstable, with fairly rapid changes among democracy, single-party authoritarianism, and military rule. Starting independence with a lively competitive party democracy, Ghana switched to single-party rule in 1964 largely as a result of what Dennis Austin refers to as "Nkrumah's pathological distaste for any manifestation of opposition."[26] Single-party rule lasted until the military overthrow of the regime in 1966 and still represents Ghana's only experiment with this type of system. Since then Ghana has alternated military rule with periods of democratic revival. The first period of military rule lasted from 1966 until 1969, when the military government handed over power to a freely elected civilian government led by Dr. Kofi Busia. This government survived for three years until 1972, when a further military coup under General Ignatious Acheampong brought the military back to power. This time the army stayed in power for seven years, although there were several intramilitary coups. A further revival of democracy took place in 1979, but lasted only until New Year's Eve 1981, when the military under Jerry Rawlings displaced it. Here we will be concentrating on the events leading up to the second revival of democracy of Ghana's Third Republic, on the revival itself, and finally on the reasons why it collapsed. However, some understanding of the earlier period is necessary to put the later events into historical perspective.

In 1947 the postwar development of nationalism resulted in the formation of the United Gold Coast Convention (UGCC), led by J. B. Danquah. The party was composed mainly of well-educated and middle-class Ghanaians and took a relatively moderate stance, seeking the ending of colonial rule through negotiation. Kwame Nkrumah was appointed its full-time secretary but tensions rapidly developed between him and the rest of the UGCC leadership. In 1948 anticolonial strikes and riots took place. The more radical Nkrumah was anxious for the party to become associated with these events, but his colleagues favored a more cautious approach. In 1949 Nkrumah broke away to form his own Convention People's Party (CPP). From then until independence, the major feature of politics was competition to decide which party was to form the first postcolonial government. Nkrumah's personal charisma and his ability to organize mass support for the CPP led to the victory of his more radical wing of the nationalist movement in free elections. In the elections of 1954 and 1956, the CPP emerged as the most popular party, although support was far from monolithic. It never won as much as sixty percent of the votes cast and support was regionally uneven, being strongest in the south and in Accra and weakest in the north and in Ashanti. Nkrumah's boast that "the CPP is Ghana: Ghana is the CPP," was always an exaggeration.

From 1957 until the overthrow of Nkrumah by the military in 1966, the political system of Ghana grew increasingly authoritarian. In 1958 a Preventitive Detention Act, allowing for arrest without charge and five years detention without trial was passed. Danquah was only one of those who died in prison without ever being charged. This was followed by a new sedition act which allowed for fifteen years' imprisonment for anybody making statements likely to injure the reputation of the government. Strict controls were placed on the media, the trade unions, the university, and the chiefs which made public opposition to the government possible. Nkrumah became life chairman of the CPP and, with the introduction of the single-party state in 1964, president for life of Ghana. A massive personality cult was developed around Nkrumah which had the effect of distancing him from reality as he became increasingly surrounded by sycophants and Ghana crumbled into inefficiency and corruption. However, if this is the negative side of Nkrumah, it is important to remember the positive side of the man who became the symbol of a wider African nationalism in his (ultimately unsuccessful) search for Pan-African unity and dignity. The paradox of Nkrumah is accurately captured by Ali Mazrui when he writes that:

> Nkrumah was African first and Ghanaian second. This combination was both Nkrumah's strength and weakness. His dreams about the continent and its place in world

*affairs captured one of the fundamental urges of modern
Africans in different parts of the continent. . . . He became
the ultimate symbol of the defiant assertion of African
dignity. . . . but his commitment to Africa was not matched
by a similar consideration for Ghanaians. Within Ghana
he drifted towards policies of bungling through and left
Ghanaians much poorer and, as individuals, less free than
he found them. It would be foolish to say that Nkrumah
did not love Ghana. A man of such political sensitivities
in a nationalist sense could not escape the more immediate
patriotic ties. But it is true that he put greater emphasis
on African dreams than on Ghana's realities.* [27]

Kwame Nkrumah died in exile in 1972 but he lives on as an
inspiration for African nationalists and the goal of African unity. Unfortunately, his record in Ghana did not match his con-
tinental preeminence.

The one institution in Ghana that Nkrumah failed in his
attempts to control was the army. [28] To counteract this he established a body known as the President's Own Guard Regi-
ment (POGR) which was loyal only to him and also much better
paid and equipped than the regular army. Partly in response
to this, the army ousted Nkrumah in a coup in February 1966.
The coup met virtually no resistance and was generally welcomed in Ghana. [29]

Following the coup, a National Liberation Council (NLC)
consisting of soldiers and police under the leadership of Major-
General J. A. Ankrah (later replaced by Brigadier A. A. Afrifra)
was established to administer the country until new elections
could be held. Although there was an attempt at a further coup
in 1967 competitive elections were held in 1969. The major
parties in this election were the Progress Party (PP) led by Dr.
Kofi Busia, an academic who had been a member of the opposition to Nkrumah before it was banned, and the National
Alliance of Liberals (NAL) led by Komla Gbedemah, a former
CPP man who had broken with Nkrumah in the early 1960s.
The election was peaceful and the PP won fifty-nine percent of
the vote (gaining 105 seats), the NAL thirty percent (twenty-
nine seats) with eleven percent (six seats) going to minor parties. The PP performed very strongly in Akan areas while the
NAL triumphed amongst the Ewe. In power the Busia govern-

ment appeared biased in favour of its Akan supporters: when five hundred members of the bureaucracy were purged, none were Akan. In 1971 a dramatic fall in world cocoa prices severely damaged the economy. The Second Republic lasted three years, but was overthrown by a further coup under General Ignatious Acheampong in 1972. This coup was motivated almost entirely by the selfish interests of those staging it. Decalo describes it as an "officers amenities coup" which was "unaccompanied by any attempt to camouflage the new clique's desire to redress both personal and military grievances."[30]

During the first couple of years of the Acheampong regime, the Ghanaian economy enjoyed a period of unexpected buoyancy due to a rise in the world price of cocoa. However, after that the progress of the regime, both economically and politically, was strictly downhill. Acheampong and his government grew increasingly unpopular as manifestations of large-scale corruption, financial mismanagement, and a heavy-handed authoritarianism became more open and obvious. From around 1975 onward demands for a return to democratic civilian rule grew, especially, though not exclusively, from the educated middle class. In 1977 the Ghana Bar Association and the Ghana Medical Association staged national strikes to support their demands. Large-scale demonstrations by students and others supported the call for democratization, but they were often dealt with in a very coercive manner. This continuing demand for democracy has been a central feature of Ghanaian politics throughout the postindependence period, despite several attempts to force it out of existence. As Anthony Kirk-Greene has remarked, "whatever the pessimist is prompted to think about the democratic process in independent Ghana he cannot doubt the continuing faith of the electorate in the fundamental legitimacy of the ballot box."[31] Faced with continuing economic deterioration and growing pressure for the restoration of democracy, Acheampong's response was a form of union government (referred to in Ghana as UNIGOV) which would, in theory, have meant government in the hands of a triumvirate of army, police, and civilians.[32] The proposals allowed for elected elements in the civilian segment, but precluded the formation of political parties to contest the elections. This scheme was widely resented in Ghana for falling far short of the demands for democracy and being instead a method by which army rule was to be maintained in a fairly transparent disguise. In March 1978 the government organized a referendum to "test support" for the proposals. The public debate preceding the vote was distorted by the government, which used all the resources of the state to encourage support for UNIGOV and to harass those who opposed it by beatings and jailings. The official result of the referendum was a small majority in favor of the UNIGOV proposals. Opponents of the idea refused to accept this result however, arguing correctly that the whole exercise had been rigged. Those organizing the referendum had been detained at one stage to make clear that the government were only interested in the "correct" (i.e., supportive) result. Following the announcement of the result, many democratic opponents of UNIGOV were detained in an attempt to silence criticism of the idea.

The UNIGOV proposals were never implemented. In July 1978 the seeming impasse was broken by a further coup, led by Lieutenant General (later General) Fred Akuffo, which finally put an end to the Acheampong regime. Whatever his personal feelings, Akuffo, faced with a disintegrating economy, army, and political system, had little choice but to face the necessity of presiding over an interim regime and preparing for a return to democratic civilian rule in 1979. Preparations were thus made for elections, but before the elections could be held, a series of events took place that Hansen and Collins accurately describe as "rivalling in sense of drama only the extravagences of the James Bond films."[33] In May 1979 a hitherto-unknown junior officer in the Ghana Airforce, Flight Lieutenant Jerry Rawlings, burst onto the Ghanaian political stage with an attempted seizure of power. At this first attempt, Rawlings failed and was arrested and brought to trial for subversion. Rawlings was not against a return to civilian rule but protested at the nature of the proposed handover. His main arguments concerned the character and, more especially, the personnel of the military regime from 1972 onwards. His case was that during the 1972–1979 period the senior members of the military regime, together with some of their civilian cohorts, had neglected any semblance of national interest and had been engaged in massive corruption which had had a cancerous effect on Ghanaian society. For Rawlings it was a matter of total injustice that such people should be allowed to calmly retire to live off their ill-gotten gains: any return to civilian rule had to be proceeded by a massive "house-cleansing" of Ghanaian public life. Rawlings's tirade against the kleptomania of the Acheampong and Akuffo regimes struck a very responsive chord in many sectors of Ghanaian society, not least among the junior officers and lower ranks of the armed forces who had suffered from the declining prestige of the service and who had gained nothing personally from the causes of that decline. In June armed supporters of Rawlings released him from detention and this time his attempt at a coup d'etat was successful.

The first Rawlings period lasted for three months. The approach of his armed forces revolutionary council was summed up best in terms of metaphors concerning "rotten apples" and the result was a series of measures against the individuals seen as responsible for Ghana's plight. Hasty and secret "revolutionary trials" were held, and a number of people associated with previous regimes were executed. Among the latter were not only Achaempong and Akuffo but also Lieutenant General Afrifra who had headed the military regime that had handed over power to Busia. Thus, three ex-heads of state were executed in a single week.[34] The response to the problem of black-market prices of essential commodities was to completely destroy the main market in Accra and inflict severe retribution on the (mainly female) market traders, leaving the real causes of the problem untouched. Perhaps the most surprising aspect of the whole affair was that, apart from causing some minor delay, it had no effect on the timing of the recivilianization of the Ghanaian political system. Chazan notes that this "is a credit not only to Rawlings, but also to the centrality of notions of civil rights that have become such a part of Ghanaian politics."[35] Retrospectively, it might be argued that the prospects for the Third Republic might have been improved if some delay had taken place in the process of demilitarization. In 1979 the political system of Ghana was in an extremely turbulent and unsettled state that did not provide a secure base from which to launch a return to democratic civilian rule. Perhaps a longer-term, more carefully staged, transfer of power, such as had taken place in Nigeria, would have produced longer-lasting results. All this, of course, is to be wise after the event. By 1979 Ghanaians were heartily sick of military rule and longed for a return to democracy, a fact which had been clearly demonstrated over the previous few years by the widespread and courageous opposition to Acheampong. Although Rawlings was a genuinely popular figure, any perpetuation of military rule could quite easily have led to even greater political instability in Ghana at that time.

As in Nigeria there was never any doubt that the Third Republic should represent a competitive party political system. Having experienced the disasters of single-party rule under Nkrumah, the people of Ghana had no wish for a rerun. Unlike the Second Republic, the new constitution made provision for an executive presidency directly elected by a majority of voters. It has been suggested that this decision reflected similar developments in Nigeria. Even if this is true it was a limited influence because, in most other ways, the Ghanaian constitution was quite different from that of Nigeria with a less complex institutional structure reflecting the smaller size of Ghana. Whereas Nigeria is a federal system, Ghana is unitary; where Nigeria had a bicameral legislature at the center, Ghana's was unicameral, with a single 140-member parliament elected on a single-member, first-past-the-post basis. The constitution also tried to ensure the independence of the judiciary and guaranteed a long list of human rights. At the behest of the military, some restraints were introduced relating to political parties and candidates, but they were not as severe as those already examined in the Nigerian case. The reestablishment of parties that had competed in any previous Ghanaian election and the adoption of their names and symbols were prohibited. The regulations also precluded anybody who had previously been found guilty of corruption or any public malfeasance from standing for office or holding an official party position; a review tribunal was established to judge individual cases. The regulations also included some fairly undemanding requirements relating to the establishment of a minimum number of regional party officers, residency requirements, deposits, and candidate qualifications. No political party of any significance had any difficulty in meeting these requirements, although some individuals were debarred by the review tribunal.

When the ban on political parties was lifted, one was able to witness rapid formation, splitting, and realigning similar to that in Nigeria but on a smaller scale. Over twenty parties were launched, but only seven were finally registered and of these one dropped out before the election.[36] Of the remaining six, the two most important could be regarded in part as exhibiting some lineal connections with previous parties, although in an informal and unofficial manner. The People's National Party (PNP) had organizational and personnel links with the old CPP of Nkrumah, but was ideologically much more pragmatic and also had a wider ethnic and regional base and a large number of new younger party adherents. The moving force behind its formation was Imoru Egala, a veteran political heavyweight from the north of the country. Egala, however, fell foul of the review tribunal and was prevented from standing for office. Leadership of the PNP and its presidential nomination passed to Dr. Hilla Limann, who was Egala's nephew, a little known but intellectually able diplomat who was not associated directly with any past regime. In terms of organization the PNP was the best equipped of the parties and in the election campaign its policy statements were pragmatic and conservative in style.

The Popular Front Party (PFP) exhibited a degree of lineal descent from the Progress Party (PP) of Kofi Busia which had been the governing party in the Second Republic. Although Busia was by now dead, many of the leaders of the PFP were men who had previously been his colleagues, its leader, Victor Owusu being a prime example. Like the old PP it drew heavily on Asante and Brong support in the Ashanti and Brong-Ahafo regions, but it was not confined to these areas. Not all of the old PP leaders were attracted to the PFP. A section of them, led by Paa Willie Ofori-Atta, an ex-minister in the Busia cabinet, formed the United National Convention (UNC). Ethnically, the UNC appeared as largely a Ga and Ewe party although it did attract some Asante support from those hostile to Owusu.

The other parties were smaller and more limited. The Action Congress Party (ACP) under the dynamic leadership of Frank Bernasko was largely based on the urbanized Fantis of the central region although it did include the noted Ewe poet Kofi Awoonor. The Social Democratic Front (SDF) represented, according to Jeffries, "too bizarre an alliance to arouse anything more than humorous derision amongst most Ghanaian voters including the unionised workers to whom it was supposedly directed."[37] The SDF was initially launched as a trade union party and, in theory, supported the creation of a socialist state, but its leadership was resolutely northern and aristocratic. Its presidential candidate was Dr. Ibrahim Mahama, a successful businessman and, more importantly, the leading member of the Andani royal family of the Ya Na chieftancy. Most clearly ideological of the parties was the small and ineffective Third Force Party (TFP) led by Dr. John Bilson, which was right wing, procapitalist and monetarist.

Among both contestants and observers of the 1979 elections there is a total concensus that they were free and fair. The campaigns were conducted in a peaceful manner and the quality of organization of the electoral exercise was very high. In a country that had become almost a byword for administrative incompetence and inefficiency, the administration of the elections provided an example of what Ghanaians were capable of when the conditions and motivations were right. The details of the parliamentary election are given in Table below.

Clearly, the PNP was the most successful party, emerging with a bare overall majority in the legislature (71 out of 140). Even more impressive was the fact that it managed to win seats in all regions of the country, something no other party managed

Table 6–6. Ghanaian Election Results, 1979							
REGIONS	PNP	PFP	UNC	ACP	SDF	TFP	IND
Central	8	0	0	7	0	0	0
Greater Accra	6	1	3	0	0	0	0
Cater	11	6	4	0	0	0	0
Ashanti	2	19	1	0	0	0	0
Brong-Ahafo	2	10	0	0	0	0	1
Volta	11	0	5	0	0	0	0
North	7	4	0	0	3	0	0
Upper	15	1	0	0	0	0	0
Western	9	1	0	3	0	0	0
TOTAL	71	42	13	10	3	0	1

to do. While it was relatively weak in the PFP heartland of Ashanti and Brong-Ahafo (although even here it won two seats in each), it was the best-supported party in all of the other seven regions. As with the NPN in Nigeria, one could see the emergence of a party with nationally based support. The second most successful party, the PFP, dominated the Ashanti and Brong-Ahafo regions, but did manage at least one seat in seven out of nine regions, failing completely only in Central and Volta regions. The UNC and ACP won thirteen and ten seats respectively, but were largely confined to their ethnic strongholds. The SDF won three seats, all in the home base of its leader. The right wing TFP failed to win a single seat. One Independent candidate won in Brong-Ahafo. In the first round of the presidential election, voting went very much along the lines of the parliamentary elections. Hilla Limann and Victor Owusu emerged as the two best-supported candidates, with thirty-six percent and thirty percent of the popular vote each. Because no candidate won an overall majority, the two best-supported were left to contest the second round. On this occasion most of the supporters of the smaller parties switched to Limann, who won with nearly two-thirds of the popular vote.

On paper, the turnout in the elections appears disappointingly low: for example, in the second presidential ballot, only thirty-six percent of the registered voters turned out. However, as Jeffries[38] suggests, this may be explained more by a grossly inflated voter register than by apathy. Under the Acheampong regime, registration officers were paid according to the number of voters they registered: it would be difficult to imagine a method more guaranteed to produce inflated figures.

On September 24, Rawlings officially handed over power to the new Limann government. Democratic rule had returned to Ghana, but in the most ominous circumstances. Following over twenty years of incompetent and often corrupt mismanagement, the economy was in ruins. The social and economic infrastructure of the country, its roads, telecommunications, schools, and hospitals, had deteriorated to such an extent that they hardly functioned. The national currency, the Cedi, was literally hardly worth the paper it was printed on and had become the joke of west Africa: at one stage the national airline refused to accept payment in the national currency, arguing quite correctly that it was worthless. The world price of the main export crop, cocoa, continued to fall as well as the amount of cocoa produced. The roads leading from the cocoa-producing areas of the interior to the coast were so bad that it became almost impossible to get out what cocoa was still being grown. Many of the cocoa growers preferred to smuggle their crop into the Ivory Coast where prices were better and paid in a currency, the CFA franc, that had some standing. Clearly any attempt to rehabilitate the Ghanaian economy would be long-term. As things worked out, the Limann government did not have a long-term future, but in the just-over-two-years that it was in power it made little progress in righting the economy. The much-needed devaluation of the Cedi was postponed for fear of political repercussions. This resulted in postponement of the IMF credit funding. As Chazan remarks, "the superficial, albeit well-intended, moves of the regime aimed at rectifying the overt rather than the deep-seated aspects of the state's malady were simply not forceful enough to make a dent in the economic morass."[39] If the government did little to make the situation worse, it did little to make it better.

Politically, the period of the Third Republic was overshadowed by the figure of Rawlings hovering in the wings. To go back to being a junior officer in the armed forces after being head of state could never be an easy transition. Rawlings had always made it clear that the civilian government was in his opinion "on probation," and in his handover speech he had suggested that it might be more appropriate to "commiserate" with Limann.[40] It would be difficult to know who was most afraid of whom; Limann of Rawlings or Rawlings of Limann. In fact they had good reason to be frightened of each other. Rawlings was forced to retire from the armed forces and there are suggestions that his assassination was planned but never carried out.[41] Perhaps a more coercive government would have killed Rawlings, but it is doubtful if the eliminiation of one man would have done more than create a martyr. As time went on, Rawlings became more openly critical of the government in his public statements,[42] dismissing them as "wig and gown people." He repeatedly rejected suggestions that he might stand as a parliamentary candidate. While he would almost certainly have succeeded in getting himself elected because of his personal popularity in the urban areas, it is more doubtful that he could have put together a political coalition that could have gained sufficient support over the length and breadth of Ghana among the rural peasant majority. If he had attempted this and failed, his national political credibility would have been dented, so he preferred not to attempt it. To claim mass popular support but to be unwilling to put such claims to the test where democratic mechanisms for doing so actually exist must necessarily raise questions about the validity of such claims. The situation remained tense. Although officially a private citizen, Rawlings was known to have very substantial support in the armed forces, especially at the more junior levels. Looking back to the executions of senior officers in 1979, few of the armed forces elite could risk being identified as anti-Rawlings. For the whole of the period of the Third Republic, the elected civilian government was working in a situation in which it felt constantly threatened. Partly because of this, it acted in an extremely tentative fashion. Given the immensity of Ghana's problems, tentative government was unlikely to provide solutions.

On December 31, 1981, the seemingly inevitable happened, and Jerry Rawlings was returned to power in yet another coup, thus becoming the first military leader in Africa to gain power this way for a second time. The institutions of the Third Republic were dissolved, the parties banned, and their leaders arrested. State power passed to a Provisional National Defence Council (PNDC) with Rawlings as its chairman. In the light of the above discussion the reasons for the overthrow of Ghana's democratic system appear obvious. During its short term in power, the Limann government was unable to arrest the almost total collapse of the economy. The resultant poverty was causing real suffering, especially in the urban areas where a day's wages were insufficient to buy a single meal. Ironically, many of the rural peasants fared better because they followed the exit option. That is, they withdrew from the "national" economy and returned to subsistence farming, growing enough food to feed themselves and their families and ceasing to rely in any significant way on the Ghanaian market economy. Such a move was facilitated, or even made necessary, by the breakdown in communications between the coast and much of the interior: in some parts of the north communications were worse than they had been in the nineteenth century. Peasants following the exit option can be denied government services but where these services are minimal to nonexistent this is a small price to pay for avoiding hunger. Ghana is not alone in having an exiting peasantry; in several other African countries the decline of the state has had similar results. Thus, the failure of the economic performance of the Limann government has to be set alongside the enormity of the problems it faced. Politically, the failure of the revival of democracy is largely explained by the Rawlings factor. With the support he undoubtedly had in the armed forces, the success of any coup attempt always looked likely. The question remains why he should have wanted to use this support to take over government power in Ghana again. Two factors may explain this. First, one has to recognize the personal safety element. There was always a distinct possibility that harsher councils would prevail in the government or elsewhere and that Rawlings would be physically eliminated. The fact that this had not happened by the end of 1981 provided no guarantees for the future. It was less risky in personal terms to return to power: in common parlance Rawlings got his retaliation in first. However compelling, such an explanation is by itself overly simplistic. One has to recognize that Rawlings really did believe that he could make a better job of governing Ghana than others had. Whether he was correct in this belief is beside the point. Although observers of military takeovers in Africa have become very cynical about the altruistic statements made by soldiers to justify their seizure of power, the evidence suggests that for Rawlings a genuine altruism was an important factor. Whatever criticisms can be made of Rawlings, he cannot be seen as just another military ruler on the make, using state power for personal aggrandizement: he is in no way a Mark II Acheampong. Rawlings had, and still has, a vision of a return to a more prosperous and more egalitarian Ghana and a belief in himself as the man who can provide the necessary leadership.

Assessments of the performance of the regime of Rawlings's "second coming" vary, but recently there has been a growing belief that in economic terms the situation is slowly improving.[43] Ironically, in view of all the revolutionary rhetoric that surrounded his regime in the early stages, Rawlings has followed a relatively orthodox, almost right-wing economic path over the past few years, including a drastic reduction in the public sector and close relations with the World Bank and the

IMF. Such policies have cost him the support of many of his erstwhile left-wing supporters, many of whom have gone into exile and, as Rado notes, "landed up in capitalist London where they mingle in reasonable amnity with right-wing opponents of the regime."[44] If the economic sphere in Ghana gives scope for some tentative hopes of a slow incremental improvement,[45] the political sphere remains much more uncertain. Since 1981 the regime has been threatened by a number of attempted coups and coup plots which it has managed to survive.[46] Exile groups like the Campaign for Democracy in Ghana and the Ghana Democratic Movement continue their external opposition. As yet no clear picture of what future political institutions of Ghana may look like has emerged and Rawlings seems uncommitted to a return to civilian rule at a specified date. While it is not impossible that democracy could be revived again in Ghana's future, it does not seem likely in the short term unless Ghanaian politics changes dramatically. Of course, dramatic changes in Ghanaian politics are not unknown.

Chapter • 7

More Doubtful Cases

Uganda, Liberia, Sudan

NIGERIA AND GHANA can be seen as examples of the failure of the consolidation of democracy, because in both cases the democratic system was subsequently overthrown through military intervention. In spite of this, the periods of the Second Republic (Nigeria) and the Third Republic (Ghana), which lasted for fifty-one months and twenty-eight months respectively, were clearly examples of functioning democracy, albeit with attendant problems. The shadow cast by their demise is real enough, but while they lasted, their classification as democratic revivals was clearly appropriate. In both cases the 1979 elections were not only genuinely competitive but remarkably free and fair. Despite the emergence of some electoral malpractice in the 1983 Nigerian elections, the results gave a clearer picture of the balance of electoral support within the country than is ever possible in the pseudocompetitive elections of the single-party states. In some areas the voice of the electorate was muffled, but in most it was clearly heard. In neither state was there any attempt to extinguish opposition parties to give the ruling party an unchallenged and unchallengeable hold on state power. In both Nigeria and Ghana the opposition parties continued to provide open criticism of the central government, and in Nigeria, because of its federal system, opposition parties actually held power at the level of the individual state. In some cases, like Lagos State, it is generally acknowledged that the national opposition performed well as rulers and administrators.

The next three cases to be examined are much less clear cut and seem to belong to a slightly different category. All three are further examples of demilitarization. In each case competitive party systems were revived and some of the other features associated with democracy were also reintroduced. And yet, for a variety of reasons, these must be regarded as more doubtful examples of democratic revival. The evidence that they present raises the question as to whether they should be viewed as imperfectly functioning democracies or whether the ambiguities which they present take them over that very imprecise line which circumscribes the democratic category. The only reasonable way to proceed is to examine each case individually because the three exhibit very marked differences: all may be described as doubtful cases but they are doubtful for quite different reasons and in quite different ways. As will be shown, all three revivals were created in extremely difficult circumstances for the state involved. It is well to remember that there was no preordained reason why the attempt to revive a competitive party system had to be made: the alternative choices of continued military rule or the creation of a single party state were obviously available, even though at the time they were not taken up. The fact that it was the more democratic alternative that was chosen does tend to indicate the strength of supportive feeling for democracy that exists in Africa even in the most difficult circumstances. Although the actual realization of democracy in these states is certainly questionable, the broad-based normative support for it was considerable and undeniable even if not universally shared by all those involved.

UGANDA

Winston Churchill once referred to Uganda as the "pearl of Africa." At the time of independence in 1962 this description did not seem too farfetched. With a propitious climate, fertile soils, and a sound infrastructure Uganda had a strong economic base. It was the home of Makerere University, perhaps the finest in Africa at the time, and partly because of this had a well-educated and talented elite. There was also a hard-working entrepreneurial Asian minority within the population.[1] However, whatever form of analysis one might choose, there is no way of disputing the fact that since independence things have gone horribly wrong in Uganda. Nowadays the name most clearly associated with Uganda is that of Idi Amin. Even though Amin himself has now left the Ugandan political stage (one must hope permanently) the country has become a by-word for political violence, instability, and state collapse. The once-prosperous economy is in ruins and hundreds of thousands of Ugandans have been tortured and butchered in the two and a half decades since independence. In this context the revival of a competitive party system in 1980 may be regarded as just one more failed attempt to restore Uganda to something resembling a functioning political entity.

With the benefit of hindsight the situation in 1962 can be seen as less promising than it appeared at the time. Even then the political system contained serious unresolved tensions. Like most African states the raison d'etre of Uganda was colonial convenience rather than natural homogeneity.[2] The territory included several powerful kingdoms—Buganda, Bunyoro, Ankole, Toro and others—and a larger number of smaller, less centralized population groups. Of these the kingdom of Buganda was the most important. Ethnically, it was much the largest single group and its elites were among the richest and best educated in the country. Politically, its level of organization made it virtually a state within a state, and in the 1950s there had been strong moves for the creation of an independent Buganda state quite separate from the rest of Uganda. While these moves were temporarily defused by the colonial administration, the longer-term issue remained unresolved. The tensions that existed in Uganda at independence called for considerable political skill, tact, and sensitivity from the leadership if chaos and turmoil were to be avoided. Unfortunately, none of Uganda's postindependence leaders appear to have been blessed with these particular attributes.

The preindependence elections of April 1962 proved inconclusive in that they did not result in any party gaining an overall majority in the legislature. The Uganda People's Congress (UPC), led by Milton Obote emerged with thirty-seven seats. The Democratic Party (DP) led by Benedicto Kiwanuka, which had strong support from the Catholic church, held twenty-two seats and the Kabaka Yekka (KY-king alone) had twenty-one. The KY was a strongly traditionalist royalist party formed to support the position of the Kabaka of Buganda. Although the UPC formed a coalition government with the KY in the immediate postindependence period, the relationship quickly deteriorated and Obote turned on the Bugandan supporters of KY. He used the army to storm the royal palace and the Kabaka, Sir Edward Mutesa, was forced to flee into exile in Britain where he later died. The institutions and symbols of the Bugandan government were banned and many Baganda leaders were arrested or killed. In the late 1960s Obote turned to increasingly authoritarian methods in his attempts to stay in power, including the banning of opposition parties and the creation of a single-party state. In his campaign of repression in Uganda, Obote became increasingly dependent on his personally selected army leader, Idi Amin, who dealt ruthlessly with the president's political opponents. The relationship between Obote and Amin has strong echoes of the Frankenstein story. Obote was responsible for creating the monster which first turned on its creator and then went on the rampage. By 1971 Obote was feeling increasingly threatened by Amin's growing power and decided to get rid of him. Before leaving for the Commonwealth Conference in Singapore in January 1971, Obote left orders that Amin was to be arrested and charged with corruption and murder. However, to protect himself Amin struck first and staged a coup d'etat to remove Obote and place himself as head of state of Uganda. Obote went into exile in Tanzania with his close friend Julius Nyerere. At this stage the coup was not unwelcome in all quarters. Some western governments were pleased to see Obote ousted and miscalculated the effects of the new regime. The Baganda were also pleased to see the back of Obote and were permitted to bring back the Kabaka's remains and bury them in the ancestral tomb. Such optimistic feelings were singularly short-lived.

The story of Amin's brutal, oppressive, and arbitrary reign in Uganda has been reported so widely as to make detailed restatement here unnecessary.[3] In the eight years before his overthrow in 1979 Amin and his henchmen turned Uganda into "a massive grave of rotten flesh."[4] Unknown numbers of Ugandans, certainly running into the hundreds of thousands, were slaughtered. Apart from those who fled into exile, almost the entire educated Ugandan elite was massacred, along with vast numbers of ordinary peasants. The Asian community was expelled en bloc in 1972[5] and their assets, worth an estimated 850 million dollars, were divided up by Amin and his supporters. Amin treated Uganda as his own personal property and state assets were used for his personal gratification or for rewarding those whose services he relied on. Corruption is too mild a word to describe such activities. The once-prosperous Ugandan economy was reduced to a devastated shambles. The social and communications infrastructure decayed and collapsed as any government spending not designed to keep Amin in power was virtually abandoned. By the end, the Ugandan state had collapsed and functioned only as an instrument of oppression in the hands of its tyrannical leader. Amin proved a quite remarkable survivor and numerous attempts at assassination and coups by his opponents failed as the Ugandan army broke apart. He was finally undone by his expansionist territorial ambitions. In October 1978 he invaded Tanzania in an attempt to annex the Kagera salient, claiming at the time that Tanzanians had provoked the fighting.[6] The years of turmoil had left the Ugandan army in no fit state to embark on international adventures and the attack on Tanzania was largely ineffectual. The response it provoked was far more important, and in January 1979 the Tanzanian army marched into Uganda. The Tanzanians were assisted by two small armies of Ugandan exiles led by David Oyite-Ojok and Yoweri Museveni, united under the banner of the Uganda National Liberation Army (UNLA). Amin's fractured army offered little resistance to the Tanzanian invasion and fled further north, looting as they went. An airlift of 1,500 Libyan troups to support Amin did little to help and by April Kampala had been captured by the anti-Amin forces of Tanzania and the UNLA. Amin himself fled to Libya and later moved on to Saudi Arabia where he still resides, promising a comeback in Uganda.

Uganda then embarked on a period of transition back to civilian rule. Despite widespread jubilation at the overthrow of Amin, this transitional period proved to be fraught with conflict and difficulty. Fighting continued in many parts of the country, involving not just the remnants of Amin loyalists but numerous armed gangs of little or no political allegiance. The transitional government became an arena of great conflict. A broad-based umbrella organization called the Uganda National Liberation Front (UNLF), which had been formed in Tanzania by various Ugandan exiles in 1979 took over the reins of government with its leader, Yusufu Lule, in control. Lule lasted just ten weeks in office before he was peacefully ousted and replaced by Godfrey Binaisa. The latter came into conflict with the powerful chairman of the military commission of the UNLF, Paulo Muwanga. In May 1980 Binaisa was in turn ousted and replaced as head of government by Muwanga. The latter had the responsibility of organizing new elections which were initially supposed to take place in September but which were then postponed until December. The fact that Muwanga was well known as a strong supporter of Obote did not get the process off to the best of starts.

In the end four political parties contested the election. Two were direct continuations from the pre-Amin period. Milton Obote returned from exile in Tanzania to lead his UPC, and Paul Ssemogerere took over the leadership of the reconstituted DP. Both party leaders had some difficulties in explaining away the past political record of their parties. Obote denied accusations that he had been responsible for creating Amin, arguing that this was just one, unfortunate, appointment he had made.[7] He even denied that he had created a single-party state in the previous period, arguing that the banning of opposition parties had been a temporary measure, that would rapidly have been reversed if he had not been ousted, and that he had never wanted a single-party state anyway. He stated that the decision had been taken by his cabinet when he was absent due to illness.[8] Obote's projection of himself as a born-again democrat did not convince everybody. Ssemogerere rejected suggestions that the DP had originally welcomed the Amin coup. He argued that it was Obote's banning of opposition in the First Republic that had led to the deep divisions within Uganda and, like Obote, he confirmed his unconditional support for a multi-party state and free elections. Ideologically, both parties were very bland. Obote abandoned his earlier left-wing rhetoric, and both leaders, not unreasonably, stressed the priorities of creating conditions of peace and reconstructing the country. The other two parties were smaller and less well organized. The Conservative Party (CP), led by Joshua Mayanja-Nkangi, was to some extent a revival of the old KY and what support it had was largely confined to the Baganda. It espoused the creation of a federal system in Uganda with a significant devolution of power. The fourth party was the Uganda Patriotic Movement (UPM), led by Yoweri Museveni. Lacking the organizational structure of the larger parties, it was a more radical grouping that was supported mostly by younger elements and those who had fought with the Tanzanians to bring down Amin. More than anything, the UPM represented an attempt to break away from the old ethnic and regional patterns of the past.

The election campaigns were marked by some violence, although it has to be remembered that Uganda was still a country in which violence existed irrespective of the elections. One DP candidate was assassinated and the party claimed that in seventeen constituencies it had been prevented from lodging its nomination papers. Doubts over the fairness of the elections increased when, while the counting of votes was taking place, Paulo Muwanga announced that the offical proclamation of results could only take place after he (rather than the electoral commission) had scrutinized them. At that time there were strong rumors that the DP had won a majority. Muwanga later withdrew this announcement, but the damage had been done to the credibility of the elections. The official results gave Obote's UPC a sizeable majority with seventy-two seats, including the uncontested ones where the DP claimed it had been prevented from standing. The DP won fifty-one seats, and the smaller parties registered little support, with the UPM picking up one seat and the CP none: It is difficult to know how much credence to give these results, but the evidence suggests that even though some malpractices had taken place, the results were broadly representative of real support. The Commonwealth Group of Observers announced that they were broadly satisfied that the election was about as fair as possible under the circumstances. Sathyamurthy suggests that the UPC would almost certainly "have won without resorting to foul means."[9] It is quite possible that Muwanga's heavy-handed and ineffectual intervention only served to reduce the legitimacy of the candidate he supported. Museveni refused completely to accept the results and returned to the bush to organize his National Resistance Army (NRA) and promote violent opposition to Obote. The DP, on the other hand, opted to accept the role of official opposition under the new system. On December 15, 1980 Milton Obote was sworn in as president (the first African leader to make such a come-back) with Paulo Muwanga as his vice-president and minister of defense.

The second Obote period of four years and six months lasted until July 1985 and cannot be considered a success. The economy did improve slightly, but improvement on the Amin record was from a very low baseline. The security situation in Uganda hardly improved at all, and numerous armed groups controlled different parts of Uganda. Some, like Museveni's NRA were highly motivated politically and surprisingly well-disciplined, but others can only be described as gangs of bandits. Obote's army, based on the UNLA which was supposed to help in restoring law and order, was itself undisciplined and did more to increase chaos than to control it. While Obote depended on his army to protect his position, he had in fact very little control over it. The obvious comparison between the disciplined and committed troups of the NRA and the shambolic and brutal performance of other armed groups, including the UNLA, was not lost on the Ugandan population, which increasingly supported Museveni's men. Government attempts to crush the NRA more often resulted in attacks on innocent civilians and the looting of their property which further increased NRA support. Independent bodies like Amnesty International provided abundant evidence of the terror tactics of government forces. While it would be difficult to completely exonerate Obote in connection with these developments, he increasingly appeared as a relatively weak and impotent bystander, and Uganda continued to suffer. The opposition DP had even less control over events. Perhaps surprisingly the party held together remarkably well: by the end of the period the large majority of DP MPs had stayed loyal and only a handful had defected to the UPC while a couple more had gone into exile and two had been killed. In July 1985 Obote was deposed by the army and replaced as head of state by Lieutenant General Tito Okello. The latter tried to patch together a ruling coalition by including civilian politicians in his cabinet. The DP leader, Paul Ssemogerere, became minister of the interior and the government also included three other DP politicians, a couple from the UPC and even one from the small Conservative Party. The period of rule of this government was very brief. The strength and popular support of the NRA increased and on January 27, 1986, it took control of Kampala. Two days later Museveni was sworn in as the new president to the accompaniment of considerable rejoicing in Uganda. At the time of writing, the new government (which includes representatives from the political parties) has still not managed to gain full control over all parts of Uganda but the country is less lawless than it was previously. The possibility of a new beginning once again exists in Uganda although the problems facing President Museveni are daunting. Whether the NRA can serve as a vehicle for the creation of some meaningful semblance of national unity remains to be seen. Ethnically the NRA is broadly based: Museveni is a Munyankole but his support base includes most groups in Uganda. Museveni has pledged to restore democracy to Uganda in four or five years' time, but it is obvious that if democracy is to have any real chance of success, very considerable preparatory work will have to be undertaken.

The reasons for the failure of the revival of democracy in Uganda appear to be fairly clear. Much less clear is the question of whether this can be seen as a failure of democracy as such or whether the inherited problems were so great as to have made the success of any system improbable at that time. It would appear highly unlikely that a continuation of military rule in 1980 or any attempt to impose a single party state would have fared any better or produced successful solutions to Uganda's gigantic problems. Museveni's commitment to a return to democracy in the future (whether or not this actually takes place) would seem to suggest that democracy itself is not to be held to blame. The single most important cause of the failure of the second Obote period was the legacy of the Amin period. As Decalo writes, "Amin's brutal nine-year reign left nothing but massive social and economic devastation and dislocation that taxed the resources of the successor Obote regime until its own collapse."[10] By 1980 no coherent state structure was in existence in Uganda. The nature of the transitional period from Amin to the revival of democracy both exposed and created further problems. What should have been a steady development toward recivilianization in an atmosphere of calm (as, for example, in Nigeria) was anything but. Instead, the process took place in a hopelessly confused and conflict-ridden atmosphere in which two further coups (the ousting of Lule and Binaisa) took place and military leaders battled among themselves for positions of power. In such a situation it was a necessary (although not sufficient) condition for any chance of success that the basis of legitimacy for the new government should be well established through the electoral process. Perceptions of electoral malpractice were based in reality, however exaggerated sometimes. Thus, the underpinning of legitimacy through the ballot box which might have helped sustain the system was uncertain and ambiguous.

If democracy is to be successfully restored in Uganda in the 1990s, all of these imperfections will have to be rectified. The Museveni government will have to ensure that law and order is returned to Uganda and that the various armed groups which still exist are disarmed and broken up. In setting a longer schedule for redemocratization, Museveni has made it possible for a more orderly and gradual process to take place. Ensuring that the elections are free and fair when they do take place will be difficult, but other African military regimes have demonstrated that it is not impossible. Whether or not the Museveni regime has the strength and determination to fulfil all of these conditions, only time will tell, but there is no doubt that Uganda needs relief from the traumas of the first quarter century of independence.

LIBERIA

The small west African state of Liberia may accurately be described as the most doubtful of our doubtful cases. Although a new multi-party constitution was approved in 1984 and competitive party elections were held in 1985, leading to the installation of a new government in 1986, the actual functioning of the system has been marred by a great many undemocratic features. The election was almost certainly subject to malpractice, and opposition parties and their leaders have been constantly harassed by government forces. There is no doubt that the operation of a democratic system has been seriously impeded by the attitudes and actions of President Samuel Doe and that Liberia presents a good case study of how vulnerable democracy is to the motivations of an authoritarian leadership. However, on a more positive note, Liberia does possess a framework for democracy that enjoys popular support. It also has a number of able opposition figures, some of whom are in detention at the time of writing, who continue to struggle to make democracy a reality in their country in spite of the obstructions placed in their way and the considerable personal cost to their own lives and safety. If these forces were to triumph, the transformation of Liberia from a pseudo to a genuine democracy is a distinct possibility. It remains to be seen whether or not this can be done without the violent overthrow of Doe.

Liberia has a history which makes it unique in Africa. Founded in 1822 by the American Colonization Society as an African homeland for freed slaves, it became an independent republic as long ago as 1847. It was never incorporated into any of the European colonial empires, although in purely economic terms it was as closely tied to America as the other African states were to their European masters. The Americo-Liberians (descendants of the freed slaves) enjoyed a relationship of dominance to the indigenous inhabitants which in many ways parallels the relationship of European colonizers to Africans in other colonies. The fact that they were black instead of white made little practical difference. Although Lowenkopf has correctly pointed out that this group was not quite as impervious to assimilation as may have been argued[11] they did form a very cohesive group that dominated Liberian society politically, economically, and socially until the last decade. Their True Whig Party (TWP) was the longest ruling party in the world. Coming to power in 1877, it controlled the government until the Doe coup of 1980, despite the fact that the Americo-Liberians numbered around one percent of the population.[12] For most of this long period of TWP dominance, the political system was formally one of democratic multi-partyism, but in practice it rarely operated as even a close approximation to this model. Periodic attempts to develop opposition parties were met with considerable harassment and they were often banned before they could fully develop. The franchise was extremely limited and a property qualification favored the richer Americo-Liberian elite. Elections were rigged to a staggering extent. In the 1927 election the opposition People's Party candidate was declared to have received 9,000 votes. With a qualified electorate of 15,000 this might appear a substantial victory, if it were not for the fact that the incumbent President King of the TWP was credited with 243,000 votes. This election enjoys the dubious distinction of being included in the *Guinness Book of Records* as the most corrupt election ever held anywhere. Earlier, in 1923, President King had somehow managed to secure 45,000 votes from a 6,000 electorate.[13]

It was not until the 1970s that the Americo-Liberia TWP dominance was significantly threatened. In 1971 President William Tubman, who had been in power since 1947, died and was replaced by William Tolbert. The latter was a member of the same elite ruling group but was less opposed to reform than his predecessors. Although the Americo-Liberians remained in a majority in Tolbert's cabinet, there was some attempt to ameliorate the situation by bringing in some people from outside this group. However, Tolbert's tentative reforms proved to be too little and too late, and in the second half of the 1970s opposition to the regime grew rapidly. Two major organizations formed in opposition to the TWP government. The first was the Movement for Justice in Africa (MOJA) which had strong support amongst younger intellectuals and was led by Doctor Togba Nah Tipoteh, who had previously been professor of economics at the University of Liberia until he was dismissed for political reasons in 1974. The other was the Progressive Alliance of Liberia (PAL), led by Gabriel Baccus Matthews, which briefly transformed itself into an opposition political party, the Progressive People's Party. As a party it survived just four months before it was banned and its leaders arrested.

In 1979 the regime was severely shaken by massive riots over an increase in the price of rice, the staple food of the poorer urban dwellers, which left up to 150 people dead. Although the initial response of the regime to the riots was one of brutal suppression, it later backed down over the price increase, a very rare example of a west African government changing its policy as a result of riots.[14] During the riots serious splits appeared in the Liberian army between the officers, who were mainly Americo-Liberians, and the other ranks, which consisted almost entirely of men from outside this group. President Tolbert was forced to use troops sent by President Sekou Toure of Guinea to control this situation. This crushing of opposition unrest proved to be very temporary. In 1980 the Tolbert regime continued its suppression of anyone associated with opposition movements and of "unreliable" sectors of the armed forces. In April 1980 the end finally came for the TWP's century-old supremacy. A military coup, staged by NCOs and lower ranks, and led by a previously unknown Master Sergeant Samuel Doe overthrew the Tolbert regime. Leading members of the latter, including President Tolbert, were publicly executed or privately butchered in an outburst of bloody vengeance that sent shock waves throughout west Africa and beyond.

In the end, the toppling of the TWP regime proved comparatively easy. But it left a thoroughly confused situation in Liberia, with government power residing in the hands of a group of predominantly young, ill-educated, and totally inexperienced as soldiers. Awash in a sea of revolutionary rhetoric, Doe established the military People's Redemption Council (PRC) to rule the country. The leading figures in this body, apart from Doe himself, were Sergeant (later Major General) Thomas Weh Syen and Sergeant (later Brigadier General) Thomas Quiwonkpa, both of whom were subsequently killed trying to oust Doe. In an attempt to secure army loyalty, the new government immediately doubled the pay of the soldiers. Doe also established a council of ministers which was predominantly composed of civilians, including most of the prominent opposition figures of the late 1970s. Matthews of PAL was appointed minister of foreign affairs, Tipoteh of MOJA became minister of economic affairs and planning, and another senior MOJA figure, Henry Fahnbulleh, became minister of education. This combination of radical, well-educated civilians and illiterate and nonideological (despite the rhetoric) soldiers made for a curiously unbalanced ruling group in which it was never clear quite who was using whom. The civilians hoped to be able to use their relationship with Doe to control the policy-making arena and move toward fairly rapid social change. The soldiers hoped that through the use of the civilians they could attain international respectability for the regime and a degree of ad-

ministrative competence in government. The hopes and expectations of the radical civilians and those outside of Liberia
who supported them soon proved to be illusory, and within a
comparatively short period of time they had all resigned or
been dismissed by Doe, who dropped his revolutionary rhetoric
in favor of a very conservative image. Symbolically, Doe abandoned his battle fatigues for expensive tailored suits and the
slim young coup leader was transformed into a rather portly
middle-aged politican.

Early on in his rule, Doe announced his intention of returning Liberia to civilian rule under a democratic system as soon
as possible. As early as 1981 a start was made in drawing up
a new constitution, and the final version was put to a national
referendum in July 1984. The new constitution finally abol-
ished the anachronistic property qualifications for voters that
had existed in the past and reduced the presidential term from
eight to four years, but in most other ways was not very different from what had existed before the coup. Elections to the
bicameral legislature were to be held on the basis of multi-
party competition. A rather ominous provision that political
parties could not advance ideologies "alien to Liberia's way of
life" was included. It was never made clear what might happen
if the referendum went against the proposed constitution but
in the end a huge majority voted in favor (540,113 to 7,771).
Following this the PRC was dissolved and a new interim national assembly was formed to rule in the transitional period.
The members of the assembly were chosen by Doe and included
both soldiers and civilians. A surprising number of the latter
were prominent survivors of the old TWP. At the end of July
the ban on political parties was lifted and from then until October 1985, when the elections were held, the focus of interest
was on the extent to which competition for power would operate in a democratic fashion. It rapidly became apparent that
Doe had no intention of withdrawing from power and simply
presiding over the choice of a successor regime as, for example,
the military elite in Nigeria had done in 1979. Rather it became
clear that he regarded himself as a contestant in the forthcom-
ing elections. While there was nothing illegal or unconstitutional in this, nor necessarily anything undemocratic, the
question remained as to how far Doe could or would ensure

the nonpartisan operation of the competitive system in which he himself was a competitor.

Unfortunately for democracy in Liberia, it transpired that the answer to this question was largely, though perhaps not entirely, negative. While Doe's own party, the National Democratic Party of Liberia (NDPL), experienced no difficulties in registering with the Special Elections Commission (SECOM), all the opposition parties had great difficulty in ensuring their registration. There is no doubt that SECOM acted in a way that was intentionally obstructive toward the opposition, and although, by the time of the election, three opposition parties had succeeded in registering, other potentially important ones had failed. During this period the press in Liberia was heavily constrained by the government, many opposition leaders were periodically taken into detention and some beaten up by the soldiers. The two parties that were outgrowths of the left-wing opposition movements of the late Tolbert period failed in their attempts to gain registration. The Liberian People's Party (LPP), led by an academic, Dr. Amos Sawyer, and based on the MOJA group, and the United People's Party (UPP), led by Gabriel Baccus Matthews of the former PPP, were unable to contest the election. The three opposition parties that did contest the election were all relatively weak, which is perhaps one of the reasons they were allowed to participate. They were the Liberian Action Party (LAP), led by Jackson Doe (not a relative), which included several old TWP figures, the Unity Party (UP) led by Edward Kesselly, another old TWP man who had been detained earlier in the year, and the Liberia Unification Party (LUP), led by Gabriel Kpolleh, a leader with no great political experience.

On October 25, 1985, election day finally arrived. For many Liberians who had previously been disenfranchised by the property qualifications in operation during the TWP period this was the first time they had ever had an opportunity to vote. Vast numbers turned out to vote and many spent hours queuing in the hot sun in order to exercise their democratic rights. Certainly the imperfections of the election cannot be blamed on the indifference or apathy of the mass of the Liberian people, who patiently and peacefully participated as best they could. Unfortunately, there is abundant evidence to suggest that the way the voters actually cast their votes bore only a limited relationship to the official results later announced. By putting the running of the election into the hands of his own supporters, Doe diminished any faith that observers might have had in the results. Numerous reports of burnt ballot papers, missing boxes, extra unexplained boxes turning up, and deliberate miscounting all reduced confidence in the official results in a self-defeating way that seriously undermined the legitimacy of the declared winners. While democratic elections contribute to the legitimacy of the government that results, popular perceptions of serious irregularities in an election have the opposite effect.

In the presidential elections Samuel Doe was officially credited with 50.9 percent of the total votes, an exaggerated figure no doubt, but one which appears almost moderate in comparison with the presidential election results of the 1920s discussed earlier. Jackson Doe was second, with 26.4 percent and Kpolleh and Kesselly almost level, with 11.5 percent and 11.1 percent respectively. Table 7-1 shows the results in the legislative election.

All the opposition parties claimed the results were invalid and demanded that the elections be declared void, but with Samuel Doe's placemen controlling SECOM, there was no chance of this happening. The LAP claimed to have won sixty-three percent of the votes in the legislative election. While it is obviously impossible to substantiate this claim, there is no doubt that the votes actually cast by the Liberian electorate for the opposition parties were much greater than the official results suggested.

Table 7–1. Liberian Legislative Election Results, 1985		
PARTY	SENATE	HOUSE OF REPRESENTATIVES
NDPL	22	51
LAP	2	8
LUP	1	3
UP	1	2

Within a couple of weeks of the election, political events in Liberia took another dramatic turn. On November 12 Brigadier General Quiwonkpa, an erstwhile colleague of Doe, launched an attempted coup using doubts about the elections as a justification. He promised that new elections would be held and that genuine democracy would be installed in Liberia. At first it appeared that the coup had been successful and there were reports of widespread rejoicing on the streets of Monrovia. Such joy was shortlived. Doe rallied enough of his bitterly divided army to beat off the challenge and the coup attempt was put down at an estimated cost of 1,000 Liberian deaths. Quiwonkpa's badly mutilated body was put on public display in Monrovia. On January 6, 1986, Samuel Doe was sworn in as the new president of Liberia in a flamboyant ceremony that was boycotted by most of the opposition MPs.

Since then the three opposition parties have united to form "a grand coalition" and have continued to call for the resignation of Doe and the holding of free and fair elections. In his relations with the opposition Doe has alternated somewhat erratically between stick and carrot methods to try to persuade them to tone down opposition to his rule. Several attempts have been made to co-opt the opposition leaders by offering them a role in government, but so far these attempts have failed. In September 1986 the ban on the UPP was lifted but Matthews proved no more compliant than the other opposition leaders. Over the same period all of the latter have spent time in detention.

Parallels with the later TWP period appear strong despite the fact that the social background of Doe is quite unlike that of his Americo-Liberian predecessors. Corruption and economic mismanagement are rife. In his refusal to allow the democratic system to operate as it was designed to and in his oppression of opposition, Doe appears to be denying the chance of a legitimate basis for government power in Liberia and foreclosing all peaceful options for change. If this situation continues, the chances of a repeat of the violent retribution meted out to President Tolbert in 1980 will remain a distinct possibility. Doe-mocracy is no substitute for democracy.

SUDAN

It must be stressed at the outset that Sudan is a very different case from both Uganda and Liberia. Although it would appear fair and accurate to describe Sudan as a "doubtful" case of democratic revival, the doubts arise from circumstances quite unlike those in the other two. In April 1986 genuinely competitive elections were held involving a number of political parties, and the victors formed a new civilian government which is still in place at the time of writing. The outgoing military leaders did not seek to influence the outcome of the election (as arguably they did in Uganda) and even less did individuals in the military seek to reestablish themselves in power through the electoral process (as happened in Liberia). The doubts surrounding the Sudanese case arise from the fact that in 1986 the electoral process was not in operation throughout the entire country. With a debilitating civil war still rumbling on in parts of the south the security situation meant that in some constituencies it was impossible to organize an election and polling had to be postponed indefinitely. Viewed from a national perspective, postponements accounted for only a relatively small proportion of the constituencies. Out of 301 demarcated constituencies, the election took place in 264, or just under ninety percent. From a regional perspective the problem was more serious as the postponements were confined entirely to the southern constituencies where elections were possible in under half; thirty-one out of sixty-eight. Certainly the organizers of the elections can justifiably claim that the fact that the elections were incomplete was due to circumstances entirely outside their control and did not represent any desire on their part to obstruct or restrict the democratic process, but the gaps must be seen as limitations on the revival of democracy in Sudan. The revival also faced other enormous problems. The collapse of the Sudanese economy and the widespread drought and famine that became a focus of global concern hardly presented a conducive environment. On top of this Sudan has become, not altogether willingly, the center of a massive refugee problem. Refugees from conflicts in Ethiopia, Uganda, and Chad have poured into Sudan. Reliable figures are impossible to obtain in such confused circumstances, but it is estimated that the country is home to at least one million refugees and quite probably very many more. Acting as host to such vast numbers of displaced foreigners not only places enormous strains on the already stretched Sudanese infrastructure, but tends to lead to political complications both internally and with Sudan's neighbors, further exacerbating the already major problems of the country.

As well as being the largest state in Africa (967,500 square miles) Sudan is one of the most socially diverse and one of the least well-integrated. The country forms a bridge between Arab Africa and Black Africa and fits easily into neither category. The most fundamental division is between the North, which is Arabic and Islamic and the South, which is distinctly black African and non-Islamic, with most people following Christianity or a variety of traditional indigenous religions. However, this simple dichotomy cannot disguise the existence of many further cleavages and neither the North nor South can be viewed as homogeneous entities. The Northerners are divided along ethnic and ideological lines and though Islam acts as a unifying force where relations with the South are concerned, the Muslim community is split into numerous sects and groups. The South is an ethnic and tribal mosaic with up to 572 different groups identified.[15] The nature of colonial rule exacerbated the social divisions of Sudan. Administratively there was no real attempt to unite the North and South and they were run on quite separate lines. Economic and educational development was confined almost entirely to the North, creating a serious imbalance in the country which left the South in a disadvantaged position. The paucity of communications further divided the North and South. Road links were little developed in the colonial period and since independence improvements in the communication infrastructure have been extremely modest.

Like is the case with so many other African states, the existence of Sudan is based on the rather arbitrary structures of colonial rule which have survived with difficulty in the postindependence period. The relationship between the North and South has fluctuated between uneasy peace and outright war throughout the period since independence in 1956. Starting at that time, an active secessionist struggle took place until peace was restored by the Addis Ababa agreement of 1972 which allowed for some degree of southern regional autonomy. However, by the 1980s the situation had once again deteriorated, due largely to the increasingly authoritarian rule of President Numeiri from Khartoum. In 1983 civil war resumed. Under the leadership of John Garang, the Sudan People's Liberation Army (SPLA), military wing of the Sudan People's Liberation Movement (SPLM), began a policy of armed struggle against the Khartoum regime. Although its support is confined to the South, the SPLM is not strictly speaking a secessionist movement because it advocates a high degree of regional autonomy within a united Sudan rather than the creation of a separate breakaway state in the South.[16] It also advocates a totally secular state in Sudan. This war continues despite numerous attempts to arrive at a solution. We shall return to the question of relations between the SPLA and the post-Numeiri elected government a little later.

Even without the North–South conflict, the immediate post-independence period in Sudan would have been one of great political instability with a high level of military involvement in politics. In 1969 Gaafar Mohamed Numeiri seized power in a military coup and, despite several further attempted coups, survived in power until 1985.[17] Numeiri attempted to give his basically military regime a civilian gloss by the creation of a single-party state in which his own Sudan Socialist Union (SSU) was the sole legal party. Throughout his time in power the regime remained a highly personalized autocracy. Despite some early success, most notably the Addis Ababa agreement that temporarily ended the civil war, Numeiri gradually became more and more isolated and his regime became more and more repressive. Several actions of Numeiri led to a breakdown of the agreement he had negotiated with Southern leaders. The decision to redivide the Southern region into three governmental regions, Upper Nile, Bahr al-Ghazal, and Equatoria, was widely seen as an attempt at divide and rule and a unilateral breaking of the 1972 agreement. More devastating to North–South relations was the introduction of Islamic Sharia law which included amputating the limbs of offenders. Such an imposition was totally unacceptable to the largely non-Muslim Southerners and served to promote the cause of John Garang and the SPLM. Although the introduction of Sharia law was popular with some Northern Muslims of a fundamentalist persuasion, it was viewed with suspicion by many others. As one writer put it, "many Muslims in Northern Sudan saw its harsh application as an attempt to legitimize repression in an increasingly shaky regime."[18] If, as appears likely, Numeiri's aim was to unite the North behind him even if this meant alienating the South, it was one doomed to failure. Opposition from many groups grew in the North only to be met with increased repression. The public execution in 1985 of seventy-six-year-old Mahmoud Mohamed Taha, a highly respected but nondogmatic Koranic theologian, was bitterly resented by all but a few on the far right of the political spectrum. By April 1985 the repressive nature of the regime and the accompanying economic crisis and food shortages led to large antigovernment strikes and riots in Khartoum and other parts of the country. On April 6, with Numeiri out of the country on a visit to the United States, the army, under its commander Lieutenant General Siwar al-Dhahab, deposed him in a bloodless and widely popular coup. It was, as one commentator put it, "both a coup and more than a coup,"[19] combining army and mass civilian opposition to the Numeiri regime.

The new regime pronounced itself merely a transitional one and identified its main task as preparing the way for the restoration of democratic civilian government within one year of the coup, a commitment which was adhered to. John Garang and the SPLA announced a seven-day cease fire and demanded that the new regime should relinquish power within that time. Predictably, Siwar al-Dhahab replied that it was quite impossible to complete the process of demilitarization within such a short space of time and rejected Garang's quite unrealistic demand. It is hard to believe that Garang expected his demand to be taken seriously and it appears to have been an exercise in political rhetoric rather than a practical proposal. At the end of the week the SPLA resumed hostilities in the South. Siwar al-Dhahab announced the formation of a Transitional Military Council (TMC) to rule Sudan in the period leading up to the restoration of democracy and began negotiations with civilian leaders, including most of those who had opposed Numeiri. After two weeks an interim cabinet was formed to take charge of administration during the transitional period. The fifteen-member cabinet was predominantly civilian with only the ministries of defense and the interior controlled by soldiers. Three non-Muslim Southerners were included, with the veteran Dinka politician Samuel Aru Bol as deputy prime minister. John Garang refused a seat in cabinet despite conciliatory moves by the government that included offers to cancel the redivision of the Southern region and modify Sharia law with special provisions for non-Muslims. Having failed to secure a peace in the South, the transitional regime began making arrangements for democratic multi-party elections. The ban on the formation of political parties that had existed under Numeiri was lifted and a large number began to form, representing a variety of ideological and regional bases of support. Some were a reincarnation of older parties like the Umma Party and the Sudanese Communist Party, but many others were new to the Sudanese political scene.

Many commentators expressed doubts as to whether the elections would take place, given the enormous economic and security problems that Sudan was facing. Some feared that Siwar al-Dhahab might use the problems as an excuse to postpone the revival of democracy and prolong military rule. In the end, these doubts and fears proved groundless, and in April 1986, just one year after the coup, the elections were held. Over forty parties contested the elections, which passed off peacefully despite the necessary postponement in thirty-seven of the Southern constituencies. The military made no attempt to interfere with the elections or determine their outcome. The results[20] in the 264 constituencies where voting took place are shown in Table 7–2.

Although the UP, DP and NIF clearly emerged as the major parties no party had anything like an overall majority and negotiations began to set up a coalition government. The key role was played by the leader of the UP, Dr. Sadiq el-Mahdi, a longtime opponent of Numeiri who had spent several periods in prison, the most recent from 1983 to 1985. He put together a coalition government dominated by his own UP and the DUP which included representatives of many of the minor parties including representation for Southern parties. He was later to claim[21] that his coalition represented around ninety percent of electoral votes. The most notable omissions from the coalition were the parties of the far right and the far left. From the right the NIF was excluded. Standing for hardline Islamic fundamentalist values, the NIF, led by Dr. Hassan el-Turabi, who was defeated in his Khartoum constituency, supported total

Table 7-2. Sudanese Election Results, 1986	
PARTY	ASSEMBLY SEATS
Umma (People's) Party UP	99
Democratic Unionist Party DUP	63
National Islamic Front NIF	51
South Sudan Political Alliance SSPA	9
Sudanese National Party SNP	8
Progressive People's Party PPP	5
Sudanese African People's Congress SACP	5
Sudanese Communist Party SCP	3
Sudanese African Congress SAC	2
Others	19

retention of the Sharia laws and rejected UP and DUP concessions on this key issue. On the left the Sudanese Communist Party was excluded from the coalition. The exclusion of the ideological extremes made any unified action by the opposition parties unlikely. In May 1986 Sadiq el-Mahdi was sworn in as prime minister and the military regime of Siwar al-Dhahab stood down in favor of the newly elected civilian government. Sharif Zayn al-Abidin al-Hindi of the DUP became deputy prime minister and also gained the foreign affairs portfolio.[22]

There is no doubt that the elections were marred by the absence of polling in the thirty-seven Southern constituencies. As long as the war continues there is little prospect of that situation being rectified. Since coming to power the Sadiq el-Mahdi regime has made several attempts to attain a political solution but without success. The problem is complicated by the wider regional conflict in that part of Africa which has become significantly internationalized, with world powers as well as regional powers taking part. Garang receives considerable support from the Ethiopian regime which perceives its interests to lie in the destabilization of Sudan. The war has become a debilitating stalemate with little prospect of outright victory for either side. While the revival of democracy and the ousting of Numeiri have removed some of the grievances that originally fueled the support for the SPLA, the reluctance of the latter to participate in the democratic process has made a political solution elusive. Meanwhile, the economic situation in Sudan remains precarious. The democratic system is better placed to solve these problems than the authoritarian alternatives of military or single-party rule that have failed Sudan in the past, but it remains to be seen if solutions can be found and, if not, whether the democratic system will be able to survive.

Chapter • 8

Ephemeral and Partial Cases

Burkina Faso, Central African Republic, Mauritania

THE CASES OF DEMOCRATIC REVIVAL following periods of military rule dealt with so far have all been full-blown examples of that phenomenon despite their imperfections and variety. To conclude the examination of demilitarization and democratization three further cases can be briefly examined. Realistically, these three cannot in themselves be said to provide particularly convincing evidence in support of the contention that democracy remains a viable force in Africa. At best they can be seen as minor examples of a largely submerged democratic impulse in three further state systems. The revival of democracy in Burkina Faso (the name which means "the land of men of integrity" was adopted in 1984 to replace the old colonial name of Upper Volta) and the Central African Republic (briefly titled Central African Empire from 1976 to 1979) was both partial and ephemeral. That in Mauritania is partial: whether it will also be ephemeral or whether it might lead to a fuller restoration of democracy remains to be seen.

BURKINA FASO

The remote, landlocked state of Burkina Faso is one of the poorest and least well-endowed in the world, with no real prospect for any significant improvement. It is the birthplace of the great precolonial Mossi Kingdoms, but during the colonial period it enjoyed a fluctuating existence. At times the territory was divided between neighboring colonies and its present borders were acquired in 1947. The territory appears devoid of any useful natural resources. It has a weak agricultural economy, mainly of a subsistence type, but even this has been plagued by almost constant drought. In spite of this the territory is relatively densely populated (nearly eight million in 109,869 square miles). One of the results of this imbalance between resources and population is that many of the most able-bodied in the population are forced to seek work in the more prosperous Ivory Coast. It has been estimated that at any given time around one million are in the Ivory Coast, some of whom have more or less permanently abandoned their luckless homeland. Since independence in 1960 the country has had a very high level of political instability, with frequent changes from one authoritarian regime to the next. Opposition parties were declared illegal shortly after independence, and the military has been prominent in the political arena ever since. However, in the late 1970s an attempt was made to revive some sort of democracy, although even this was subject to limitations. In November 1977 a referendum on a new civilian constitution was held in which 97.75 percent voted in favor. The constitution allowed for multi-party competition but attempted to limit the competition to three parties. Although no restriction on party formation was to operate in the first instance, the initial election was to provide the basis for eliminating smaller parties. After the election only the three parties that obtained the largest number of votes would be permitted to continue. The idea behind this entirely arbitrary device was to prevent a proliferation of parties, but to permanently ban those that failed to generate enough support in a single election has to be seen as a considerable restraint on democratic choice, especially since given the unsettled history of the country and the previous restraints on political association, parties in the first election were bound to be fairly ad hoc affairs. In the end seven parties were formed to contest the elections. All were centered around individual political leaders in the capital Ouagadougou and had little in the way of grass-roots support or organization in the countryside. Under the circumstances it is difficult to see how it could have been otherwise.

The legislative elections took place in April 1978. Only around forty percent of registered voters turned out to vote and it is recognized that the registration process had failed to register many who would have been entitled. In the elections the Union Democratique Voltaique-Rassemblement Democratique Africain (UDV-RDA)[1] won twenty-eight seats, the Union Nationale pour la Defense de la Democratie (UNDD) won thirteen, the Union Progressiste Voltaique (UPV) won nine, the Parti du Regroupement Africain (PRA) won six, and the Union Nationale des Independents (UNI) won just one. Two other parties, the Parti du Renouveau National (PRN) and the Groupement d'Action Populaire (GAP), together with a number of independent candidates, won none. Thus the UDV-RDA narrowly failed to win an overall majority. In May the presidential elections were held. The most controversial candidate was the incumbent military ruler, General Aboubakar Sangoule Lamizana, who had twice seized power through coup d'etat in 1966 and 1974. Lamizana was adopted by the UDV-RDA as its candidate, a move that caused splits in the newly formed party so that a breakaway faction put up a candidate to oppose him. All the other candidates argued that Lamizana should retire from the army before contesting the election, but he refused to do so. The first round of voting on May 14 proved inconclusive and so the two best-supported candidates went to a final round on May 28. On this occasion Lamizana gained 711,722 votes against 552,956 for the UNDD candidate Macaire Ouedraogo and secured the presidency, although he still refused to resign his army post. In 1979 all but the three largest parties were outlawed, as had been decreed by the constitution, although some individuals from the minor parties joined those that survived.

In November of the following year the partial and somewhat tentative democratic experiment was brought to an end by yet another military coup. The leader of the coup, Colonel Saye

Zerbo arrested Lamizana and banned all political activities. Since then the dismal picture of coup, counter coup and plotted coup has continued in Burkina Faso. In one attempt to quantify military intervention in Africa since 1980 through a "total military involvement score," the country is placed right at the top of the African league.[2] In 1983 Captain Thomas Sankara became the latest in the chain of military leaders. The youthful Sankara, an exponent of radical populism, survived in power despite an abortive coup in 1984 and a border war with neighboring Mali at the end of 1985, but in October 1987 he was ousted and killed in yet another bloody coup.

CENTRAL AFRICAN REPUBLIC

The revival of democracy in the CAR was even more partial and even more ephemeral than that in Burkina Faso. Since independence, this remote, backward, and sparsely populated state has had a most unfortunate political history.[3] In 1959, the year before its independence, the state was deprived of its most popular and credible leader, Barthelemy Boganda, by his death in a car crash. As a substantial producer of diamonds, the CAR has some economic advantages over Burkina Faso, but too often the focus of interest in the diamond industry has been theft and corruption rather than its contribution to the economic well-being of the country. Few outside of a small elite and some foreign participants have received any benefits. Politically, the country is most closely associated with the somewhat ludicrous figure of Jean Bedel Bokassa who overthrew his cousin David Dacko (himself a rather authoritarian and unpopular leader) in a coup in 1966 and ruled until 1979. During this period Bokassa created "a highly personal and increasingly abusive regime that exhibited marked features of tyranny."[4] In 1976 Bokassa, who was a great admirer of Napoleon, declared the end of the Republic and the creation of the Central African Empire in its place. The main, and perhaps the only, reason for this move was that an empire necessitated an emperor. In December 1977 Bokassa crowned himself emperor. His coronation, a surrealistic extravaganza, cost around $20 million and was received by most of the rest of the world with disbelief and derision. To see Bokassa merely as a pathetic megalomaniac and figure of fun is however, to miss the point.

His regime became increasingly authoritarian and brutal, cul-
minating in 1979 with the murder of over 100 schoolchildren
in which, it is reported, Bokassa personally participated. By
this stage Bokassa had become a source of deep embarrass-
ment to his major foreign backers, the French, and his removal
seemed convenient. In September 1979 French paratroops deposed him and installed, once again, David Dacko as president.
The imperial designation was abandoned and CAE returned to
being the CAR. Although the downfall of Bokassa was generally
welcomed, the new regime had a weak basis of legitimacy and
was opposed by many. In an attempt to create a more secure
basis for government, a new democratic constitution was drawn
up. In February 1981 the constitution was put to a referendum
which returned 97.4 percent of the votes in favor. It was, however, never properly implemented. In March 1981 presidential
elections were held but they were marred by violence and strong
claims that French troops interfered to support Dacko. There
were five candidates, four representing hastily created political
parties and one independent. They were David Dacko (Central
African Democratic Union), Agne Patasse (Movement for the
Liberation of the Central African People), Francois Penua (Independent), Henri Maidou (Republican Progress Party) and
Abel Goumba (Oubanguien Patriotic Front). Dacko was officially credited with 50.23 percent of the vote: less than fifty
percent would have necessitated a second round of voting. The
results were greeted by strikes and rioting and Dacko declared
a state of seige and arrested most of the opposition party leaders. Legislative elections were due in May but Dacko canceled
them until the following year: they were never to take place.
In September 1981 the army, under General Andre Kolingba
overthrew the Dacko regime and the country returned to military rule. The opposition leaders supported the coup but called
for a rapid return to democracy.

Democratization in the CAR was even more partial and
ephemeral than it was in Burkina Faso. Legislative elections
that would have tested levels of popular support for the parties
were preempted by the overthrow of the regime and there is
simply no way of knowing whether they might have been conducted fairly or what results might have ensued. However, despite the differences there do appear strong parallels between
the two cases. Both indicate a recognition of the belief that

competitive democratic elections provide a way of reestablishing a regime with a basis of legitimacy following periods in which the legitimacy of both the regime and the state system have been undermined by idiosyncratic authoritarian rule (which in the case of the CAR had reached unusual proportions). While this belief was not held ubiquitously and thus proved problematic in implementation, its presence is unarguable. In both cases political parties rapidly formed to take part in the process. In spite of the hasty and ill-planned nature of the exercise, it is obvious that, even in these early stages, there was no shortage of participants eager to play a role, thus further undermining the argument that the single-party state is "natural" in Africa. Even at the bottom end of the market of democratic revival this type of argument is demonstrably false. In neither case were those in control of the apparatus willing to let the system operate as it was designed to and as a substantial number of people wanted it to. This resulted in the willful frustration of democratic expectations and, as a direct consequence, the overthrow of those responsible for that frustration. The implied decision, by both Lamizana and Dacko, to treat the process as a zero sum game led directly, if not immediately, to their winning nothing.

MAURITANIA

At the time of writing the most recent example of democratic revival is to be found in the seemingly unlikely setting of Mauritania. The preliminary steps in the process are rather limited, but further democratization is planned. During the colonial period Mauritania was little more than an administrative appendage of Senegal from where it was governed by the French who did nothing to develop the territory. Since independence Mauritania has experienced a lengthy period of single-party rule, which lasted until 1978, followed by a series of fragile and fluctuating military regimes changed by frequent, but on the whole fairly bloodless, coups.

Mauritania is very large, over 620,000 square miles in size, but is reckoned to be the least densely populated state in Africa. No census has been conducted since 1976, but the 1984 UN estimate of population was 1,832,000. Much of the population is traditionally nomadic, but years of serious drought have been reducing the numbers involved in this way of life and the capital city Nouakchott especially has been rapidly expanding. Racial and religious divisions, between an Arabic north and a black south are reminiscent of Sudan but the political consequences have been far less severe. Tensions between the two communities have produced periodic riots, but there has been no development of a secessionist movement. For a considerable period, Mauritania was directly involved in the war in the Western Sahara, laying claim to part of the territory of the old Spanish Sahara. In 1979 Mauritania decided to abandon its participation in the war and renounced its territorial claims, leaving Morocco to battle it out with the Polisario front.

In December 1984 the newly installed military government of President Ould Taya announced its intention to move towards a democratization of Mauritanian politics. A general amnesty was granted to all political prisoners, and opponents living abroad were invited back to participate in the new moves. An incremental revival of democracy that would begin at the lower levels of the political system was planned. In December 1986 the first stage of the revival took place with municipal elections in each of the thirteen towns which act as regional headquarters. The elections were on a party list proportional representation basis. A maximum of four party lists was permitted in each town and party activity was restricted to the particular town so that national party activity was not allowed. If more than two party lists were put forward the two receiving most support proceeded to the second round of voting while the others were eliminated from the election (but not banned). In nine of the thirteen towns it was unnecessary to proceed to a second round: in three of these only one party list was presented and in the other six there were just two. In a further three towns three parties contested the election which necessitated a second round. Only in Nouakchott, which is very much larger than the rest, were there four parties. Seats on the municipal councils were awarded in proportion to the number of votes received by each party, whether in a single round or in the second round. The newly elected councils are responsible for local matters such as health, sanitation, local transport, and security. This partial revival of democracy was implemented without problems. One observer reported that "electoral campaigns were non-violent and spirited with large crowds participating in the colorful rallies. . . . discussions with participants indicated an earnest commitment to this small democratic opening."[5]

The revival of democracy in Mauritania is obviously fairly limited in extent at present. Although extensions are planned for the future, it is not yet clear when this will be applied to the level of national government, which is still controlled by an unelected military elite. Clearly the municipally based parties could form the starting point for the creation of new national parties if and when the opportunity arises. However it should be stressed that, within the limits laid down, competitive democracy appears to have operated freely and fairly in Mauritania. The elections were not rigged and there is no indication that the military attempted in any way to influence their outcome. For the first time since independence the Mauritanian electorate, or that section of it living in the towns at least, has been able to exercise some real choice over how it is governed by participation in a competitive democratic electoral process.

Chapter • 9

Democratization without Military Intervention

Senegal

UP TO THIS POINT the cases of democratic revival we have looked at have all been clearly associated with the process of demilitarization. Although some of Africa's military rulers seem determined to stay in power indefinitely, a good number have handed power back to civilians. Where this has taken place it has most commonly been accomplished through democratization. It has become clear that this is not necessarily a permanent change and that democratic revivals following demilitarization do not, so far, have a very good record of further survival. In a majority of cases the military have reintervened within a few years. The coup d'etat is now the most usual way in which democracy is eclipsed, although the eclipse itself may also be less than permanent. In the 1960s the most common way in which democracy was ended was through the creation of a single-party state, but this is now a rare occurence.

Zimbabwe may be proceeding in this direction, but having gained its independence twenty years after most African other states, it may well be following their pattern two decades later.

It does appear to be the case that once the military has intervened in the politics of a state there is a certain propensity for it to continue to do so, providing a succession of democratic and nondemocratic phases. It is not yet altogether clear whether this might be best thought of as democracy with authoritarian interludes or as authoritarianism with democratic interludes. What makes the Senegalese case especially interesting is that it represents the only example so far of a revival of democracy in which the military played no part at all. As will be seen, Senegal went through a period of undemocratic rule from the mid-1960s to the mid-1970s but then embarked on a process of democratic revival. Although this process was partial at first, it gradually expanded, with the eventual creation of the open and competitive system that exists in Senegal today. As a revived democracy it has already established a longer period of continued existence than the other revivals examined, although the nature of African politics precludes the possibility of giving any guarantee of permanency. Senegal is therefore critical for any study of the role of democracy in Africa. Questions about the long-term future of African democracy are bound up with the question of how many more Senegals we are likely to see.

By African standards the Republic of Senegal is a medium-sized state with an area of 75,750 square miles and a population of just under seven million.[1] It borders Mauritania, Mali, Guinea, and Guinea Bissau and is almost bisected by The Gambia. To the south of The Gambia the Casamance region has remained comparatively isolated from the rest of Senegal and a somewhat sporadic secession movement has existed for a number of years. Since independence Senegal has retained close ties with France in the economic, military and diplomatic fields, although the relationship is not quite as close as it was because the Senegalese have developed their contacts with other Western and some Arab states. Economically, the country is largely dependent on agriculture, which is prone to drought but has been developing its phosphate mining and fishing sectors. Groundnuts provide the main export crop. Around forty percent of the population are Wollof, with smaller numbers of Serer, Lebu, Tukulor, and, in Casamance, Jola, Mandinka, and

Fula. Around eighty percent of the population can speak Wollof, but French remains the official national language. Islam is the dominant religion, accounting for ninety percent of the population, and is increasing.[2] Some five percent of the population are Christian, mainly Roman Catholic, living largely in the urban areas and enjoying better than average educational standards. In general, Senegalese politics has been largely free from serious conflicts among the different ethnic and religious groups, and a tolerant and amiable relationship has existed between the different communities. President Leopold Senghor, who dominated Senegalese politics until his retirement at the end of 1980, was a Roman Catholic leader of a predominantly Muslim population.

During the French colonial period Senegal was of key importance. The capital, Dakar, was the administrative center for the whole of French West Africa. French policies of assimilation were followed more seriously here than elsewhere and African political advance in the urban areas (Dakar, Goree, Rufisque, and Saint-Louis, known as the "four communes") led the way in the European colonial empires. By the time of the French revolution, Saint-Louis and Goree already had African mayors. In 1914 Blaise Diagne became the first black African to sit as a deputy in the French Assembly.[3] A later deputy, Lamine Gueye, was a member of the executive of the French Socialist Party in the post-1945 period. The exposure to, and involvement in, modern electoral politics of Senegal's black urban population was far more advanced and extensive than anywhere else in black Africa. The contrast with anglophone Africa (or even more with Belgian or Portuguese Africa), is very marked. However, outside of the urban areas, the situation was very different and democratic participation was not possible for most of the colonial period. Suffrage was not extended to the rural areas, where the majority of the African population lived, until 1946. This disparity had important ramifications for the development of Senegalese politics. Gellar argues that "the great disparity in colonial status between citizens and subjects gave rise to two markedly different styles of political leadership. . . . In the communes the prototype of the political leader was the urbane western educated Senegalese intellectual: in the countryside it was the marabout."[4] The legacy of this situation can still be seen in contemporary Senegalese politics where the power of Islamic leaders in the rural areas is of great significance.[5]

Linking the late colonial period and the postindependence period and for much of the time dominating both is the impressive figure of Leopold Sedar Senghor, one of the continent's intellectual and political giants. Senghor was, and in many ways still is, a man of many parts and paradoxes. He was both a lofty intellectual and a highly skilled grass-roots politician. His philosophical formulation of negritude was one of the most influential to come out of Africa. Stressing the unique value of the African personality, negritude can be seen as a precursor of modern black consciousness and did much to undermine myths of white superiority.[6] Senghor was a Catholic leader who forged links with the leaders of the Islamic brotherhoods. He was also an autocrat who instituted the revival of democracy in his country and who became the very first civilian African president to voluntarily give up power and retire gracefully from office. Although he is no longer center stage in Senegalese politics, it has to be recognized that he did more to shape the political life of the country than any other individual. By the time of independence in 1960, Senghor's political party, the Union Progressiste Senegalaise (UPS), was dominant and assumed control of government, although a significant opposition was still operating. Between 1960 and 1966 the opposition parties were increasingly harrassed and most were banned, although Senghor managed to entice some of their leaders into his own UPS. From 1966 to 1974 Senegal became a de facto single-party state: in practical terms it was impossible for legal opposition to exist although the country never formally adopted a constitutional single-party system.[7]

In 1974, however, Senghor embarked on the process of liberalization which was eventually to lead to the extension of political pluralism and the revival of democracy in Senegal. In July of that year the Parti Democratique Senegalaise (PDS) of Abdoulaye Wade was legally recognized. This cautious first step reflected not just a belief in the desirability of democracy and political freedom on the part of Senghor, but a growing confidence on the part of the regime and a recognition of the fact that if opposition is to exist (which seems inevitable in Senegal), it is safer for it to do so in public than through the formation of clandestine underground organizations. In April 1976 the provision for opposition parties was extended through a new and rather curious constitutional amendment. The new formulation allowed for three parties but made it obligatory for each party to adopt one of three designated ideological positions; liberal, socialist, or Marxist-Leninist. Senghor insisted that his own party was to occupy the socialist slot, and Wade rather grudgingly accepted the liberal label for his PDS. The communist Parti Africain de l'Independence (PAI) of Majhmout Diop became the third recognized party. Although political ideology is an important concern for some of the urban intellectuals, it is largely irrelevant to the rural masses and this attempt to construct an ideological party system in Senegal appeared to have little connection with political reality, although it did allow Senghor to claim possession of what was probably the least undesirable of the ideological labels. In November 1976 the first elections under this arrangement were held at the municipal level and resulted in landslide victories for the UPS, although the PDS managed to gain control of two rural councils. In December 1976 Senghor's UPS, having gained admission to the Socialist International changed its name to the Parti Socialiste (PS), by which it has been known ever since. In February 1978 the first national elections under the three-party system were held and resulted in a landslide victory for the PS. In the presidential election Senghor won eighty-two percent of the vote, the rest going to his only opponent, Abdoulaye Wade. In elections to the national assembly the PS gained eighty-three seats and the PDS seventeen, while the PAI won none. While it does appear that there was some element of electoral malpractice, the enormous superiority of the PS electoral machine was largely responsible for the size of its victory.

Meanwhile, new opposition groups were attempting to gain legal recognition and registration as political parties. At the time this was hampered by the rules limiting parties to fixed numbers with prescribed ideological positions. But Senghor's victory over his opponents in the 1978 election had increased his confidence and clearly shown that the strength of the PS was not unduly threatened. In December 1978 a further concession was made to the strong desire in Senegal for a more open and freely competitive party system. The constitution was amended to allow for the legalization of a party representing a right-wing ideological stance. The Mouvement Republicain Senegalais (MRS), led by Boubakar Gueye, nephew of the late great nationalist leader Lamine Gueye, became the fourth party in the system. The new party, which had been established in 1977, had a monetarist economic policy and supported an increase in Islamic piety in Senegal. Despite this further concession, the basic structure of the rules limiting parties remained intact at this stage. Another new party, the Rassemblement National Democratique (RND), led by the eminent Senegalese academic, Cheik Anta Diop, was refused recognition under the rules. As the RND was a party of the left, it was argued by the government that this position on the ideological spectrum was already occupied by the PAI and that leaders and supporters of the new party should simply join in the PAI if they wished to participate in competitive electoral politics.

Although in democratic terms the system was a distinct advance on the previous de facto single-party rule in Senegal it was, by the late 1970s, starting to look rather cumbersome and restrictive. Its ideological categories did not appear to coincide well with Senegalese political reality, and pressure was building up for further liberalization. Having experienced a partial extension of democracy, there was a strong feeling that the reforms should be taken further. At the end of 1980 President Senghor announced, to the surprise of many, that he would retire from politics at midnight on December 31. This was a surprising decision, not least because he was the first civilian president in postindependence Africa to retire voluntarily. (Since then, a number of others have followed his example: Ahidjo in Cameroon, Nyerere in Tanzania, and Siaka Stevens in Sierra Leone). His decision was totally unforced and his comment, that "in politics you should know when to go,"[8] is probably the key to his exit. Although in his mid-seventies his health was good for a man of his age. The Senegalese political system appeared stable and secure and he had been grooming his successor for a number of years; it is rather pointless to groom a successor if you never allow him to succeed. The chosen successor was Abdou Diouf, who was some thirty years younger than Senghor. Diouf had been head of Senghor's private office from 1963 to 1965, secretary general of the presidency from 1965 to 1968, minister of planning and industry from 1968 to 1970 and prime minister since 1970. Under the Senegalese constitution it is the prime minister who succeeds a retiring president. On January 1, 1981, he was sworn in as president for the remainder of the five-year term Senghor had won in 1978. Two weeks later Diouf also succeeded Senghor as general secretary of the ruling PS. Clearly it was not going to be easy for Diouf to follow a man of Senghor's stature, and a number of commentators expressed uncertainly about whether he would be able to cope despite his acknowledged record as a fine administrator. Two writers summed this up when they wrote that "there are doubts as to whether or not Diouf has the political acumen to weld together the disparate ethnic, religious and economic interest in Senegal to long survive Senghor's passing."[9] However, any notion that Diouf might just be a stop-gap replacement, soon to be swept away by the rough and tumble of Senegalese politics, has long since disappeared. Since 1980 Abdou Diouf has quite remarkably increased his stature within his own party, within the Senegalese political system, and as an actor on the international stage. It would appear that Senghor made an astute choice in his successor and helped to launch a statesman with a stature directly comparable with his own.

As a reforming president, Diouf made a decisive start by confronting the problem of the extension of democracy in Senegal. Soon after taking over, he scrapped all the remaining restrictions on the existence and recognition of political parties. In April 1981 a new constitutional amendment made possible the free formation of parties to oppose the government as they wished. As in the case of several of the other democratic revivals, parties were still forbidden to restrict themselves to a single ethnic, language, religious, or regional grouping. This method of attempting to control the divisive potentialities of socially pluralistic African states appears to have become a common feature of the revival of democracy on the continent. Any party which was funded from abroad was also to be denied recognition. The reasoning behind this was rather more specific. At that time there was strong evidence to suggest that Ghadaffi's Libya was attempting to destabilize a number of west African states by financing antigovernment groupings. Not unnaturally, Diouf was unwilling to permit the opening up of democracy in Senegal only to see it become a vehicle for use by Libyan oil money to subvert the system. Subsequently

Diouf confirmed his antiLibyan stance by refusing to attend the OAU summit when it was held in Tripoli.

Diouf's desire to democratize as fully and as quickly as possible took most commentators by surprise because a more hesitant and cautious start to his presidency had been expected. In one sense his actions might be seen as a logical continuation of the process that had been started by Senghor in the mid-1970s, but there was nothing inevitable or predetermined about this extension of democracy. It can, of course, be argued that Diouf is a committed democrat and was merely availing himself of the first opportunity to turn his ideas into reality, while at the same time demonstrating that he was his own man and that the old order had changed. A timid maintenance of the status quo would have been interpreted as weakness on his part, now that his long-term patron had left active politics, whereas positive action on a popular issue disarmed his potential critics and signaled that he was a force to be reckoned with in his own right. It is also quite probable that a certain amount of astute political calculation lay behind Diouf's move, although one should beware too much use of the benefits of hindsight. It could well be argued that paradoxically, the decision to give more freedom to the opposition was designed to weaken them rather than strengthen them. By removing the restrictions on the number of opposition parties, Diouf could be seen as giving them full scope to engage in the sort of internecine conflict which would result in splintering and the creation of more but smaller and weaker opposition parties. The penchant of the urban-based intellectuals, who constitute the main opposition leaders, to engage in suicidal political and ideological squabbling was not entirely unpredictable. So long as Diouf was confident of maintaining the unity of the PS, at least in broad terms, there must have seemed a good chance that greater democratization was unlikely to pose much of a threat in the short term. As will be shown, to the extent that such calculations lay behind Diouf's decision, he proved to be astute at predicting the consequences of his actions. The relative importance of the idealism and Machiavellianism that lay behind Diouf's thinking at this time are of course impossible to assess precisely.

As was expected, there was a rapid rush of new parties wishing to register. Cheik Anta Diop's RND, which had been rejected under the previous arrangement, was among the first into the ring. Another party of political significance was the Mouvement Democratique et Populaire (MDP), led by Mamadou Dia who had been Senegal's first prime minister after independence but who had been sacked and detained following allegations of a coup plot. There were a number of other smaller parties of a mainly Marxist orientation including Maoist, pro-Soviet, and pro-Albanian varieties which seemed from the start to be of doubtful interest to the mass of the Senegalese electorate.

Having made this reforming, democratizing beginning, the first major test for Diouf was to come with the 1983 elections. These were the first post-Senghor elections and the first since independence in which the free formation of opposition parties had been permitted. The Senegalese electorate were to be invited to pass judgement on the new leadership of the ruling PS in a context in which a wide range of alternative choices were open to them. In the elections for the presidency a system similar to the Gaullist model in France was used and for the 120 seats in an enlarged national assembly a system of proportional representation similar to the West German model applied. The president was to be elected by an absolute majority on a national basis. In the event of no candidate achieving an absolute majority, a second round of voting was to take place. For the national assembly half the deputies were to be elected by majority poll at the departmental level and half by proportional representation at the national level. Both lists were to be included on the same ballot paper. It is generally believed by psephologists that proportional representation benefits smaller parties, although no system can do much for really miniscule parties. For the 1983 elections a number of smaller parties which had formed following the liberalization did not have the organization or the wealth to fight an election campaign and did not put forward candidates. In the end, eight parties contested the legislative elections but only five of these put up presidential candidates. The election campaigns passed off in an orderly and peaceful manner, and the opposition was given free access to the national media to state their respective cases to the electorate.

Both the presidential and legislative elections were held on

February 27, 1983, and marked a resounding victory for Diouf and his PS. Tables 9-1 and 9-2 present the results of the presidential and legislative elections.

The results of the presidential and legislative elections were very similar to each other and to the results of the 1978 elections. Most of the new, smaller parties were inconsequential in electoral terms; only the PDS (which had existed in 1978) and the RND (which had not) offered any real challenge to the PS. In the presidential election Diouf did marginally better than his party did in the legislative elections and marginally better than Senghor had done in 1978 when Wade had been the only opponent. In spite of the changes, the overall support for the PS candidates remained almost static between 1978 and 1983. The only difference in 1983 was that the opposition vote was spread more thinly around a wider number of parties and candidates. As mentioned earlier, the possibility of this sort of outcome may well have been a part of the reason for Diouf's decision to abandon restrictions on the opposition parties. If he really had calculated that the extra freedom given to the opposition would result in its fragmentation, then the doubts previously expressed about his political acumen would appear singularly inappropriate and the opposition parties have only themselves to blame for falling into the trap.

After the election both the ruling party and the opposition accused each other of electoral malpractice,[11] but the supreme court declared the process and the results valid. At first both the PDS and the RND said they would boycott the national

Table 9–1. Senegalese Presidential Election Results, 1983		
CANDIDATE	NUMBER OF VOTES	PERCENTAGE OF VOTES
Abdou Diouf (PS)	908,879	(83.45%)
Abdoulaye Wade (PDS)	161,067	(14.79%);
Mamadou Dia (MDP)	15,150	(1.39%);
Oumar Wone[10] (PPS)	2,146	(0.2%);
Majhmout Diop (PAI)	1,833	(0.17%).

assembly. Almost immediately the PDS changed this decision and its eight deputies took their seats. The situation concerning the single RND seat was more prolonged, but in April 1984 Babacar Niang, the deputy secretary general of the party, who had been on the parties' electoral list, took the seat. Because of disagreement within the RND, Niang broke away to form yet another new party, the Parti pour la Liberation du People (PLP). In February 1986 the RND leader, Cheikh Anta Diop, died, and his distinguished intellectual reputation produced glowing tributes from the government.

There is no doubt that the weaknesses and divisions within the opposition contributed significantly to the electoral success of Diouf and his party. The PS was clearly a much more organized and disciplined party and fought a really professional campaign. The petty ideological squabbling of the opposition might have been of some interest to the electorate in the urban areas, but was largely irrelevant in the rural areas where most of the voters are located and where the PS machine reigned supreme. In the rural areas the PS benefited enormously from the continuing support of most of the major Islamic leaders and teachers. Diouf was able to continue where Senghor had left off in these relationships, with the added advantage that unlike Senghor, Diouf was himself a Muslim. As Creevey comments, "the marabouts of all the major brotherhoods supported Diouf in the 1983 elections."[12] In African states in which competitive party politics are practiced, elections are won and lost in the rural areas where most of the electorate reside. It is the peasant rather than the urban dweller whose vote is crucial. Until such time as the Senegalese opposition can generate a strong rural support base, the electoral dominance of the PS seems assured. It is a recurring feature in Africa's competitive democracies that the opposition tends to be predominantly urban-based.

In April 1987 Diouf faced a quite different test of his leadership when the Senegalese police force went on strike. The issue that brought about the strike was the imprisonment of seven policemen who had been found guilty of seriously mistreating a prisoner four years earlier. The strike was illegal (as in many countries, the Senegalese army and police are not allowed to strike) and the issue was one that generated no public sympathy for the police. Striking police were involved

Table 9–2. Comparison of Senegalese Legislative Election Results, 1983 and 1978

PARTY	NUMBER OF VOTES IN 1983	PERCENTAGE OF VOTES IN 1983	PERCENTAGE OF VOTES IN 1978	NUMBER OF SEATS IN 1983	NUMBER OF SEATS IN 1978
Parti Socialiste (PS)	869,107	79.92%	82.45%	111	83
Parti Democratique Senegalaise (PDS)	151,970	13.98%	17.12%	8	17
Rassemblement National Democratique (RND)	28,520	2.62%	—	1	—
Mouvement Democratique et Populaire (MDP)	12,447	1.14%	—	—	—

League Democratique Mouvement pour le Parti du Travail (LD-MPT)	12,204	1.2%	—	—	—
Parti de l'Independence et du Travail (PIT)	5,929	0.55%	—	—	—
Parti Africaine d'Independence (PAI)	5,148	0.47%	0.32%	—	—
Parti Populaire Senegalaise (PPS)	2,128	0.2%	—	—	—

in rowdy demonstrations in Dakar, calling for the release of their colleagues even though their guilt was not challenged. Diouf responded by dismissing the entire police force and temporarily handing over normal policing duties to the Gendarmerie. The sacked police were allowed to reapply for their jobs on an individual basis.

Once it became clear that Diouf was not to be intimidated, this challenge to the rule of law by those employed to uphold it rapidly disintegrated. By the end of the year the majority of policemen had been reengaged, but the reconstituted force was one-third smaller than before the strike. Diouf's strong but astute handling of the problem did nothing to harm his chances in the elections constitutionally due the following year.

The Senegalese electorate went to the polls again in February 1988 in competitive presidential and parliamentary elections. By 1988 there were sixteen opposition parties in existence, but many were too small to make it worthwhile for them to attempt any sort of electoral challenge. In the end, only four parties contested the presidential election and six, the parliamentary elections. The decision of many of the smaller opposition parties not to contest had the effect of focusing the election rather more, and it developed predominantly into a two-party contest between Abdou Diouf and his PS and Abdoulaye Wade and his PDS, thus emphasizing the trend evident in 1983. Once again, support for Diouf from the Muslim brotherhoods was a crucial factor in much of rural Senegal as was the superior organization of the PS. The PDS, with its slogan of *Sopi* (Wollof for "change") campaigned better in Dakar and in Casamance, where separatist sympathies counted against the ruling party. The electronic media were made available to contestants on an equal basis: all presidential candidates were given five minutes each day on radio and television, and parties contesting the parliamentary elections had three minutes each.

The elections once again brought victory to Diouf and the PS, although a drop in support since 1983 was evident. Table 9–3 shows the full results.

The results clearly indicate that, in essence, the presidential election had been a two-candidate contest and the parliamentary election a two-party contest. Other candidates and parties had little support. Because the opposition parties had not engaged in formal electoral pacts, one can say that it was the

Table 9–3. Senegalese Presidential Election Results, 1988		
CANDIDATE	VOTES	PERCENTAGE OF SHARE
Abdou Diouf (PS)	828,301	73.2
Abdoulaye Wade (PDS)	291,869	25.8
Landing Savane (AJ-MRNDO)	2,849	0.25
Babacar Niang (PLP)	8,449	0.75

voters who dictated the duopolistic nature of the election. It is possible to speculate that if the development of pacts by those opposed to the PS had taken place, it might have increased the opposition vote even further. Wade and his PDS did best in Dakar and Casamance. In Ziguinchor province, which comprises half of Casamance, Wade defeated Diouf in the presidential election.

Some opposition leaders, including Wade, bitterly claimed that the official figures misrepresented the true picture, and riots broke out in Dakar involving mainly young people and students. Wade was arrested and charged with incitement to riot. He was found guilty by the courts, given a suspended sentence, and released. Although there was no evidence that the government had intervened, the leniency of the sentence made good political sense and shortly afterwards Wade entered

Table 9–4. Senegalese National Assembly Election Results, 1988			
PARTY	VOTES	SHARE	SEATS
PS	794,559	71.43	103
PDS	275,552	24.75	17
LD-MPT	15,664	1.41	0
PLP	13,185	1.18	0
PIT	9,304	0.84	0
PDS-R	5,481	0.49	0

into talks with Diouf. There is little doubt that the accusations of malpractice and the subsequent rioting marred the democratic character of the elections, although the South African claim that this proved that black Africans could not handle democracy has to be seen as unwarranted. All significant commentators agreed that, even allowing for the possibility of some electoral malpractice, the PS still enjoyed clear majority support in most of Senegal.

The revival of competitive democracy in Senegal has done little to dent the hegemony of the PS and its leader. Having been granted the opportunity to choose, the bulk of the Senegalese electorate have, so far, chosen to maintain the political status quo.

Chapter • 10

CONCLUSIONS

Explaining the Survival and Revival of Democracy and a Look Toward the Future

IN REASSESSING the place of democracy in Africa, the detailed experiences of a significant number of individual states have been examined. This is as it should be because they represent diverse sets of circumstances and outcomes rather than a single coherent form. Nevertheless, despite the inescapable difficulties involved in the process, some attempt at generalization must be made if one is to understand why it is that democracy has continued to play a role in African politics, in empirical contradiction of endless attempts to write it off, and how it may fare in the future. It would be unhelpful and tedious to repeat the details of the experiences of individual states here and no attempt will be made to do so. Rather, certain factors which appear to be supportive of democracy in Africa will be suggested.

In examining the reasons for the survival and revival of democracy in Africa, the main considerations appear to be political rather than economic or social. From a global perspective there appears to be a clear, though not deterministic, relationship between levels of economic development and the existence of democracy. Such a relationship is difficult to find *within* Africa. By world standards, all African states can be seen as underdeveloped, and yet some function on a democratic basis. There does not appear to be any connection between levels of economic development and the existence of democracy. For example, it does not appear to be the case that more economic development in some states has enhanced the prospects for democracy when compared with less economically developed states. Kenya, Cameroon, Malawi, and Ivory Coast have all enjoyed relative economic prosperity in comparison with, for example, The Gambia, and yet they have not been democratic. The only exception to this general picture is that democracy does not appear to survive in those states which have experienced total economic collapse. A large degree of social pluralism is generally seen as dangerous to democracy, and yet in Nigeria, where this is found to the greatest extent, the democratic impulse, despite setbacks, appears stronger than in ethnically homogenous states like Swaziland and Somalia. It is thus difficult to explain convincingly the survival and revival of democracy through social and economic factors, and it becomes necessary to turn to political factors.

A short time ago I was interviewing President Dawda Jawara of The Gambia and asked him directly why he had thought it important to maintain a democratic system. He looked at me for a few seconds, then smiled and in his usual quiet, thoughtful way replied, "if you look at the alternatives I think you can see why." This reply sums up nicely one of the main reasons why, despite difficulties, democracy continues in Africa. The reason is a negative one. The political experience of more authoritarian types of rule, whether single-party or military, has in general not been a happy or successful one in terms of performance indicators like stability, efficiency, development, or human rights. It is this failure of authoritarian alternatives that has kept democracy alive. In the first few years after independence a sense of disappointment was common. Freedom from colonial rule had for most people failed to live up to expectations as the benefits promised by nationalist politicians failed to materialize. Although the mood was open to a fair amount of cynical manipulation by self-seeking politicians, there was also a more genuine belief that many problems were the fault of the inherited political systems. Oppositions parties especially were blamed for promoting divisive tendencies and hindering progress, and it was felt that a strong, united government and political system might be more appropriate to tackle what were, quite genuinely, immense problems of nation-building and development. When many of the resulting single-party states also failed to provide solutions, the military often stepped in. Once again there was an initial period of optimism. The military were seen as a strong, disciplined, coherent group with a pronounced sense of national purpose and an appropriately technocratic approach to the problems of development. Impressed by the altruistic pronouncements made by the soldiers to justify the forceful overthrow of civilian governments, many observers looked to a new dawn. Unfortunately it never materialized. Once the soldiers were in office the unreality of many of the assumptions made about African armies became apparent as they showed themselves to be just as incompetent and corrupt as their predecessors. Frequently they soon proved to be even more faction-ridden than the civilians. The disciplined unity of many armies proved to be a sad myth, a fact that led to many violent struggles and counter coups within the army.

Single party and military rule necessitate some sacrifice of political rights and civil liberties. Opponents of the government are forbidden to organize even peacefully, and the electorate is denied the choice of voting for such opponents. However, in too many cases, the price, in terms of rights and liberties, has been paid but the benefits have not been delivered. Authoritarian regimes have in the main failed to provide commensurate gains in stability, national order, and economic development. Often there is little or no check on a self-centered bureaucratic elite tied to a ruling party or military junta. Corruption has been increasingly recognized as a major problem in many African states, including, it must be said, some democratic ones. However, it would be ludicrous to argue that the incidence of corruption would be lessened by the absence of free opposition to check and criticize the government. In authoritarian states would-be critics of disastrous economic policies find themselves powerless against the uncontestable power of ruling elites who devise and benefit from such policies. The major sufferers are frequently the rural peasant masses. In all African states the peasants are the majority of the population, and where democracy exists, their votes are necessary to any ruling group hoping to stay in power or any opposition trying to replace them. Thus, the fact that neglect of peasant wishes and interests would amount to electoral suicide inhibits the development of too extreme an urban bias. In authoritarian states where the votes of the peasantry are not needed to survive, governments are at liberty to emphasize urban interests (including the army) which offer more of a political threat.

Nor have authoritarian states been more stable than democratic ones. The most common result of the introduction of the single-party state is the military coup; the most common result of the coup is a series of countercoups. Although democracies are sometimes overthrown by the military, evidence suggests that they are less prone to this than other forms. One recent study, based on a major statistical survey, concluded that "African states that have either maintained or restored some degree of party competition have considerably less military involvement than more authoritarian states."[1] Party competition is seen as "strongly stabilizing." The relationship between the lack of democracy and instability is not only concerned with military intervention. The old view that public contestation when allied to social pluralism would lead to the breakup of African states, appears to have little empirical support. One might correctly view the emergence of significant secession movements and consequential civil war as the maximum level of instability because the very existence of the state as a unit is called into question. Given the arbitrary nature of colonial state demarcation in Africa, one might have imagined that this would become a common feature of African politics, but this has not happened. Most conflict within states has been for control of the existing state, not the creation of a new one. However, it is noticeable that where significant secession movements have arisen, they have not done so within in states that proclaim to be democratic but within states that (at the time of attempted secession) were highly authoritarian (e.g., Biafran secession during the military period in Nigeria, in southern Zaire, and at the present time in several parts of Ethiopia).[2] Insomuch as secession is linked with legal and legitimate public contestation, it is the absence of the latter that appears a contributory factor, not its presence.

The negative learning experience associated with authoritarian rule is related to the periodization of democratic decline and revival outlined earlier. Disenchantment with what were thought to be the failures of democracy was rife in the 1960s and helped its decline. However, by the later 1970s even greater disenchantment with authoritarianism contributed to the continuing phenomenon of democratic revival in a number of states. Although it cannot be proved, it seems likely that if authoritarian government had been widely successful, the abandonment of democracy in Africa might have continued as the dominant theme. However, as Jawara said "look at the alternatives."

In spite of this I would not wish to argue that positive beliefs in democracy are solely determined by the experience of its absence. This would be to neglect the importance of democratic ideals and ideas. All but the most committed materialist would recognize the importance that ideas have in political life. In spite of the difficulties that democracy has faced in Africa, an undeniable feature of the debate has been the continuing strength of support at both elite and mass levels for the idea of free and open democratic competition: what one might justifiably call the persistence of the democratic alter ego. For the electorate it is hardly surprising that they prefer a real choice that makes governments more accountable to them. The mute testament of long lines of African peasants queuing in the hot sun to take part in competitive elections supports this. To argue that the mass of the population in Africa does not understand or value democracy is patronizing and wrong, even when such views are propounded by some African leaders. To argue that avoidance of starvation and poverty is more important for the African masses than the niceties of democracy may be true, but it is irrelevant because it is to assume that they are mutually exclusive alternatives. It is simply not true to say that the denial of political rights and the removal of civil liberties is likely to make most of the people better off in a material sense.

Support for democracy in Africa is certainly not ubiquitous, but it is found widely at all levels of society. Calls for a restoration of democracy where it has been denied are very widespread, even though political elites do not necessarily respond to such calls. We have already seen how a firm belief in democracy by such as Khama, Masire, and Jawara has facilitated democratic survival. In recent years support for democracy which involves competition has also come from some more surprising sources. In a remarkable speech in Lusaka, Zambia, in June 1986 ex-president of Tanzania Julius Nyerere said that since retiring as head of state, he had studied his own structure and concluded that there were serious flaws that made him doubt the viability of a single-party political system.[3] He argued that the single-party system bred complacency among elected representatives because "there is an absence of political challenge to keep the leaders of the ruling party on their toes."[4] He also said that he had told Robert Mugabe of Zimbabwe of the "negative aspects of the single-party state." *The Times of Zambia* said in an editorial that "Mr. Nyerere's expressed misgivings should be ringing in our ears." In the longer term it will be interesting to see what effects this change of heart by Nyerere has on political developments. In the past his status has meant that much of the moral basis of support for single-party rule rested on his advocacy.

Vitriolic attacks on the single-party system and strong defense of competitive democracy have also come from the radical Tanzanian Marxist Abdul Rahman Mohmed Babu. The latter had previously been a supporter of the single-party state in Tanzania. He was at one time minister of economic development, but later his radicalism led to his detention and subsequent exile. Babu has argued that "loyal opposition is an essential and indispensable aspect of the political life of the nation. . . . a one-party system is not and by definition cannot be democratic."[5] He has also called for "a struggle for the abolition of the repressive system of one-party states" which has "more than anything else contributed to the economic and political stalemate in Africa."[6] The same writer also attacked the view that Africans are not yet ready for democracy, a view that has been proposed by some leaders of authoritarian regimes in Africa. He wrote that "they are in effect justifying the Bothas' and Smiths' claim that Africans are not yet ready for complete freedom; unwittingly they are reflecting the same fascist and racist frame of mind."[7] More recently the veteran Kenyan politican and ex-vice-president Oginga Odinga broke seven years' political silence when, in an open letter to President

Daniel Arap Moi, he bitterly criticized the single-party state and called for a restoration of a multi-party system.[8] The possibilities of this taking place are reduced by Moi's previously stated opposition to a multi-party state. He has said that "many people even in Kenya do not realise how much we owe our progress to the one party system. . . . it is within the multi-party democracies in this continent that anarchy has re-emerged most frequently."[9] The evidence strongly suggests that this linkage of democracy and anarchy is false and that by refusing to countenance constitutional opposition from people like Odinga, Moi is merely fueling support for violent and clandestine opposition groups.

It is clear that support for democracy in Africa is found across the broad range of the ideological spectrum including not only the liberals one might expect, but also radical socialists like Odinga and Marxists like Babu.

The continued existence of the partially submerged democratic alter ego can also be witnessed in some very unlikely places. Even in some of the most resolutely authoritarian states, leaders often express the view that competitive democracy is what *ought* to exist, even if present circumstances, so they argue, make it impossible. In a practical sense the short-term ramifications of such a position may not be great, but it is a further indication of the importance of democracy as an idea despite its difficulties in Africa. It is very frequently the case that military leaders, when ousting a government through an unconstitutional coup d'etat, promise a later return to democracy. Whether they eventually achieve this, or indeed whether they stay in power long enough to do so, is, of course, a different matter, but it is curious that what is the least democratic of acts is often accompanied by a restatement of a belief in democracy as the ideal, even though it has not been the norm in postindependence Africa. Siaka Stevens who introduced a particularly authoritarian single-party system when he was president of Sierra Leone, has stated that "I sincerely hope that our people will adopt the multi-party parliamentary system when the long and painful process of fully integrating and unifying our nation has been successfully completed."[10] This is, of course, the "Africans are not yet ready for democracy" argument that Babu and others (including this author) strongly dispute, but it is interesting to see competitive democracy remaining the ideal even in the unpromising context of Sierra Leone. It is also ironic that Stevens was himself the first African leader of an opposition to come to power through electoral victory, even though in his case the intervention of the military was needed to facilitate the transfer of power. Unsurprisingly, Stevens had previously been an outstanding advocate of the importance of a legal opposition.

These few examples, which could be multiplied many times over, should be seen as an indication of how widespread the existence of the democratic alter ego is in African politics. While this study has concentrated on democratic survival and revival it should not be thought that support for the idea that democracy is the way in which politics ought to be organized is restricted to those cases alone.

Although protestations of democratic intent made by military governments may at times be spurious,[11] this is, obviously, not always the case. It has been clearly shown that demilitarization provides much the most common route to the revival of democracy in Africa, providing all but one of the cases of this phenomenon. However, revival of democracy brought about by a return to the barracks cannot simply be explained by an attachment to democratic ideas on the part of some military elites, however genuine they may be. It is also necessary to take into account the political dilemmas that face military regimes. It is generally accepted that although it is easy for the military to seize power, it is difficult for them to handle it in the long term. Sooner or later the question arises as to how long a particular military regime wishes to stay in power. Unless it is brutally repressed, there is normally a buildup of civilian demands for a return to civilian rule. In addition to this, experience has shown that the longer a military regime stays in power, the more susceptible it is to a countercoup arising from divisions within the army. These divisions may be of a sectional nature (ethnic, regional, religious, etc.) or they may simply reflect the fact that even under a military government the majority of the soldiery are not involved in the processes of government. Jealousy and resentment often build up among the majority of the armed forces against the small minority actually exercising state power. Such countercoups can be very bloody. Thus, rational calculations of personal safety may predispose military governors to withdraw. Sometimes even the members of a military government may be split on this issue. Although military leaders can still decide to try and retain a military form of government, perhaps with a little civilian gloss, it is a risky business and it is not surprising that prudence leads many to the decision to hand back power to civilians. The attempt at the halfway house of UNIGOV suggested by Achaempong in Ghana was never implemented and ultimately led to his overthrowing and subsequent execution.

Once the decision has been taken to return power to civilians, the question inevitably arises as to which civilians to hand power back to (this problem of the transfer of power is almost identical to the one faced in the late colonial period). The choice then lies between attempting to impose a particular civilian regime or allowing the electorate to select one through the ballot box. While the first alternative of imposing a regime of the military's choosing has some attractions, it also has a number of drawbacks from the point of view of the soldiers. Where there is strong pressure from civilian groups for military withdrawal, such groups are unlikely to be placated if, as their final act, the military handpicks its successors. Also, if the military elite nominates a successor government, it then becomes directly implicated in any of the failings that government may display in the future, which could turn out to be dangerous. Because they did not do this, Obasanjo in Nigeria and Rawlings in Ghana could escape responsibility for the failings of the Shagari and Limann regimes.

The process of military withdrawal from power is clearly problematic and entails a number of difficult decisions along the way. Even to propose a hand-over period of a few years risks being interpreted as a desire to cling to power for as long as possible. The decisions of the military are not predetermined and can go in a number of directions but, as has been shown, the logic of the situation has led to a number of cases in which the military, as a way out of the dilemma they face, decide on a revival of democracy in which the question of the successor government is left in the hands of the electorate. It is something of an irony that a quarter of a century after independence, African armies pose the greatest threat to democracy on the continent[12] and at the same time provide the most common route to its revival. Although the military often make return to democracy possible, they pose serious problems for its consolidation because of their propensity to reintervene. This situation is enhanced by the fragmented nature of so many African armies. The military threat to democracy emanates not from a single source but from a multiplicity of sources. These sources are mutually hostile, lacking formal overt structure, and tend to be defined retrospectively as a result of action or inaction. As such they are virtually impossible to guard against. Democratic civilian regimes can try to avoid giving too easy an excuse for military intervention (for example, by minimizing the extent of corruption and by adhering to constitutional procedures), but ultimately there is probably nothing they can do to make themselves "coup proof."

Finally it can be argued that a competitive party system is more natural in that is reflects the plural nature of all African states. The evidence suggests overwhelmingly that unless steps are taken to prohibit the free formation of parties, more than one will emerge. In some cases, such as Botswana, The Gambia, and Senegal, one particular party has risen to dominance while opposition parties have remained fairly weak, but nevertheless opposition has persisted. Justifications of the single-party state that claim it represents a natural unity of the citizenry do not bear close examination: the only way to achieve the authoritarian single party is forcibly to impose it. To pretend otherwise is to falsify the reality of political life in Africa.

THE FUTURE

In reassessing the role of democracy in black Africa over the past quarter of a century or more, the conclusions presented here have clearly been more positive and optimistic than is usually the case. The overly pessimistic view that competitive democracy cannot exist in Africa has been shown to be contradicted by the evidence: democracy can exist, and it does. Democracy is not the rule in Africa, but neither is it so very exceptional. However, even this positive view cannot hide the fact that it would be naïve to suggest that in the foreseeable future all or most African states are likely to emerge as stable democracies. The heady optimism of the independence period is unlikely to be repeated: a quarter of a century on, Africa is a sadder and wiser continent. However, the disappointments of independence have led to an overreaction on the part of observers of Africa. Most of the recent literature has concentrated almost entirely on negative aspects and has been filled with a profound doom and gloom. The need now is for a more balanced view which can combine optimism with realism and which pays as much attention to democracy's successes in post-independence Africa as to its failures. It is in this spirit that I will attempt to make some tentative predictions about what role democracy is likely to play in the foreseeable future. Political prediction in Africa is fraught with problems, but so long as it is based on a realistic assessment on what has already taken place it is not worthless.

It does appear that predicting what is likely to take place on a general level in Africa can be done with more confidence than predicting what will happen in individual states, in which a combination of local factors, perhaps as yet unknown, can prove conclusive. For those states currently practicing democracy, dangers still exist, greater for some than for others, and it seems probable that not all will succeed in maintaining a democratic system. Experience would seem to support this contention. Equally, experience suggests it is very probable that in some states that currently have authoritarian systems, democracy is likely to be revived. In other words, although some democracies may well collapse they are likely to be replaced by others, thus keeping alive the democratic alternative in Africa. To predict the moderate persistence of democracy in Africa is more realistic than to predict its total eclipse. It is surprising how often the collapse of a democratic government is interpreted as definitive proof that democracy is not a viable form of politics in Africa, whereas the equally frequent collapse of a single-party state or military government is not interpreted in the same way. The future of African democracy is likely to be patchy and changeable but persistent.

From the evidence, it would also seem likely that democracy within particular African states will be part of a cyclical process in which it alternates with more authoritarian forms. It has already been suggested that the poor performance of authoritarian regimes enhances the image of democracy and contributes to its revival. It follows logically that when a democratic government performs poorly the chances increase that it will be overthrown (Africa still being very short of peaceful changes of government through the ballot box, although this could also be subject to change). Although the poor performance is more likely to be in spite of democracy than because of it, disillusionment can settle in. Social and economic conditions are not deterministic, but they do act as factors that can be supportive or nonsupportive of democracy, and in Africa it must be admitted they have often been of the latter type. Although the position will be mixed, there does not seem any great prospect for the continent as a whole that these conditions will change dramatically in the near future. Even though only a small number of African states have achieved dramatic economic growth, the number that have maintained a steady state, with perhaps a little progress in some sectors, do outnumber those in which economic collapse has occurred, even if it is the latter type that grab the headlines. There is evidence to suggest that in a number of cases the lessons of past economic experience are being learned and that changing policies and priorities could allow for moderate economic improvement. Social pluralism, the inheritance of arbitrary colonial division, will also continue to be a feature, but not in an unchanged way. The political role of class has often been overstated by various writers on the left, but it appears likely that it will grow in importance, even if it continues to operate alongside more traditional cleavages rather than replacing them. The evidence of Mauritius suggests that where this happens, communal cleavages become more blurred and less of a threat to democracy.

Even if it is right to be cautious about the prospects for significant economic and social change, the predictions for democracy in Africa do not have to be gloomy as political factors play a more crucial role. If developed economies, first-rate infrastructures, high standards of universal education, and homogenous populations were necessary preconditions for democracy, it would not exist in Africa or anywhere else in the Third World.

What then will the political map of Africa look like a decade from now? The best guess might be that it will still represent a patchwork of different types of authoritarian and democratic regimes. Authoritarian regimes will still be in the majority, but perhaps in a smaller majority than today. It is even possible that the Republic of South Africa will have joined the democratic group of African states. For this to happen, major changes will have to occur, but a democratic South Africa would be a great boost to African democracy.

Notes

Chapter 1. Democracy as Choice and Competition in an Imperfect World

1. The use of a referendum does incorporate an aspect of direct democracy.

2. Martin Staniland, "Democracy and Ethnocentrism," *Political Domination in Africa: Reflections on the Limits of Power*, ed. Patrick Chabal (Cambridge: Cambridge University Press, 1986), p. 57.

3. Ibid., p. 56.

4. To dichotomize the roles played by the participants in a political system as being those of either politicians or voters is, of course, misleading. What exists is a spectrum of political activism ranging from top members of the political elite to the individuals whose only political act is to cast a vote,—with a wide range of modes of political participation in between.

Chapter 2. The Conditions for Democracy?

1. See, for example, S. E. Finer, *Comparative Government* (London: Penguin, 1970).

2. See Philip O'Brien and Paul Cammock, *Generals in Retreat: The Crisis of Military Rule in Latin America*, Manchester University Press, 1985.

3. See, for example, M. Angulu Onwuejeogwu, *The Social Anthropology of Africa* (London: Heinneman, 1975).

Chapter 3. An Overview of Democracy in Africa: The Transfer of Power and Beyond

1. See R. W. Johnson, "Guinea" *West African States: Failure and Promise*, ed. John Dunn (Cambridge: Cambridge University Press, 1978), pp. 36–65.

2. See Nyerere's collected speeches in *Freedom and Unity, Freedom and Socialism* and *Freedom and Development*, (Oxford: Oxford Uni-

versity Press: 1966; 1968; and 1973). See also Cranford Pratt, *The Critical Phase in Tanzania, 1945–1968* (Cambridge: Cambridge University Press, 1976); John Hatch, *Two African Statesmen* (London: Secker and Warburg, 1976); Andrew Coulson, *Tanzania: A Political Economy*, (Oxford: Clarendon Press, 1982).

3. See Issa G. Shivji, *Class Struggles in Tanzania*, (London: Heinemann, 1976).

Chapter 4. The Unambiguous Cases: Botswana, The Gambia, Mauritius

1. See, for example, Christopher Colclough and Stephen McCarthy, *The Political Economy of Botswana: A Study of Growth and Distribution* (Oxford: Oxford University Press, 1980); Penelope Hartland-Thunberg, *Botswana: An African Growth Economy* (Boulder, Colo.: Westview Press, 1978); Charles Harvey, ed., *Papers on the Economy of Botswana* (London: Heinemann, 1981). For a critical study of one aspect of wealth distribution see Lewis A. Pickard, "Bureaucrats, Cattle and Public Policy: Land Tenure Changes in Botswana," *Comparative Political Studies*, Vol. 13, No. 3: (October 1980), pp. 313–356.

2. This is a point which readers lacking experience in Africa may not fully appreciate. In most African states the reliability of such facilities is woeful.

3. I. Schapera, *A Handbook of Tswana Law and Custom*, (London: Frank Cass, 1938).

4. For a fascinating study of this group see Margot and Martin Russell, *Afrikaners of the Kalahari: White Minority in a Black State*, (Cambridge: Cambridge University Press, 1979).

5. See Ranwedzi Nengwekhulu "Some Findings on the Origins of Political Parties in Botswana," *Pula: Botswana Journal of African Studies*, Vol. 1, No. 2 (1979), pp. 47–75.

6. The origins of the nickname are not totally clear but the most widely accepted story is that some of the party's older supporters had difficulty in pronouncing "democratic" and the result was akin to "domkrag". This is an Afrikaans word meaning "jack," especially the sort used for wagons. The name was adopted by the party which uses it as a symbol of its ambition to "jack up" (i.e., develop) the country.

7. For a detailed study of this area, see John A. Wiseman, "Conflict and Conflict Alliances in the Kgatleng District of Botswana," *Journal of Modern African Studies*, Vol. 16, No. 3 (1978), pp. 487–494.

8. James H. Polhemus, "Botswana Votes: Parties and Elections in an

African Democracy," *Journal of Modern African Studies*, Vol. 21, No. 3, (1984), p. 410.

9. See, for example, Gwendolen M. Carter and E. Philip Morgan, eds., *From the Front Line: Speeches of Sir Seretse Khama*, (London: Rex Collings, 1980).

10. The total of those registered to vote has steadily increased throughout the period, reflecting population increase and improved administration in compiling the register.

11. The 1984 figure, for example, compares very favorably with British general elections.

12. See, for example, the most recent *Republic of Botswana: National Development Plan 1985–91* (Gaborone, Botswana: Government Printer, 1985).

13. See Richard Wiesfelder, "Human Rights in Botswana, Lesotho, Swaziland and Malawi," *Pula: Botswana Journal of African Studies*, Vol. 2, No. 1 (1980), pp. 5–32.

14. John D. Holm and Richard G. Morgan, "Coping with Drought in Botswana: An African Success," *Journal of Modern African Studies*, Vol. 23, No. 3 (1985), pp. 463–482.

15. Ibid., p. 467.

16. Ibid., p. 487.

17. See, for example, details on the treatment of the Northwest in John A. Wiseman, "The Opposition Parties of Botswana," *Collected Papers, Vol. 4*, Centre of Southern African Studies, (York: University of York 1979), pp. 183–193.

18. Op. cit., p. 417.

19. This is a topic in which I have been extremely interested and which has involved me in conflict with other commentators. Over ten years ago I suggested that the relationship between modern politicians and chiefs was the key political issue in Botswana and that the chiefs were the major potential threat to the BDP and the only group that could seriously threaten its supremacy, and that this was recognized by the party. John A. Wiseman, "Multi-Partyism in Africa: The Case of Botswana," *African Affairs*, Vol. 76, No. 302 (1977). I was roundly condemned for this by two other writers who suggested that the chiefs were a spent force and that I overrated their influence. Christopher Stephens and John Speed, "Multi-Partyism in Africa: The Case of Botswana Revisited," *African Affairs*, Vol. 76, No. 304 (1977). A decade

later I felt gratified to see that Pickard, the most prolific writer on modern Botswanan politics, had adopted a position on this issue (although I must say, not on all issues) remarkably similar to my own. He writes that "Political elites in Botswana have continued to perceive the greatest potential threat to be discontented traditional authorities who could use their influence to create a rural resistance to the BDP." Pickard in Louis A. Pickard, ed., *The Evolution of Modern Botswana*, (London: Rex Collings, 1985) p. 181. In Africa it is seldom wise to underrate the power and influence that traditional leaders still retain.

20. For an assessment see John A. Wiseman, "Botswana: The Achievement of Seretse Khama," *The Round Table* (October 1980), pp. 409–414.

21. For details see Wiseman, "Opposition Parties," op. cit.

22. See Joseph Hanlon, *Beggar Your Neighbours: Apartheid Power in Southern Africa* (London: James Currey, 1986) p. 225. Hanlon also suggests that "Botswana shows that a unified government and people are better able to resist South African government pressure," p. 129.

23. Polhemus, op. cit., p. 426.

24. Richard Weisfelder in Pickard, ed., op. cit., p. 290.

25. For details of the early history, see Harry A. Gailey, *A History of The Gambia* (London: Routledge and Kegan Paul, 1964). This is still the best overall survey of preindependence Gambian history.

26. See Patience Sonko-Godwin, *Ethnic Groups of the Senegambia: A Brief History*, (Banjul, The Gambia: Book Production and Material Resources Unit, 1985).

27. For details of the development of political parties in The Gambia see S. S. Nyang, "The Historical Development of Political Parties in The Gambia," *African Research Bulletin*, Vol. 5, No. 4 (1975); S. S. Nyang, "Politics in Post-Independence Gambia," *A Current Bibliography on African affairs*, Vol. 8, No. 2, (1975); Arnold Hughes, "From Green Uprising to National Reconciliation: The Peoples Progressive Party in The Gambia," *Canadian Journal of African Studies*, Vol. 9, No. 1 (1975); Arnold Hughes, "From Colonialism to Confederation: The Gambian Experience of Independence, 1965 to 1982" in ed. Robin Cohen, *African Islands and Enclaves*, (London: Sage, 1983).

28. For details, see Hughes, "From Colonialism to Confederation," op. cit.

29. Whenever I visit N'Jie, his opening comment is usually "have you been to see the monkey (his term for Jawara) yet?".

30. Hughes, "From Colonialism to Confederation," op. cit., p. 65.

31. See John A. Wiseman, "The Social and Economic Bases of Party Political Support in Serekunda, The Gambia,", *The Journal of Commonwealth and Comparative Politics*, Vol. 23, No. 1 (1985), pp. 3–29.

32. For details, see John A. Wiseman, "Attempted Coup in The Gambia: Marxist Revolution or Punk Rebellion?" *Communist Affairs*, Vol. 1, No. 2 (1982) and John A. Wiseman, "Revolt in The Gambia: A Pointless Tragedy," *The Round Table*, No. 284 (1981).

33. While it is possible to explain, but not justify, the attempted seizure of power, I still find myself at a loss to comprehend the huge extent of random violence that took place. It seems to contradict everything I know about The Gambia and the Gambian people. Many of my Gambian friends also still find it impossible to come to terms intellectually or emotionally with this element of random and often gratuitous violence.

34. When I discussed this with Camara he jokingly suggested that, as he was not exactly a fit young athlete, there may have been some sinister motive in trying to get him to play football.

35. For details, see John A. Wiseman, "The Gambian Presidential and Parliamentary Elections of 1987," *Electoral Studies* (December 1987).

36. In an interview I had with Sallah and Sarr they both stressed their opposition to any idea of imposing rule through a coup and argued that the democratic process in The Gambia provided the only acceptable route to power.

37. See R. H. Jackson and C. G. Roseberg, *Personal Rule in Black Africa: Prince, Autocrat, Prophet and Tyrant* (Berkeley and Los Angeles: University of California Press, 1982).

38. A feature which explains in part, why so many opposition politicians have ended up in the PPP.

39. The term "political elite" is too imprecise for a definitive number to be given, but I imagine that observers familiar with The Gambia will probably see this estimate as about right.

40. See Margaret Peil, *Cities and Suburbs: Urban Life in West Africa* (New York: Africana Publishing Co., 1981), pp. 149–151 and 209–214.

41. At the time of writing The Gambian government has embarked on an economic recovery program in an attempt to sort out the most urgent problems.

42. The major exception to this is the political historian Adele Smith Simmons whose interest in pluralism in new states led her to move on from Kenya to study Mauritius in the 1960s. Her work produced the standard book on Mauritian political history up to the time of independence. See Adele Smith Simmons, *Modern Mauritius: The Politics of Decolonisation*, (Bloomington, Ind: Indiana University Press, 1982). Any scholar trying to come to terms with the politics of Mauritius is of necessity indebted to this work.

43. Noting this parallel, Christopher Clapham suggests that "Mauritius is in almost every respect a Caribbean island transported to the Indian Ocean." See Clapham, *Third World Politics: An Introduction* (London: Croom Helm, 1985), p. 15.

44. See Jean Houbert, "Mauritius: Independence and Dependence," *Journal of Modern African Studies*, Vol. 19, No. 1 (1981), pp. 75–105.

45. Cited in Simmons, op. cit., p. 77.

46. For details, see Alfred Latham-Koenig, "Mauritius: Political volteface in the 'Star of the Indian Ocean,'" *The Round Table*, No. 290 (April 1984), pp. 166–173.

47. Houbert, op. cit., p. 100.

Chapter 5. Democracy under Threat

1. Terence Ranger, *Peasant Consciousness and Guerrilla War in Zimbabwe* (London: James Currey, 1985) and David Lan, *Guns and Rain: Guerrillas and Spirit Mediums in Zimbabwe*, (London: James Currey, 1985).

2. Ranger, op. cit., p. 25.

3. Ibid., p. 178.

4. The army was seventy percent black.

5. For details of the conference, see Jeffrey Davidow, *A Peace in Southern Africa: The Lancaster House Conference on Rhodesia, 1979* (Boulder, Colo.: Westview Press, 1984).

6. In August 1987 this anomaly was scrapped when parliament voted, by an overwhelming majority, to end separate white representation. Eight white MPs voted with the government for the change. It will be interesting to see if white Zimbabweans follow the example of white Batswana in participating in party politics on an equal nonracial basis.

7. For a warning against analyzing African politics in Zimbabwe too much in terms of bipolar tribalism, see John Day, "The Insignificance of Tribe in the African Politics of Zimbabwe," ed. W. H. Morris-Jones, *From Rhodesia to Zimbabwe* (London: Frank Cass, 1980), pp. 69–109.

8. For details of the elections, see Henry Wiseman and Alistair M. Taylor, *From Rhodesia to Zimbabwe: The Politics of Transition*, International Peace Academy, (Sevenoaks, Kent: Pergamon Press, 1981).

9. See Anthony Lemon, "The Zimbabwe General Election of 1985," *Journal of Commonwealth and Comparative Politics*, Vol. 26, No. 1 (1988).

10. For the background to this, see the personal account in Joshua Nkomo, *Nkomo: The Story of My Life*, (London: Methuen, 1984). This book provides fascinating insights into many of the issues discussed here, even if a level of personal bias has to be allowed for.

11. For details, see Richard Hodder-Williams, *Conflict in Zimbabwe: The Matabeleland Problem*, (London: Institute for the Study of Conflict, 1983).

12. Ibid., p. 17.

13. See Richard L. Sklar, "Reds and Rights in Zimbabwe's Experiment," ed. Dov Ronen, *Democracy and Pluralism in Africa*, (London: Hodder and Stoughton, 1986), pp. 135–144.

14. Cited in William H. Shaw, "Towards the One Party State in Zimbabwe: A Study In African Political Thought," *Journal of Modern African Studies*, Vol. 24, No. 3 (1986), p. 375. This article contains a most useful discussion of the movement towards a single-party state and a critical analysis of the arguments being used to justify it.

15. See Shaw, op. cit.

16. Ibid., p. 376.

17. Nkrumah's oft-vaunted claim that "the CPP is Ghana: Ghana is the CPP," comes strikingly to mind. When Nkrumah was overthrown by the army in 1966, the CPP disappeared with hardly a voice raised in its defense.

Chapter 6 Democratization without Consolidation: Nigeria and Ghana

1. Much of the literature is cited below, but see also Robin Luckham, *The Nigerian Military: A Sociological Analysis of Authority and Revolt*

1960–67, (Cambridge: Cambridge University Press, 1971); Theophilus Olatunde Odetola, *Military Politics in Nigeria: Economic Development and Political Stability*, (New Brunswick: N.J., Transaction Books, 1978); Keith Panter-Brick, ed., *Soldiers and Oil: The Political Transformation of Nigeria*, (London: Frank Cass, 1978); Anthony Kirk-Greene and Douglas Rimmer, *Nigeria Since 1970: A Political and Economic Outline*, (London: Hodder and Stoughton, 1981); J. Isawa Elaigwu, *Gowon: The Biography of a Soldier Statesman*, (Ibadan, Nigeria: West Books, 1986).

2. Michael Crowder, *The Story of Nigeria*, (London: Faber and Faber, 1978), p. 224.

3. K. W. J. Post and Michael Vickers, *Structure and Conflict in Nigeria, 1960–65*, (London: Heinemann, 1973), p. 43.

4. Oyeleye Oyediran, ed., *Nigerian Government and Politics under Military Rule, 1966–79*, (London: Macmillan, 1979), p. 7.

5. C. S. Whitaker, *The Politics of Tradition: Continuity and Change in Northern Nigeria, 1946–66*, (Princeton: Princeton University Press, 1970), p. 305.

6. For a full list of members, see C. Alex Gboyega, "The Making of the Nigerian Constitution," in Oyediran, op. cit., p. 244.

7. They wrote that "there shall be political parties and these are major political institutions essential for systematic organised popular participation in democratic government." O. Osoba and Y. B. Usman, *A Draft Constitution for the Federal Republic of Nigeria—A Minority Submission*, p. 14. More generally, see O. Osoba and Y. B. Usman, *A General Support on the Work of the Constitution Drafting Committee: A Minority Submission*. To the best of my knowledge these documents were never officially published, but they were quite widely available in mimeo form. My personal copies were given to me by one of my students at Ahmadu Bello University. See also Y. B. Usman, *For the Liberation of Nigeria*, (London: New Beacon Books, 1979).

8. B. O. Nwabueze, *The Presidential Constitution of Nigeria*, (London: C. Hurst and Company and Enugu and Lagos: Nwamife Publishers, 1982), p. 483. For other useful discussions of the 1979 constitution, see E. Michael Joye and Kingsley Igweike, *Introduction to the 1979 Nigerian Constitution*, (Nigeria and London: Macmillan, 1982); S. Egite Oyovbaire, *Federalism in Nigeria*, (London: Macmillan, 1985); Abubakar Yaya Aliyu, ed., *Return to Civilian Rule*, (Zaria, Nigeria: The Institute of Administration, ABU, 1982). For a comparative study of all Nigeria's constitutions, see B. O. Nwabueze, *A Constitutional History of Nigeria*, (Essex: Harlow, Longman, 1982).

9. Margaret Peil, *Nigerian Politics: The People's View*, (London: Cassell, 1976).

10. Ibid., pp. 110–111.

11. The full constitution was published as a series of extended supplements in the *New Nigerian* newspaper (published in Kaduna) from September 28 to October 4 1978 and these details are taken from that source.

12. The former NPC had in its constitution that "the membership of the congress is open to all people of *northern* Nigerian descent," Billy Dudley, *An Introduction to Nigerian Government and Politics*, (London: Macmillan, 1982), p. 182.

13. Nwabueze, op. cit; Joye and Igweike, op. cit; Oyovbaire, op. cit.

14. For a detailed discussion see L. Adele Jinadu, *The Federal Electoral Commission*, ed. Oyeleye Oyediran, *The Nigerian 1979 Elections*, (Nigeria and London: Macmillan, 1981), pp. 17–39.

15. Ibid., p. 39.

16. Quoted in *West Africa*, November 13, 1978.

17. For a detailed account of party formation, see Richard A. Joseph, *Democracy and Prebendel Politics in Nigeria*, (Cambridge: Cambridge University Press, 1987).

18. Dudley, op. cit., pp. 188–189.

19. Ibid., p. 190.

20. For details, see Oyediran in Oyediran, ed., op. cit. "Elections," pp. 56–65.

21. See Paul M. Lubeck, *Islam and Urban Labour in Northern Nigeria*, (Cambridge: Cambridge University Press, 1986).

22. Often referred to by Nigerian wits as Outer Gongolia.

23. Chinua Achebe, *The Trouble with Nigeria*, (London: Heinemann, 1983).

24. Ibid., p. 40.

25. See, for example, Samuel Decalo, *Coups and Army Rule in Africa: Studies in Military Style*, (New Haven: Yale University Press, 1976).

26. Dennis Austin, *Ghana Observed*, (Manchester: Manchester University Press, 1976), p. 8.

27. Alia A. Mazrui, *Africa's International Relations: The Diplomacy of Dependency and Change*, (London: Heinemann, 1977), pp. 42–43.

28. For a useful study of Nkrumah's relations with the army, see Simon Baynham, *The Military and Politics in Nkrumah's Ghana*, (Boulder, Colo.: Westview Press, 1988).

29. See Austin, op. cit., pp. 102–110.

30. Decalo, 1976, op. cit., p. 31.

31. Anthony Kirk-Greene in Peter Duignan and Robert H. Jackson, *Politics and Government in African States 1960–85*, (London, Croom Helm, 1986), pp. 38–39.

32. See Maxwell Owusu, "Politics without Parties: Reflections on the Union Government Proposal in Ghana," *African Studies Review*, Vol. 22, No. 1 (1979), pp. 89–108.

33. Emmanuel Hansen and Paul Collins, "The Army, the State and the Rawlings Revolution in Ghana," *African Affairs*, Vol. 79, No. 314 (1980), p. 3.

34. Others who were executed included Major General Utuka, Major Robert Kotei, Air Vice Marshall George Boakye, and Rear Admiral Joy Amedume.

35. Naomi Chazan, *An Anatomy of Ghanaian Politics: Managing Political Recession 1969–1982*, (Boulder, Colo.: Westview Press, 1983), p. 285.

36. For details of the parties and of the 1979 elections, see Richard Jeffries, "The Ghanaian Elections of 1979," *African Affairs*, Vol. 79, No. 316 (1980), pp. 397–414.

37. Ibid., p. 400.

38. Ibid., pp. 406–407. Jeffries reported that in his own survey a very high percentage (approaching eighty percent) considered the elections vital and intended to vote.

39. Chazan, op. cit., p. 314.

40. For a full text of the speech, see Barbara E. Okeke, *Fourth of June: A Revolution Betrayed*, (Enugu, Nigeria: Ikenga Publishers, 1982), pp. 160–163.

41. See Donald I. Ray, *Ghana Politics, Economics and Society*, (London: Francis Pinter, 1986), pp. 24–25.

42. A number of the statements are published in Okeke, op. cit.

43. See, for example, Emile Rado, "Notes Towards a Political Economy of Ghana Today," *African Affairs*, Vol. 35, No. 341 (October 1986), pp. 563–572.

44. Ibid., pp. 568–69.

45. Such hopes must be tentative. Cocoa exports are still less than one-third of the mid-1960s' figure and the industry is operating at less than one-quarter of its capacity.

46. For details of the coup plots and attempts, see Ray, op. cit., pp. 103–112.

Chapter 7. More Doubtful Cases: Uganda, Liberia, Sudan

1. See *Expulsion of a Minority: Essays on Uganda Asians*, ed. Michel Twaddle, (London: Althone Press, 1975).

2. For useful surveys of Uganda's early political development, see Peter M. Gukiina, *Uganda: A Case Study in African Political Development* (Notre Dame: University of Notre Dame Press, 1972); Jan Jelmert Jorgensen, *Uganda: A Modern History* (London: Croom Helm, 1981); S. R. Karugire, *A Political History of Uganda* (London: Heinemann, 1980); T. V. Sathyamurthy, *The Political Development of Uganda 1900–1986* (Aldershott: Gower, 1986); A. F. Robertson, ed., *Uganda's First Republic: Chiefs, Administrators, and Politicians 1967–1971* (Cambridge: Cambridge African Studies Centre, 1982).

3. See, for example, Judith Listowel, *Amin* (London, IUP Books, 1973); David Martin, *General Amin* (London: Faber and Faber, 1974); Samuel Decalo, *Coups and Army Rule in Africa: Studies in Military Style* (New Haven: Yale University Press, 1976), pp. 173–230; Henry Kyemba, *State of Blood: The Inside Story of Idi Amin's Reign of Fear* (London: Corgi Books, 1977); Peter F. B. Nayenga, "Myths and Realities of Idi Amin Dada's Uganda," *African Studies Review*, Vol. 22, No. 2, (1979), pp. 126–138. See also, Jorgensen, op. cit and Sathyamurthy, op. cit.

4. Nayenga, op. cit., p. 137.

5. See Twaddle, op. cit.

6. For a discussion of the attack and subsequent Tanzanian response, see Tony Avirgan and Martha Honey, *War in Uganda: The Legacy of Idi Amin* (London: Zed Press, 1982).

7. Interviews with Milton Obote and Paul Ssemogerere in *Africa*, London, September 1980.

8. Ibid., p. 18.

9. Sathyamurthy, op. cit., p. 708.

10. Samuel Decalo, "Military Rule in Africa: Etiology and Morphology," ed., Simon Baynham, *Military Power and Politics in Black Africa* Beckenham, (Kent: Croom Helm, 1986), p. 55.

11. See Martin Lowenkopf, *Politics in Liberia* (Stanford, California: Hoover Institution Press, 1976).

12. For studies of Americo-Liberian dominance, see Lowenkopf, ibid. See also Yekutiel Gershoni, *Black Colonialism: The Americo-Liberian Scramble for the Hinterland* (Boulder, Colo.: Westview Press, 1985); Merran Fraenkel, *Tribe and Class in Monrovia* (London International African Institute, 1964); Christopher Clapham, *Liberia and Sierra Leone: An Essay in Comparative Politics* (Cambridge: Cambridge University Press, 1976); Stephen S. Hlophe, *Class Ethnicity and Politics in Liberia* (Washington D.C.: University Press of America, 1979); Anthony J. Nimley, *The Liberian Bureaucracy* (Washington, D.C.: University Press of America, 1977).

13. See Lowenkopf, op. cit., pp. 114–115.

14. For details, see John A. Wiseman, "Urban Riots in West Africa 1977–85," *Journal of Modern African Studies*, Vol. 24, No. 3 (1986), pp. 509–518.

15. See Dunstan M. Wai, *The Southern Sudan: The Problem of National Integration* (London: Frank Cass, 1973).

16. See Philippa Scott, "The Sudan People's Liberation Movement and Liberation Army," *Review of African Political Economy*, No. 33 (August 1985), pp. 69–82.

17. For a useful discussion of the tactics used by Numeiri to retain power in this period, see the section on him in Robert H. Jackson and Carl G. Rosberg, *Personal Rule in Black Africa*, (Berkeley and Los Angeles: University of California Press, 1982), pp. 130–142.

18. Peter Woodward, "Sudan After Numeiri," *Third World Quarterly*, Vol. 7, No. 4 (October 1985), p. 960.

19. Ibid., p. 958.

20. *Keesings Archives*, Vol. 32 (August 1986), p. 34530.

21. Interview in *New African*, No. 235 (April 1987).

22. In September 1987 this coalition broke up with the withdrawal of the DUP.

Chapter 8. Ephemeral and Partial Cases: Burkina Faso, Central African Republic, Mauritania

1. The RDA was the interterritorial francophone political movement led by Felix Houphouet-Boigny of the Ivory Coast in the postwar, preindependence, period.

2. See Pat McGowan and Thomas H. Johnson, "Sixty Coups in Thirty Years: Further Evidence Regarding African Military Coups d'etat," *Journal of Modern African Studies*, Vol. 24, No. 3 (1986), p. 544.

3. For a useful general survey of CAR, see Thomas O'Toole, *The Central African Republic: The Continent's Hidden Heart*, (Boulder, Colo.: Westview Press, 1986). In the colonial period the territory was known as Ubangi-Shari.

4. Jackson and Rosberg, op. cit., p. 242.

5. Lyse Doucet, "Fragile Politics", *West Africa*, 19 January 1987, p. 110.

Chapter 9. Democratization without Military Intervention: Senegal

1. For a good general introduction to Senegal, see Sheldon Gellar, *Senegal: An African Nation Between Islam and the West* (Boulder, Colo.: Westview Press, 1982).

2. In 1900 only fifty percent were Muslim.

3. For a detailed account of this period, see G. Wesley Johnson Jr., *The Emergence of Black Politics in Senegal: The Struggle for Power in the Four Communes 1900–1920* (Stanford: Stanford University Press, 1971).

4. Gellar, op. cit., p. 11.

5. For a detailed background, see Donal B. Cruise O'Brien, *The Mourides of Senegal: The Political and Economic Organisation of an Islamic Brotherhood* (Oxford: Oxford University Press, 1971) and *Saints and Politicians: Essays in the Organisation of a Senegalese Peasant Society* (Cambridge: Cambridge University Press, 1975).

6. For studies of Senghor and the concept of negritude, see Irving Leonard Markovitz, *Leopold Sedar Senghor and the Politics of Negritude* (London: Heinemann, 1969) and Jacques Louis Hymans, *Leopold Sedar Senghor: An Intellectual Biography* (Edinburgh: Edinburgh University Press, 1971).

7. For a useful background on this period, see Edward J. Schumacher, *Politics, Bureaucracy and Rural Development in Senegal*, (Berkeley and Los Angeles: University of California Press, 1975).

8. Quoted in Kin-Kiey Mulumba, "Exit Senghor, Enter Diouf" *Africa*, London, February 1981, p. 25.

9. Pamela Cox and Richard Kessler, "Apres Senghor: A Socialist Senegal?" *African Affairs*, Vol. 79 (1980), p. 334.

10. Oumar Wome, leader of the Parti Populaire Senegalais, was the only contestant not referred to here and was of minimal significance. In *West Africa*, the journalist Adama Gaye commented, before the election, that "if he had not offered himself at the presidential elections, Oumar Wome would have remained as obscure as his party and his private medical clinic." *West Africa*, 28 February 1983, p. 537. The candidacy of Mamodou Dia surprised many commentators as he was well into his seventies and almost completely blind.

11. The consensus among observers of the elections was that while some electoral malpractice probably did take place, it had no real effect on the overall outcome of a resounding PS victory.

12. Lucy A. Creevey, "Muslim Brotherhoods and Politics in Senegal in 1985," *Journal of Modern African Studies*, Vol. 23, No. 4, 1985, p. 720. See also her "Muslim Politics and Development in Senegal," *Journal of Modern African Studies*, Vol. 15, No. 2 (1977), pp. 261–277. On the elections, see also Christopher Harrison, "The Marabout Factor," *West Africa*, March 14, 1983, p. 644.

Conclusions: Explaining the Survival and Revival of Democracy and a Look Toward the Future

1. Thomas H. Johnson, Robert O. Slater, and Pat McGowan, "Explaining African Military Coups d'Etat 1960–1982," *American Political Science Review*, Vol. 70, No. 3 (1984), p. 634. It might be noted that the phrase "maintained or restored" has strong echoes of my "survival and revival."

2. In Sudan the democratic government inherited the secession movement from a more authoritarian period. In Mozambique and Angola the civil wars are complicated by South African involvement

on the side of rebel groups, but one might ask whether the refusal of the governments of those two states to countenance democratic competition hinders, rather than assists, in the search for a solution.

3. Reported in "Nyerere Doubts on One-Party System," *The Guardian*, London, June 11, 1986.

4. Ibid.

5. Abdul Rahman Mohmed Babu, "A Conversation on Democracy," *Africa Now* (November 1982), p. 65.

6. Babu, "Militancy in Africa," *Africa Now* (August 1982), p. 47.

7. Babu, *African Socialism or Socialist Africa?* (London: Zed Press, 1981), p. 170. This view accords well with the critique of bogus Afrocentrism in the first chapter of this book.

8. Reported in "Kenyan Dissident Returns to Politics," *The Guardian*, London, July 2, 1987.

9. Moi, *Kenyan African Nationalism: Nyayo Philosophy and Principles* (London: Macmillan 1986), p. 173.

10. Siaka Stevens, *What Life Has Taught Me* Bourne End, (Bucks: Kensal Press, 1984), p. 408.

11. Even when they are spurious, it is still interesting to ask why they are made. It is the very wide strength of the attachment to democracy as the legitimate form of politics that leads some military leaders to attempt to legitimize their own actions by appealing to democracy. If this were not so, declarations of democratic intent would be quite pointless.

12. For the first half of this period it was the single party state that proved the greatest threat. Since then, the possible example of Zimbabwe notwithstanding, this threat has largely receded.

Bibliography

Achebe, Chinua. *The Trouble with Nigeria*. London: Heinemann, 1983.

Aliyu, Abubakar Yaya. *Return to Civilian Rule*. Zaria, Nigeria: ABU, 1982.

Amonoo, Benjamin. *Ghana 1957–1966: The Politics of Institutional Dualism*. London: George Allen and Unwin, 1981.

Austin, Dennis. *Politics in Ghana: 1946–1960*. Oxford: Oxford University Press, 1970.

———, *Ghana Observed*. Manchester: Manchester University Press, 1975.

Avirgan, Tony and Martha Honey. *War in Uganda: The Legacy of Idi Amin*. London: Zed Press, 1982.

Babu, Abdul Rahman Mohammed. *African Socialism or Socialist Africa?* London: Zed Press, 1981.

Baynham, Simon. *The Military and Politics in Nkrumah's Ghana*. Boulder, Colo.: Westview Press, 1988.

Baynham, Simon, ed. *Military Power and Politics in Black Africa*. London: Croom Helm, 1986.

Carter, Gwendolen and E. Philip Morgan, eds. *From the Front Line: Speeches of Seretse Khama*. London: Rex Collings, 1980.

Chabal, Patrick, ed. *Political Domination in Africa: Reflections on the Limits of Power*. Cambridge: Cambridge University Press, 1986.

Chazan, Naomi. *An Anatomy of Ghanaian Politics: Managing Political Recession 1969–1982*. Boulder, Colo.: Westview Press, 1983.

Clapham, Christopher. *Liberia and Sierra Leone: An Essay in Comparative Politics*. Cambridge: Cambridge University Press, 1976.

———. *Third World Politics: An Introduction*. London: Croom Helm, 1985.

Colclough, Christopher and Stephen McCarthy. *The Political Economy of Botswana: A Study of Growth and Distribution.* Oxford: Oxford University Press, 1980.

Collier, Ruth Berins. *Regimes in Tropical Africa: Changing Forms of Supremacy.* Berkeley and Los Angeles: University of California Press, 1982.

Coulson, Andrew. *Tanzania: A Political Economy.* Oxford: Clarendon Press, 1982.

Cox, Pamela and Richard Kessler. "Après Senghor: A Socialist Senegal." *African Affairs*, Vol. 79, No. 2 (1980).

Creevey Lucy A. "Muslim Brotherhoods and Politics in Senegal." *Journal of Modern African Studies*, Vol. 23, No. 4, 1985.

———. "Muslim Politics and Development in Senegal." *Journal of Modern African Studies*, Vol. 15, No. 2 (1977).

Davidow, Jeffrey. *A Peace in Southern Africa: The Lancaster House Conference on Rhodesia.* Boulder, Colo.: Westview Press, 1979.

Decalo, Samuel. *Coups and Army Rule in Africa: Studies in Military Style.* New Haven: Yale University Press, 1976.

Diamond, Larry, Juan J. Linz, and Seymour Martin Lipset, eds. *Africa* Vol. 2, *Democracy in Developing Countries*, Boulder, Colo.: Lynne Rienner, 1988.

Diamond, Larry. *Class, Ethnicity and Democracy in Nigeria: The Failure of the First Republic.* London: Macmillan, 1988.

Dudley, Billy. *An Introduction to Nigerian Government and Politics.* London: Macmillan, 1982.

Duignan, Peter and Robert H. Jackson, eds. *Politics and Government in African States, 1960–85.* London: Croom Helm, 1986.

Dunn, John, ed. *West African States: Failure and Promise.* Cambridge: Cambridge University Press, 1978.

Elaigwu, J. Isawa. *Gowon: The Biography of a Soldier Statesman.* Ibadan, Nigeria: West Books, 1986.

Fatton, Robert. *The Making of a Liberal Democracy: Senegal's Passive Revolution, 1975–1985.* Boulder, Colo.: Lynne Rienner, 1987.

Finer, S. E. *Comparative Government.* London: Penguin, 1970.

Fraenkel, Merran. *Tribe and Class in Monrovia.* London: International African Institute, 1964.

Gailey, Harry A. *A History of The Gambia.* London: Routledge Kegan Paul, 1964.

Gellar, Sheldon. *Senegal: An African Nation Between Islam and the West,* Boulder, Colo.: Westview Press, 1982.

Gershoni, Yekutiel. *Black Colonialism: The Americo-Liberian Scramble for the Hinterland.* Boulder, Colo.: Westview Press, 1985.

Gukiina, Peter M. *Uganda: A Case Study in African Political Development.* Notre Dame: University of Notre Dame Press, 1972.

Hanlon, Joseph. *Beggar Your Neighbours: Apartheid Power in Southern Africa.* London: James Currey, 1986.

Hanson, Emmanuel and Paul Collins. "The Army, the State and the Rawlings Revolution in Ghana. African Affairs, Vol. 79, No. 314 (1980).

Hartland-Thunberg, Penelope. *Botswana: An African Growth Economy.* Boulder, Colo.: Westview Press, 1978.

Harvey, Charles, ed. *Papers on the Economy of Botswana.* London: Heinemann, 1981.

Hayward, Fred M. *Elections in Independent Africa.* Boulder, Colo.: Westview Press, 1987.

Hlophe, Stephen S. *Class, Ethnicity and Politics in Liberia.* Washington: University Press of America, 1979.

Hodder-Williams, Richard. *An Introduction to the Politics of Tropical Africa.* London: George Allen and Unwin, 1984.

———. *Conflict in Zimbabwe: The Matabeleland Problem.* London: Institute for the Study of Conflict, 1983.

Holm, John D. and Richard D. Morgan. "Coping with Drought in Botswana: An African Success." *Journal of Modern African Studies,* Vol. 23, No. 3 (1985).

Houbert, Jean. "Mauritius: Independence and Dependence." *Journal of Modern African Studies,* Vol. 19, No. 1 (1981).

Hyden, Goran. *Beyond Ujamaa in Tanzania.* London: Heinemann, 1980.

Hymans, Jacques Louis. *Leopold Sedar Senghor: An Intellectual Bi-*

ography. Berkeley and Los Angeles: University of California Press, 1975.

Hughes, Arnold. "From Colonialism to Confederation: The Gambian Experience of Independence, 1965–1982." ed. Robin Cohen, *African Islands and Enclaves,* London: Sage, 1983.

———. "From Green Uprising to National Reconciliation: The People's Progressive Party in The Gambia." *Canadian Journal of African Studies,* Vol. 9, No. 1 (1975).

Jackson, R. H. and Rosberg, C. G. *Personal Rule in Black Africa: Prince, Autocrat, Prophet and Tyrant.* Berkeley and Los Angeles: University of California Press, 1982.

Jeffries, Richard. *Class, Power and Ideology in Ghana: The Railwaymen of Sekondi.* Cambridge: Cambridge University Press, 1978.

———. "The Ghanaian Elections of 1979." *African Affairs,* Vol. 79, No. 316 (1980).

Johnson, G. Wesley. *The Emergence of Black Politics in Senegal: The Struggle for Power in the Four Communes, 1900–1920.* Stanford: Stanford University Press, 1971.

Johnson, Thomas H., Robert O. Slater, and Pat McGowan. "Explaining African Military Coups d'Etat, 1968–1982." *American Political Science Review,* Vol. 70, No. 3 (1984).

Jorgensen, Jan Jelmert. *Uganda: A Modern History.* London: Croom Helm, 1981.

Joseph, Richard A. *Democracy and Prebendal Politics in Nigeria.* Cambridge: Cambridge University Press, 1988.

Joye, E. Michael and Kingsley Igweike. *Introduction to the 1979 Nigerian Constitution.* London: Macmillan, 1982.

Karugire, S. R. *A Political History of Uganda.* London: Heinemann, 1980.

Kasfir, Nelson. *The Shrinking Political Arena.* Berkeley and Los Angeles: University of California Press, 1986.

Kirk-Greene, Anthony and Douglas Rimmer. *Nigeria Since 1970: A Political and Economic Outline.* London: Hodder and Stoughton, 1981.

Kyemba, Henry. *State of Blood: The Inside Story of Idi Amin's Reign of Fear.* London: Corgi Books, 1977.

Lan, David. *Guns and Rain: Guerrillas and Spirit Mediums in Zimbabwe*. London: James Currey, 1985.

Latham-Koenig, Alfred. "Mauritius: Political Volteface in the Star of the Indian Ocean." *The Round Table*, No. 290, (1984).

Listowel, Judith. *Amin*. London: IUP Books, 1973.

Lowenkopf, Martin. *Politics in Liberia*. Washington D.C.: Hoover Institution Press, 1976.

Lubeck, Paul. *Islam and Urban Labour in Northern Nigeria*. Cambridge: Cambridge University Press, 1986.

Luckham, Robin. *The Nigerian Military: A Sociological Analysis of Authority and Revolt, 1960–67*. Cambridge: Cambridge University Press, 1971.

Mandaza, Ibbo. *Zimbabwe: The Political Economy of Transition, 1980–86*. Dakar, Senegal: Codesria Books, 1986.

McGowan, Pat and Thomas H. Jackson. "Sixty Coups in Thirty Years: Further Evidence Regarding African Military Coups d'Etat." *Journal of Modern African Studies*, Vol. 24, No. 3 (1986).

Markovitz, Irving Leonard. *Leopold Sedar Senghor and the Politics of Negritude*. London: Heinemann, 1969.

Martin, David. *General Amin*. London: Faber and Faber, 1974.

Moi, Daniel Arap. *Kenyan African Nationalism: Nyayo Philosophy and Principles*. London: Macmillan, 1986.

Morris-Jones, W. H., ed. *From Rhodesia to Zimbabwe*. London: Frank Cass, 1980.

Nayenga, Peter F. B. "Myths and Realities of Idi Amin Dada's Uganda." *African Studies Review*, Vol. 22, No. 2, (1979).

Nengwekhulu, Ranwedzi. "Some Findings on the Origins of Political Parties in Botswana." *Pula: Botswana Journal of African Studies*, Vol. 1, No. 2 (1979).

Nimley, Anthony J. *The Liberian Bureaucracy*. Washington: University Press of America, 1977.

Nkomo, Joshua. *Nkomo: The Story of My Life*. London: Methuen, 1984.

Nwabueze, B.O. *A Constitutional History of Nigeria.* London: Longman, 1982.

———. *The Presidential Constitution of Nigeria.* London: C. Hurst, 1982.

Nyang, S.S. "The Historical Development of Political Parties in The Gambia." *African Research Bulletin,* Vol. 5, No. 4 (1975).

———. "Politics in Post-Independence Gambia." *Current Bibliography on African Affairs,* Vol. 8, No. 2 (1975).

Nyerere, Julius. *Freedom and Development.* Oxford: Oxford University Press, 1973.

———. *Freedom and Socialism.* Oxford: Oxford University Press, 1968.

———. *Freedom and Unity.* Oxford: Oxford University Press, 1966.

O'Brien, Donal B. Cruise. *The Mourides of Senegal: The Political and Economic Organization of an Islamic Brotherhood.* Oxford: Oxford University Press, 1971.

———. *Saints and Politicians: Essays in the Organization of a Senegalese Peasant Society.* Cambridge: Cambridge University Press, 1975.

Odetola, T. O. *Military Politics in Nigeria: Economic Development and Political Stability.* New Jersey: Transaction Books, 1978.

Okeke, Barbara E. *The Fourth of June: A Revolution Betrayed.* Enugu, Nigeria: Ikenga Publishers, 1982.

Omara-Otunnu, Amii. *Politics and the Military in Uganda 1890–1985.* London: Macmillan, 1987.

Onwuejeogwu, M. Angulu. *The Social Anthropology of Africa.* London: Heinemann, 1975.

O'Toole, Thomas. *The Central African Republic: The Continent's Hidden Heart.* Boulder, Colo: Westview Press, 1986.

Owusu, Maxwell. "Politics Without Parties: Reflections on the Union Government Proposal in Ghana." *African Studies Review,* Vol. 22 No. 1 (1979).

Oyediran, Oyeleye, ed. *Nigerian Government and Politics Under Military Rule, 1966–79,* London: Macmillan, 1979.

Oyediran, Oyeleye, ed. *The Nigerian 1979 Elections*. London: Macmillan, 1981.

Oyovbaire, S. Egite. *Federalism in Nigeria*. London: Macmillan, 1985.

Paden, John N. *Ahmadu Bello, Sardauna of Sokoto: Values and Leadership in Nigeria*. London: Hodder and Stoughton, 1986.

Panter-Brick, Keith, ed. *Soldiers and Oil: The Political Transformation of Nigeria*. London: Frank Cass, 1978.

Peil, Margaret. *Cities and Suburbs: Urban Life in West Africa*. New York: Africana Publishing Co., 1981.

————. *Nigerian Politics: The People's View*. London: Cassell, 1976.

Pellow, Deborah and Naomi Chazan. *Ghana: Coping with Uncertainty*. Boulder, Colo.: Westview Press, 1986.

Pickard, Louis A. "Bureaucrats, Cattle and Public Policy: Land Tenure Changes in Botswana." *Comparative Political Studies*, Vol. 13, No. 3 (1980).

————. *The Evolution of Modern Botswana*. London: Rex Collings, 1985.

————. *The Politics of Development in Botswana: A Model for Success?* Boulder, Colo.: Lynne Rienner, 1987.

Polhemus, James A. "Botswana Votes: Parties and Elections in an African Democracy." *Journal of Modern African Studies*, Vol. 21, No. 3 (1984).

Post, K. W. J. and Michael Vickers. *Structure and Conflict in Nigeria, 1960–65*. London: Heinemann, 1973.

Potholm, Christian P. *The Theory and Practice of African Politics*. Englewood Cliffs, N.J.: Prentice-Hall, 1979.

Pratt, Cranford. *The Critical Phase in Tanzania, 1945–68*. Cambridge: Cambridge University Press, 1976.

Rado, Emile. "Notes Towards a Political Economy of Ghana Today." *African Affairs*, Vol. 35, No. 341 (1986).

Ranger, Terence. *Peasant Consciousness and Guerrilla War in Zimbabwe*. London: James Currey, 1985.

Ray, Donald I. *Ghana: Politics, Economics and Society*. London: Frances Pinter, 1986.

Robertson, A. F., ed. *Uganda's First Republic: Chiefs, Administrators and Politicians 1967–71*. Cambridge: Cambridge African Studies Centre, 1982.

Ronen, Dov. *Democracy and Pluralism in Africa*. London: Hodder and Stoughton, 1986.

Russell, Margot and Martin. *Afrikaners of the Kalahari: White Minority in a Black State*. Cambridge: Cambridge University Press, 1979.

Sathyamurthy, T. V. *The Political Development of Uganda 1960–86*. Aldershot: Gower, 1986.

Schapera, I. *A Handbook of Tswana Law and Custom*. London: Frank Cass, 1938.

Scott, Philippa. "The Sudan People's Liberation Movement and Liberation Army." *Review of African Political Economy*. No. 33 (1985).

Shaw, William H. "Towards the One-Party State in Zimbabwe: A Study in African Political Thought." *Journal of Modern African Studies*, Vol. 24, No. 3 (1986).

Shivji, Issa G. *Class Struggles in Tanzania*. London: Heinemann, 1976.

Simmons, Adele Smith. *Modern Mauritius: The Politics of Decolonization*. Bloomington: Indiana University Press, 1982.

Sonko-Godwin, Patience. *Ethnic Groups of the Senegambia: A Brief History*. Banjul: Book Production and Material Resources Unit, 1985.

Stephens, Christopher and John Speed. "Multi-Partyism in Africa: The Case of Botswana Revisited." *African Affairs*, Vol. 76, No. 304 (1977).

Stevens, Siaka. *What Life Has Taught Me*. Kensal Press, Bourne End: Bucks, 1984.

Tangri, Roger. *Politics in Sub-Saharan Africa*. London: James Currey, 1985.

Tijjani Aminu and David Williams, eds. *Shehu Shagari: My Vision of Nigeria*. London: Frank Cass, 1981.

Tordoff, William. *Government and Politics in Africa*. London: Macmillan, 1984.

Twaddle, Michael. *Expulsion of a Minority: Essays on Ugandan Asians.* London: Althone Press, 1975.

Usman, Yusufu Bala. *For the Liberation of Nigeria.* London: New Beacon Books, 1979.

Vengroff, Richard. *Botswana: Rural Development in the Shadow of Apartheid.* Cranbury, New Jersey: Associated University Presses, 1977.

Wai, Dunstan M. *The Southern Sudan: The Problem of National Integration.* London: Frank Cass, 1973.

Whitaker, C. S. *The Politics of Tradition: Continuity and Change in Northern Nigeria 1946–66.* Princeton: Princeton University Press, 1970.

Wiesfelder, Richard. "Human Rights in Botswana, Lesotho, Swaziland and Malawi." *Pula: Botswana Journal of African Studies*, Vol. 2, No. 1 (1980).

Williams, David. *President and Power in Nigeria.* London: Frank Cass, 1982.

Williams, Robert. *Political Corruption in Africa.* Aldershot: Gower, 1987.

Wiseman, Henry and Taylor Alistair. *From Rhodesia to Zimbabwe: The Politics of Transition.* Oxford: Pergamon Press, 1981.

Wiseman, John A. "Multi-Partyism in Africa: The Case of Botswana." *African Affairs*, Vol. 76, No. 302 (1977).

———. "Conflict and Conflict Alliances in the Kgatleng District of Botswana." *Journal of Modern African Studies*, Vol. 16, No. 3, 1978.

———. "The Opposition Parties of Botswana." *Collected Papers Vol. 4*, CSAS. York: University of York, 1979.

———. "Botswana: The Achievement of Seretse Khama." *The Round Table*, No. 280 (1980).

———. "Revolt in The Gambia: A Pointless Tragedy." *The Round Table*, No. 284 (1981).

———. "The Social and Economic Bases of Party Political Support in Serekunda, The Gambia." *Journal of Commonwealth and Comparative Politics*, Vol 23, No. 1 (1985).

———. "Urban Riots in West Africa 1977–85", *Journal of Modern African Studies*, Vol. 24, No. 3 (1986).

————. "The Gambian Presidential and Parliamentary Elections of 1987." *Electoral Studies*, Vol. 6, No. 3 (1987).

Woodward, Peter. "Sudan After Numeiri." *Third World Quarterly*, Vol. 7, No. 4 (1985).

Young, Crawford. *Ideology and Development in Africa.* New Haven: Yale University Press, 1982.

Index